W9-BXD-278

Write for Insight

Empowering Content Area Learning, Grades 6–12

William Strong

Utah State University

Foreword by Richard Sterling, National Writing Project

PEARSON

Boston   New York   San Francisco
Mexico City   Montreal   Toronto   London   Madrid   Munich   Paris
Hong Kong   Singapore   Tokyo   Cape Town   Sydney

Safety Harbor Public Library
101 Second Street North
Safety Harbor, FL 34695
(727) 724-1525

Senior Editor: *Aurora Martínez Ramos*
Series Editorial Assistant: *Kevin Shannon*
Marketing Manager: *Jennifer Armstrong*
Production Editor: *Annette Joseph*
Editorial Production Service: *Argosy Publishing*

Composition Buyer: *Linda Cox*
Manufacturing Buyer: *Andrew Turso*
Electronic Composition: *Argosy Publishing*
Cover Administrator: *Joel Gendron*

For related titles and support materials, visit our online catalog at www.ablongman.com.

Copyright © 2006 Pearson Education, Inc.

All rights reserved. No part of the material protected by this copyright notice may be reproduced or utilized in any form or by any means, electronic or mechanical, including photocopying, recording, or by any information storage and retrieval system, without written permission from the copyright holder.

To obtain permission(s) to use material from this work, please submit a written request to Allyn and Bacon, Permissions Department, 75 Arlington Street, Boston, MA 02116 or fax your request to 617-848-7320.

Between the time website information is gathered and then published, it is not unusual for some sites to have closed. Also, the transcription of URLs can result in typographical errors. The publisher would appreciate notification where these errors occur so that they may be corrected in subsequent editions.

Library of Congress Cataloging-in-Publication Data
Strong, William
    Write for insight : empowering content area learning, grades 6-12 / William Strong.
      p. cm.
    Includes bibliographical references and index.
    ISBN 0-205-41283-1 (paperback)
    1. English language—Composition and exercises—Study and teaching (Elementary)
2. English Language—Composition and exercises—Study and teaching (Secondary)
3. Report writing—Study and teaching (Elementary) 4. Report writing—Study and teaching
(Secondary). I. Title.

  LB1576.S854 2006
  808'.042'071—dc22

2005047624

Text excerpts: pp. 9, 62, 112–113, 118, 119–120, 121–122, 126, 139: Reprinted by permission from *Coaching Writing* by William Strong. Copyright © 2001 by William Strong. Published by Heinemann, a division of Reed Elsevier, Inc., Portsmouth, NH. All rights reserved. pp. 29–34, 37–39: Reprinted with permission from the National Writing Project. Strong, William. 2003. "Writing Across the Hidden Curriculum." *The Quarterly of the National Writing Project* 25(1):2–7, 38. pp. 47–48, 90, 133–134: Reprinted from Mitchell, Diana. 1996. "Writing to Learn Across the English Curriculum and the English Teacher." *English Journal* 85(5):93–97. Copyright © 1996 by the National Council of Teachers of English. Reprinted with permission. pp. 49–50, 51–52, 54, 56–57, 88, 89: Reprinted from Gere, Ann (ed.). 1985. *Roots in the Sawdust: Writing to Learn Across the*

Disciplines. Copyright © 1985 by the National Council of Teachers of English. Reprinted with permission. pp. 69, 70, 71: Reprinted from Strong, William. 1986. *Creative Approaches to Sentence Combining.* Copyright © 1986 by the National Council of Teachers of English. Reprinted with permission. pp. 84, 85, 86: Reprinted from Pugh, Sharon, et al. 1992. *Bridging: A Teacher's Guide to Metaphorical Thinking.* Copyright © 1992 by the National Council of Teachers of English. Reprinted with permission. pp. 160–164: Reprinted from Strong, William. 1983. "Writing: A Means to Meaning or How I Got from the Tastee Donut Shop to the Inn of the Seventh Mountain." *English Journal* 72(2). Copyright © 1983 by the National Council of Teachers of English. Reprinted with permission.

Printed in the United States of America
10 9 8 7 6 5 4   RRD-IN 09 08 07

3 2206 00210 8897

For my National Writing Project colleagues, whose lives offer insights into quality instruction

and

especially for biology teacher Bob Tierney, who led the writing-to-learn movement

CONTENTS

FOREWORD

Improving the teaching of writing has been the core mission of the National Writing Project for over thirty years. Universities have pursued composition studies as a discipline for even longer. Yet we are still faced with a growing need to improve the writing abilities of young people in our schools and universities. We are witness to the growing demand for advanced literacy skills from schools and businesses, and, more importantly, we see the need for all citizens to engage in the world of ideas.

Our professional organizations, our schools of education and the world of testing and assessment all have a stake in trying to improve our ability to write, to think on paper, to solve problems and simply to communicate with each other more effectively.

So why is this so difficult? Perhaps, because through most of the twentieth century, writing was considered a skill for the few. In the past, it was possible for a young adult with a high school diploma to get a job that would feed a family. That is no longer true. Jobs in manufacturing and the new knowledge industries now require high levels of literacy. But there is another more important answer—one that may be harder to recognize: The ability to write and read is key to controlling one's life. It is as simple as that.

How do we make this idea clear for all young people? Early in my teaching career, Nancy Martin, from the London Institute for Education, visited the New York City Writing Project and began a morning presentation to teachers by announcing, "Today we're going to do something completely different." As she spoke, she handed to each teacher two or three pieces of plain stationery and a stamped envelope. "This morning I want you to think hard about someone to whom you have been meaning to write for a long, long time. Then I want you to sit down right now and write that letter, put it in the envelope, and send it."

After a stunned silence, people slowly began to write, and little by little everyone in the room became lost in the charge. Some people became emotional; some were filled with pleasure as they recalled an event that had sparked the need to write. Others became sad as they considered the lost time and connection. When people finished, they were, in a word, stunned—first, by what they had written, and second, because by writing they had recovered an important part of their lives. Nancy, in her very no-nonsense voice, said, "You see! Powerful stuff, writing, particularly when you have something you want to say."

The need to communicate is basic to human experience. Writing helps us understand the world, helps us make decisions, and, when a person is taught well, writing is a lifelong pleasure.

So again, how do we make this idea clear and how do we realize the goal of supporting strong literacy skills for all young people? Part of the answer well may lie in this book. Much space has been given elsewhere to teaching the skills needed to produce short, timed essays; complete applications for jobs; and write short answers used to test for information. But writing is so much more than those things. To write is to develop a powerful set of skills that helps us explore and make sense of the world, and to engage in and understand the ideas that have an impact on our lives.

Professor Bill Strong has been a colleague and director of the Utah Writing Project for over 25 years. He is unusual among professors in that he has spent a significant portion of his professional life working with, listening to, and engaging with school teachers of every grade and every subject. He has written many books for teachers that draw from these same experiences. This latest book draws on a deep well of knowledge, not only about the craft of writing, but also about the content of writing. The result is a text that reflects years of paying attention to what works with, and for, emerging writers.

Teachers will find in this book a rich array of materials and strategies, as well as an underlying theory of action that will serve them for many years. In this way, our profession grows stronger and we are better able to meet the changing landscape that faces each generation of students. Bill Strong's contribution to this dialogue is evidence of the richness and importance of intellectual and professional communities, like the National Writing Project, that provide the starting points for such profession-long discussions.

As Executive Director of the National Writing Project, I encourage readers of this book to visit our web site [www.writingproject.org] to learn more about the effective teaching of writing. Our web site provides links to 185 NWP local writing projects across the nation—sites that assist thousands of teachers each year with exciting opportunities for professional development. We invite your involvement.

Richard Sterling
Executive Director
National Writing Project
University of California, Berkeley

ABOUT THE AUTHOR

William Strong has worked in middle school and high school literacy instruction for four decades. Besides presenting hundreds of workshops and many conference talks, he has authored a dozen books and teacher resources, including *Coaching Writing: The Power of Guided Practice* (Heinemann, 2001). He was the consulting author in composition for the *Writer's Choice* textbooks (Glencoe/McGraw-Hill, 2001) and the series consultant for *English Matters!* (Grolier, 2000), and he served for ten years on the National Writing Project Advisory Board. At Utah State University, he founded the Utah Writing Project and directed it for twenty-five years while also teaching courses in content area literacy, English education, and writing. Both his teaching and his research have received college-level awards, and he has been honored by professional groups for his statewide leadership in pre-service and in-service teacher education. He enjoys downhill skiing, motorcycle touring, and working with school districts and National Writing Project sites. Readers can contact the author at Bill.Strong@usu.edu.

An Introduction
to Insight

All I ever know is the first line, the first sentence, the first page.
—Erskine Caldwell

First Impressions

You and I have probably never met, but we already have a relationship.

Why? Because my opening sentence, pressed with care upon the page, anchors the voice of this book. It speaks to you across great distances of time and space—and perhaps even greater distances of culture and personal experience. It invites your attention, and urges you on.

Early this morning, not long after sunrise, I thought of you as I jogged along a quiet two-lane country road in the high desert country just south of Santa Fe, New Mexico. The air was cool in the shadows of cottonwoods. I imagined your eyes gliding hawk-like across these words as you began to picture a reddish-brown landscape where nothing moved in the gray light. Would you see the old rolls of barbed wire, coiled like black tumbleweed? Would you hear the light crunch of gravel or meadowlarks welcoming the first day of summer? Would you circle back to where a hand-carved wooden cross stood among the roadside rocks and sagebrush to mark a place of tears?

You'd do none of these things, I knew, unless I could stir your imagination, with clear description and an honest voice. I wanted my words to intersect with this moment in your life, whether in a bookstore, classroom, faculty lounge, or somewhere else. First impressions matter—but especially so when personal learning, characterized by insight, is the shared work of a relationship. As used here, "insight" refers to flashes of enlightenment or surprise, a sudden "seeing from within." And to achieve insight, one must be involved, attentive, relaxed.

Like now.

This book deals with **writing as a tool for learning** in *all* content areas. By "writing," I mean activities like note-taking, drawing, summarizing, brainstorming, and metaphor-building, in addition to creating thoughtful sentences that cluster into coherent paragraphs. More specifically, this book focuses on increasing student motivation, enhancing long-term learning, and easing the workload shouldered by teachers across the middle school and high school grades. It's about working smarter, not harder.

I aim to be a friendly, thought-provoking companion to new and veteran teachers in diverse disciplines. I invite attention to strategies that support schooling's most basic aims—emotional and intellectual engagement—and I especially celebrate the work of those who teach for insight, often against daunting odds.

"Work," as Kahlil Gibran (1923/1975, p. 28) once put it, "is love made visible." To me, this is a perfect description of good teaching. It's a matter, to use Mother Teresa's phrase, of doing "small things with great love" (Scott, 2002, p. 35).

Work and Play

Now, glancing back at the paragraphs in the first section of this introduction, you can't see my spiral-bound notebook with its crossed-out sentences—and you don't know how long it took to write what you've read in moments. After all, finished text is seamless, its process of construction invisible. In my opening lines, I hoped to avoid the mind-numbing jargon of education, but I also didn't want to insult your intelligence with the kind of prose that puts its feet on the coffee table. I had no appetite for the first strategy and too much respect for the teaching profession to use the second.

Of course, I'm hardly alone in saying that careful writing is hard work—for us and for our students. Listen to a professional like John McPhee (in Murray, 1990, p. 124) who makes his living at the word processor:

> The first part—the lead, the beginning—is the hardest part of all to write. . . . You could start in any of many places. What will you choose?

Or listen to wordsmith Joan Didion (in Murray, 1990, p. 121):

> What's so hard about the first sentence is that you're stuck with it. Everything else is going to flow out of that sentence. And by the time you lay down the first two sentences, your options are all gone.

So the writing was work, but it was also fun. I liked the challenge, just as I enjoy skiing on bright winter afternoons, with my downhill shadow offering instant feedback on how I'm doing. Watching it swoop through turns, there's nowhere else I'd rather be. All that matters is paying attention. For you, the pleasure of paying attention might come from making music, shooting baskets, quilting, playing video games, doing crossword puzzles, or working at a potter's wheel. If you know the feeling of doing something for the challenge and fun of it— what psychologist Mihaly Csikszentmihalyi (1990) calls "flow"—you understand my point about mental and physical focus. Optimal experience, or flow, results from testing our own limits to see what we can do.

Skiing is one such test for me, and writing is another. I try to ski relaxed and alert, free from mental chatter and self-criticism. It's a state of mind in which I give full attention to the moment-to-moment experience—the swells and dips of the terrain, the feel of the snow—instead of worrying about how I look. The same goes for writing. I try to silence self-doubt and inner criticism by first following the thread of unfolding sentences—even though I'm unsure of their direction—and then by paying attention to their emerging meanings.

Let me explain. As I whisper what I've written, listening closely and tinkering to get the words right, language itself becomes a kind of "shadow-teacher," showing me the way. Just as I return to the same slopes in different light and snow conditions, I often revisit what I've written, seeing whether I can make the text clearer, tighter, or more vivid. It's interesting to see what I can learn.

To understand this same idea from another angle, consider the words of poet William Stafford (in Murray, 1990, p. 162), one of the great teachers of the twentieth century:

> I'm not alone when I'm writing—the language itself, like a kind of trampoline, is there helping me.

Stafford believed that the act of writing helps us "catch the bounce" of personal insights. In other words, we learn from our own writing to the extent we really pay attention to it.

So writing isn't something you learn once and for all, like the multiplication tables. It's something you continually learn how to do. For this reason, it's endlessly educational, for both teachers and students.

Learning Together

Why do I share this background? First, clear, effective writing is among the most demanding tasks most of us will ever do—and therefore it deserves special attention from those of us who presume to teach young adults. This book's ideas and writing invitations may challenge you. But as you engage honestly in writing for insight, I hope you'll come to value the content of your reflections, feel pride in the form of your work, and learn much from processes in which you participate—ones you can use in your own teaching. For example, writing a piece of your own literacy story will help you absorb the lessons of personal experience; but *sharing* that story—and hearing the stories of others—will help you become a reflective practitioner (Schon, 1983) who values student writing and uses this knowledge to excite learning in your field.

Second, this is a teacher education book with attitude. At one level, it shares a philosophy of writing instruction and practical, classroom-tested strategies for all content areas, but at another level, it's a clear call to arms that targets fakery as education's Public Enemy Number One. Visit middle school and high school classrooms as I often do, and you'll see many students who view learning as boring and pointless. Sure, they go through the motions—handing in reports, taking tests, shuffling from class to class—but the lights have gone out, and nobody's home. Often these are the same kids who were bright-eyed and eager in elementary school. But somewhere along the way, busywork and mindless activities and paint-by-numbers teaching conspired to snuff out personal insight and the joy of learning. You and I will exacerbate the problem unless we're part of the solution.

Third, this book asserts the power of the "I" pronoun as well as the power of collaboration. Both are forces for lifelong learning. Several dynamic teachers have contributed to this volume, offering useful ideas for motivating middle school and high school learners. Their ideas are showcased mainly as process writing tasks, complete with grading rubrics. While I can't offer double-your-money-back guarantees on these assignments, I think you'll find them adaptable to a range of disciplines. At the very least, these activities will stimulate your thinking about parallel approaches. Just as my voice will mentor you in this book, the voices of my teacher education students and my National Writing Project colleagues have helped shape my thoughts about the development of personal insight. I thank them for their instruction.

And now a small confession. As this book's first reader, I've reread and rewritten the words many times to get them right. Doing so, I've thought of you as an intelligent, discerning reader who often asks, "What next?" and "So what?" It's my job to respond.

As I reread the words, I can feel your identity merging with mine. It's my voice, but as I read through your eyes, I have to change words, rearrange paragraphs, add examples, and tighten language. In fact, much of my writing time is spent *reading*, not writing. The words have to make sense to me before they can make sense to you, but my anticipation of your reading has somehow enabled me to write them.

I encourage you to do as I've done—to meet the text halfway, questioning it for answers. Try to be a responsive reader, one who is intellectually open and willing to interact. Trust your responses, and write for insight at the end of each chapter. Then share your thinking with others.

Why Writing Matters

Now that you have some sense of my aims and approach, let's examine a frame of reference for this book's key ideas and recommendations. This brief section will help you understand, from a national perspective, why writing matters.

The status of secondary school writing was first revealed in a study that linked national survey research with 259 in-school observations (Applebee, 1981). The report revealed many eye-opening facts, including these two:

- Only three percent of class time in the observed classes was spent on writing of at least paragraph length.
- Thirty-two percent of the surveyed teachers said they *never* assigned such writing.

(p. 99)

The so-called "writing" activities included "multiple choice and fill-in-the-blank exercises, math calculations, and short-answer responses requiring only a sentence or two"—in other words, tasks of "mechanically 'slotting-in' the missing information" (p. 99). And incredibly, homework assignments of paragraph-length writing or more occurred only *three* percent of the time (p. 93).

As for attention to writing process—for example, helping students generate ideas or find ways to think about their topics—the average elapsed time between assignment and activity was only about three minutes (Applebee, 1981, p. 96). During these moments, teachers responded to burning student questions—"Can I use pencil? How long does it have to be?"—and writing began. And when papers came in, most teachers marked errors in mechanics (71 percent of teachers) versus engaging the ideas expressed (less than 20 percent of teachers) (p. 97).

Applebee's snapshot captured the reality of secondary school writing many years ago. But of course that was before the publication of *A Nation at Risk* (NCEE, 1983) and other hard-hitting reform documents (Boyer, 1983; Goodlad, 1984; Sizer, 1984) calling for massive overhaul of American secondary education and increased attention to writing. "Surely things have improved by now," you're thinking.

Maybe and maybe not. According to the National Commission on Writing in America's Schools and Colleges, sponsored by the College Entrance Examination Board, writing is "clearly the most neglected" of the traditional three Rs and is "increasingly shortchanged throughout the school and college years"—this despite the fact that it is "how students connect the dots in their knowledge" (CEEB, 2003, p. 3). In addition, "[m]ore than 90 percent of midcareer professionals recently cited the 'need to write effectively' as a skill 'of great importance' in their day-to-day work" (p. 11).

The same themes are echoed in an ACT report, *Crisis at the Core* (ACT, 2004). In fact, of the 1.2 million high school graduates who took the 2004 ACT assessment, only 22 percent were deemed ready for college in the basic academic areas of English, math, and science—and many did not have the skills to succeed in workforce training.

The commission argues that writing is central to education. "If students are to make knowledge their own," the authors assert, "they must struggle with the details, wrestle with the facts, and rework raw information and dimly understood concepts into language they can communicate to someone else" (CEEB, p. 9). Moreover, writing will assume increasing importance, as our technology-driven, knowledge-based economy makes new demands on workers. To summarize: "Writing today is not a frill for the few, but an essential skill for the many" (p. 11).

So once again the alarm has been sounded. Therefore, we shouldn't be too surprised that as of February and March 2005, writing tests have been added to the new ACT and SAT assessments, which are widely used for college admissions. The ACT assessment has objective items related to language skills, plus an optional 30-minute essay prompt. The writing section of the new SAT has multiple-choice items and a required 25-minute essay. Your students will find sample prompts—and test-taking advice—at the ACT and SAT web sites.

What Assessments Reveal

How are we now doing when it comes to writing instruction? Each year, the National Assessment of Educational Progress (NAEP) tests narrative, informative, and persuasive writing. Students are asked to write stories or personal essays, to share knowledge or convey messages clearly, and to take positions that they can support and develop. Most state assessments follow a similar pattern.

Drawing on NAEP progress data, there's both good news and bad news. On one hand, four out of five students can write at a "basic" level or better. On the other hand, most students "cannot write well enough to meet the demands they face in higher education and the emerging work environment." In fact, "only one-quarter [of students] at each grade level are at or above the 'proficient' level. Even more telling, only one in a hundred is thought to be 'advanced'" (CEEB, p. 16).

Let's return to the idea that writing is often shortchanged in the secondary school curriculum. In its 2002 assessment, NAEP researchers asked eighth graders how often they wrote thoughts or observations in a log or journal. The researchers then correlated these self-reports with actual writing performance (scale scores ranged from 0 to 300) and computed averages. Take a moment to compare the average scores of those who "never or hardly ever" wrote in a journal—about 36 percent of the NAEP sample—versus those who claimed to write "at least once a week," in the following table.

Journal Writing Self-Reports Correlated with Writing Proficiency

Total N = 111,216	Never or hardly ever	A few times a year	Once or twice a month	At least once a week
Average scale score	143	155	157	158
Percentage	36%	17%	17%	30%

Source: NCES/NAEP, 2002.

The NAEP researchers also wanted to know how often eighth graders were asked by their teachers to write more than one draft of a paper. They then correlated student self-reports of revision with the average scale scores in writing. Not surprisingly, those students who claimed their teachers never asked for revision did worse on the NAEP assessment than those who were often asked to revise (see following table). Good teaching tends to produce desired results.

Revision Self-Reports Correlated with Writing Proficiency

Total N = 106,722	Never	Sometimes	Always
Average Scale Score	145	150	159
Percentage	10%	51%	39%

Source: NCES/NAEP, 2002.

To conclude its landmark report, the National Commission on Writing recommends that "the nation's leaders place writing squarely in the center of the school agenda" (CEEB, p. 26). Commission authors are "troubled by findings that most students spend little time writing" and note that it is "small wonder that students do not write well" (p. 28). Three far-reaching recommendations are presented:

- **Time:** The Commission believes that the amount of time most students spend writing should be at least *doubled*. This time can be found through assignments at home and by encouraging more writing during the school day in curriculum areas not traditionally associated with it. This change alone will do more to improve writing performance that anything else states or local school leaders can do. [Italics added.]
- **Writing across the curriculum:** We strongly endorse writing across the curriculum. The concept of doubling writing time is feasible because of *the near-total neglect of writing* outside English departments. In history, foreign languages, mathematics, home economics, science, physical education, art, and social science, all students can be encouraged to write more—and to write more effectively. [Italics added.]
- **Assignments:** We suggest more out-of-school time for writing. From elementary school on, students should expect to produce written work as part of their normal homework assignments. Just 15 minutes of writing four nights a week would add 33 percent to the amount of time the average elementary student spends writing. Parents should be writing partners with their children, sharing their own writing with them and reviewing written work as their children complete it. *Research is crystal clear: Schools that do well insist that students write every day and that teachers provide regular and timely feedback with the support of parents.* [Italics added.]

(p. 28)

And in its five-point "Writing Agenda for the Nation," the commission emphasizes that "writing is every teacher's responsibility" and that "developing critical thinkers and writers should be understood as one of the central works of education" (p. 32).

Writing on the Home Front

It's the "near-total neglect of writing" in content areas outside English that has prompted me to write this book. I take the view—one supported by persuasive research (Langer and Applebee, 1987)—that writing can serve as a powerful tool for content learning, a way of empowering students to construct meaning and develop insights.

What do I mean by this? On a personal level, think about everyday activities when you've set and accomplished written goals—perhaps a shopping list, or a to-do list, or an exercise regimen. Writing gave you power, because it externalized your grocery memory, or created an errand sequence, or set up a record-keeping system for your jogs around the neighborhood. Of course, as a beginning or experienced teacher, you also use writing as a powerful planning tool, as a way of organizing instruction.

What's useful for us is also useful for students. Writing helps them collect notes, plan future action, frame questions, monitor their own learning, and engage in a rich array of imaginative and cognitive tasks. For example, as students draw a time line of events, the historical sequence becomes more organized and visual in their minds. As they write imaginatively from a character's viewpoint, they project themselves into stories or problem-solving scenarios. As they organize research notes to develop a media-assisted class report, they rehearse and refine important ideas.

In *Writing to Learn*, William Zinsser sums up the power of writing this way:

> Writing is a tool that enables people in every discipline to wrestle with facts and ideas. It's a physical activity, unlike reading. Writing requires us to operate some kind of mechanism—pencil, pen, typewriter, word processor—for getting thoughts on paper. It compels us by the repeated effort of language to go after those thoughts and to organize them and present them clearly. It forces us to keep asking, "Am I saying what I want to say?" Very often the answer is no. It's a useful piece of information.
>
> (1998, p. 49)

Although writing assists thinking in countless ways, many of us ignore this fact when it comes to schoolwork. Generally speaking, we view student writing mainly as an *assessment tool*—something students do to prove mastery or get a grade—but not as a *tool for learning* (or refining) content knowledge.

Why is this? The answer, I think, goes back to personal experience—and that it's only natural to teach as we've been taught. For many of us, "school writing" conjures up images of book reports, term papers, and essay exams—not to mention grammar worksheets and red pencil comments. Because we often associate school writing with uninspired graded tasks, we tend to discount its potential for helping students learn new ideas. Also, we may be inclined to "assign" writing but not to teach with and through it. That's a huge problem for effective instruction.

Actually, there's a big difference between **expressive writing tasks**—brief explorations that assist immediate learning—and **process writing tasks** that help kids consolidate and communicate their knowledge. This book's early chapters show how expressive work invites learners to externalize their inner speech in order to "know what they know." Typically, these are ungraded exercises that students use to connect personally to class lectures, assigned reading, or content discussions. Later chapters build on the expressive writing foundation to consider process writing tasks and ideas for coaching quality writing. Generally, these are graded activities that students develop through processes of brainstorming, researching, and organizing, and are followed by drafting, peer response, revision, and thoughtful self-assessment.

Of course, process approaches to instruction are hardly new. For example, hands-on lab activities, in-class debates, role-playing exercises, and simulations are used by many content teachers to invite active learning. Such strategies—as well as time-tested ones like study guides, vocabulary previews, and note-taking worksheets—are often called *instructional scaffolds* (Bruner, 1978). These are temporary supports that help learners construct and internalize knowledge. Thus, the teacher's role shifts from "information dispenser" to "learning facilitator"—and expert teachers are those who orchestrate interesting sequences of increasingly complex activity. They aim not so much to "cover" material as to "uncover" it. They teach for insight.

My framework for integrating expressive and academic writing is shown in Figure I-1 (Strong, 2001). It draws on the work of Fran Claggett (1996) who helped synthesize the seminal theories of James Britton (1970) and James Moffett (1983).

FIGURE I-1   Four Writing Domains

Informative/Functional Texts (*Purpose: to convey information or to explain ideas, facts, or processes*)	Literary/Poetic Texts (*Purpose: to give shape to an idea, experience, or observation*)	Argumentative/Persuasive Texts (*Purpose: to influence or convince another of one's ideas or judgments*)
School Essays description, profile/ biography, process/ procedures, information report, research report	***Narratives*** adventure/mysteries, fables/tall tales, fantasy/ science fiction, historical accounts, realistic stories	***School Essays*** literary analysis, problem/solution, controversial issue, evaluation, speculation
Real-World Discourse Forms brochures, business reports, case studies, charts, graphs, career plans, directions, guidelines, histories, holiday greetings, how-to manuals, minutes, newsletters, overviews, pamphlets, posters, resumes, regulations, rules, summaries, surveys, tables, etc.	***Poetry*** ballads, songs; concrete, visual; formula verse; free verse; rhyme formats ***Scripts*** dialogues, monologues, radio plays, video skits, hypermedia ***Practical Texts*** journals, logs, letters (all types), newspaper stories, interviews, obituaries, profiles, parodies, satires, speeches, etc.	***Real-World Discourse Forms*** advertisements, awards, tributes, commercials, complaints, cover letters, editorials, eulogies, evaluations (others), feature articles, invocations, job applications, marketing memos, petitions, proposals, rebuttals, requests, reviews (all types), self-assessments, warnings, Web pages, etc.

Expressive/Writing-to-Learn Texts (*Purpose: to discover, identify, or clarify ideas or experiences for self or for others*)

School Essays
literacy autobiography, autobiographical incident, personal reflection, multi-genre essay, triptych (memoir) essay

Discourse Forms
lists; sketches; diagrams; journal or learning log entries; notes from reading or interviews; e-mail exchanges; letters of advice, affection, apology, complaint, congratulations, invitation, protest, self-disclosure, sympathy, thanks; responses to literature, etc.

Source: Strong, 2001, p. 154.

Notice that the framework outlines four kinds of writing tasks which include many familiar assignments, or school-genre, as well as real-world types of writing. Notice too that the expressive domain has its own school-based genres—mainly narrative—as a foundation for the upper domains. Thus, *writing-to-learn work provides scaffolding for more formalized—and usually graded—tasks.* Of course, solid academic programs achieve balance across the domains.

Mapping the Terrain

This book's early chapters show how expressive writing can motivate active learning, whereas later ones emphasize how process writing can develop and extend student knowledge.

My first aim is provocative; the second, strategic. First, I hope to stimulate your interest, prompt conversation, and motivate your writing. As you discuss ideas from these chapters—and share written responses with your colleagues—you'll develop a range of insights, both personal and practical. Second, I hope to engage you in useful activities. You'll try your hand, for example, at developing imaginative writing tasks and rubrics tied to your content area—a welcome diversion from the tired approach of assigning end-of-the-chapter questions.

In Chapter 1, "Writing from the Inside Out," you'll consider the role of narrative knowledge in content learning. In particular, you'll see the usefulness of student-written learning histories in all content areas and how expressive writing can lead naturally to reflective writing. The instrumental use of narrative, with its potential to personalize learning, provides focus for this foundational chapter.

In Chapter 2, "Challenging the Hidden Curriculum," you'll reflect on teaching practices that often lead to negative outcomes (e.g., resistance from students) in traditional school writing. You'll also consider how middle school and high school teachers use learning logs to motivate expressive writing and increase in-depth learning—all with a reduction of traditional workload.

In Chapter 3, "Exploring Expressive Writing," you'll extend your learning by studying practical ideas such as guided imagery, dramatic scenarios (or "cases"), role-playing, and dialogue writing; you'll also examine brief student texts generated by these strategies. A range of engaging activities will mainly focus on ungraded writing—the kind you can assign "for fun."

In Chapter 4, "Helping Basic Writers Succeed," you'll get useful ideas about ways to help skill-deficient students write expressively. You'll see how to develop writing fluency by using strategic content-based activities and minilessons that teach skills. Here's where you search for ideas to help kids who may lack motivation and basic skills.

In Chapter 5, "Tapping the Power of Metaphor," you'll drop by my office on a snowy morning when I'm working on a couple of poems for Valentine's Day. You'll examine the soft underbelly of thought—specifically, metaphorical thinking—to see how it not only enhances expressive writing but also forges personal connections, or imaginative links, to curriculum content.

In Chapter 6, "Designing Assignments and Rubrics," you'll see how academic writing tasks can emerge from an expressive base in journals and learning logs. By attending to assignment design and grading rubrics, you'll learn how to better motivate students, invite collaboration, and help them monitor their own thinking and self-assessment processes. Additional assignments are found in Appendix D, "Content Area Writing Assignments."

In Chapter 7, "Managing the Writing Process," you'll revisit basic principles of writing process instruction and reflect on the recursiveness principle—how writers "go back" in their writing to "move ahead." You'll also learn the nuts and bolts of peer response groups and see how such activities can prompt self-assessment. This information builds on Chapter 6 and links to Chapter 8.

In Chapter 8, "Coaching and Judging Writing," you'll explore assessment. This chapter reminds you that the timing of feedback matters, and that grading doesn't have to be a black hole that sucks away all your physical and mental energy. You'll find practical, teacher-tested strategies for responding to student papers in efficient, helpful ways, plus more ideas on portfolio assessment.

In Chapter 9, "Researching Outside the Box," you'll consider alternatives to the traditional high-stakes research paper, which students pretend to write and teachers pretend to read. You'll see that high-interest formats—Saturation Reports, I-Search papers, and Multigenre Research Projects—provide exciting contexts for inquiry, documentation of findings, and related research skills.

And in Chapter 10, "Writing as a Means to Meaning," you'll travel with me to the Tastee Donut Shop in New Orleans to consider how writing can trigger insight. You'll also learn about a powerful new audio CD for assisting student writing, review key points about writing as a tool for learning, and see again that clear writing, whatever the genre, stimulates ongoing thought.

Four appendixes conclude this book. Appendix A describes a Literacy Autobiography Case Study task that you will probably find enjoyable and eye-opening. Appendix B, drawn from development work at the Northwest Central Regional Educational Laboratory (NCREL), provides generic graphic organizers that many content teachers use to support note-taking and writing. Appendix C lists Bob Tierney's "trigger words," which invite students to write metaphorically about target concepts in a discipline. Finally, Appendix D outlines several content area writing assignments (with grading rubrics) to supplement those provided elsewhere in the book.

Listening to Students

Before acknowledging colleagues who helped shape this book, I want to look back to words written 40 years ago by one of my high school students. Linda's unsolicited and unexpected letter was two pages long and neatly typed, and I've never forgotten its passionate advice to not quit teaching. Here was a quiet, almost invisible learner who understood what I was up to and wanted me to know that, yes, it *was* worth doing. Of course Linda saw my stumbles and heard the groans from some corners of her class, but through regular, ungraded writing-to-learn activities, she also saw what was at stake.

> I must commend you for making your classroom seem like a meeting of the minds more than a class. This is important. I never felt there was a prescribed course of study which had to be finished by the end of the year. Instead, I felt each day was made for discovery.

The stories drawn from my experience are used to emphasize key concepts. I also present, in abbreviated form, powerful ideas about language learning, cognitive development, and writing process. I highlight practical strategies, from ways to use learning logs to guidelines for creating effective writing tasks. And last, but certainly not least, I offer tips for managing the paper load with a smile.

For me, Linda's idea that each day is "made for discovery" remains exhilarating. As you read this book and engage in its activities, I hope you'll adopt her outlook and realize that writing for insight can enable many of your students to feel as she did. An open-minded attitude will also help with your own inevitable fatigue or impatience. Of course, I'll argue for thoughtful goal-setting and scaffolded teaching and explicit grading standards, but we both know that such aims must be enacted on your *own* terms, on your *own* turf. Good teaching is always personal.

My expression of faith is this: If you learn how to help students develop insights through writing, life-altering rewards will follow for you, just as they did for me. The first step in that learning is found in the "Write for Insight" activity at the end of this Introduction.

Acknowledgments

This book is dedicated to my National Writing Project colleagues, for all their insights into quality writing instruction—and especially to biology teacher Bob Tierney, who has been sharing writing-to-learn workshops since the early 1980s. Bob's great teaching is featured throughout this book, and I thank him for showing us the way.

Let me also thank the Utah Writing Project teachers, with whom I've been privileged to work for more than 25 years. Colleagues like Lynda Hamblin, Richard Harmston, Margaret Pettis, Nicole Robinson, Margaret Rostkowski, Jeff Stephens, Denice Turner, and Linda Warren—and others too numerous to mention—have given to the greater good without hesitation. Utah's literacy instruction would be impoverished without them.

I also need to acknowledge the students in my Utah State University classes for contributing work to this book. Support of an equally welcome kind came from convivial university colleagues who participate in a monthly writing response group. My thanks go to Christine, Brock, Keith, Ken, Lynn, Michael, Sylvia, and others who dipped into these chapters and offered helpful advice.

As for colleagues farther afield—Ann Bayer, Sheridan Blau, Rebekah Caplan, Sally Hampton, Harry Noden, Dan Kirby, Tom Newkirk, Carol Booth Olson, Sondra Perl, Will Pitkin, Tom Romano, Kathy Rowlands, Karen Spear, Nat Teich, Richard Sterling, Fran Weinberg, Jeff Wilhelm, Denny Wolfe—let me recall a fine sentence of Gabriel Garcia Marquez: "In the end all books are written for your friends."

Several outside reviewers made suggestions that improved this book's utility. I express sincere appreciation to each of them: Cathy Fleischer, Eastern Michigan University; Louel Gibbons, The University of Alabama; Stephanie Kirby, Maxwell Elementary; Carol Booth-Olson, University of California–Irvine; and Mark Reimer, Steinbach Regional Secondary School.

Kudos also go to my great editor at Allyn and Bacon, Aurora Martinez, and to editorial assistant Kevin Shannon, for their faith in this project and for shepherding the manuscript through production. I also appreciate the excellent production work of Annette Joseph and Kevin Sullivan.

Finally, and most importantly, I acknowledge Carol Strong, the woman whose insights about things that matter are both clear and true. In this book I try to honor what she has taught me.

WRITE FOR INSIGHT ACTIVITY

What thoughts did this Introduction evoke? That's a question only you can answer. As you jot responses in a learning log and compare notes with others, you might find your ideas influenced by prior experiences—such as those with textbooks (you might dislike them) or with writing tasks (you might avoid them whenever possible). On the other hand, you might already know something about instructional scaffolds in teaching or have some beliefs about the value of writing-to-learn activities.

In your Learning Log, jot down: (1) key ideas of the Introduction, (2) your insights about those ideas, and (3) your questions. As you do this writing, reflect on what you bring to the text in terms of experience. In a follow-up class session, you may be asked to share your log entry with a partner or colleague. Read what this person has to say and talk it over. Afterward, write briefly about the results of your interchange with your partner, explaining how your insights were confirmed, challenged, or extended. As you'll see, this follow-up writing serves to consolidate your learning—helping you "know what you know." Share a copy of this text (that is, two Learning Log entries) with your instructor.

1 Writing from the Inside Out

We write to taste life twice, in the moment, and in retrospection.

—Anaïs Nin

Remembered Writing

"There's a story in your picture," the nun says. Her black sleeves are like bat's wings, a whisper in passing as she swoops nearby, and her wire-framed glasses catch the light. Outside, a gray Oregon rain makes tiny, trickling rivers on the tall schoolroom windows; inside, there is radiator heat, drying wool, and fourth-grade desks in rows, bolted to long wooden runners. The desks are creaky flip-top structures of oak and iron, well-inscribed by other young scholars in parochial school uniforms.

Head on my desk, I bend to the task, leaving a world of faded pictures above a dusty chalkboard. I'm not much of a writer, but I enter a world where I'm astride a pale yellow horse—Palomino, I'll call it—with a dog at my side. The horse is rounded and solid beneath me, and my boots are gray with Texas trail-dust. It's a rocky landscape shadowed by cottonwoods, a tree I've heard about in other cowboy stories. The dog moves out ahead, and as he does, I'm remembering a story told by my father's logging partner, one about a small canyon infested with rattlesnakes. Suddenly the dog freezes, one paw raised. Hidden nearby, just off the trail, a huge rattlesnake lies coiled and hissing, ready to strike the horse. I rein him in, quiet him down. Easy, boy, easy. That was a close one.

A few days later, I am in real danger, not merely that of my imagination. I'm sent upstairs, past the office of Sister Mother Superior, to the end of the hall, the hallowed ground of seventh and eighth graders. I read my paragraphs about how the day was saved by the cowboy's trusty companion, and the nun leads a brief recitation of its virtues. As the smallest kid in fourth grade but not the dumbest, I catch the drift. Her aim is to embarrass the upper-class students into better writing. When she asks me about my inspiration, she has a mute on her hands.

It's during those days that my story appears in the school newspaper, a faded purple-ink publication run off on ditto masters. There's a secret pleasure in seeing my words in typed form. I read them over and over. To me, they look "grown up," different from the cursive writing practice that leaves a red welt on my third finger.

I take the newspaper home, knowing that being in print confers a new kind of status on my story. Maybe it *is* good, I tell myself.

My reading takes place in the kitchen, with my dad home from work in the timber, my mom fixing supper, and my sister underfoot. My dad sits at a chrome kitchen table with a laminate top. Reading to my parents feels different from reading to the kids at school. It's less scary in one sense, more scary in another. After all, I *want* them to like it. Dad nods, and I put the story away.

Somehow, it reappears on a Sunday afternoon at my grandparents' house, a small farm cottage with an oil-burning stove, a horsehair sofa, and lace doilies everywhere. The living room is filled with light and the steady ticking of an old pendulum clock. The after-dinner routine is coffee and homemade cherry pie and the adults settling in. My grandfather is lean and white-haired, a Quaker-like man with fourth-grade schooling to match mine; my grandmother is heavy-set, with blunt opinions.

"Billy's story was in the school paper," my mother says, passing it around.

My grandparents rise on cue. "Oh, a story? Let's hear it."

I'm on the spot, set up by my mother. Yet as I begin to read, I can feel myself again at the center of things, creating and sustaining a world. Dust rises from the trail. Wind moves through the cottonwood, stirring the leaves. The horse is rounded and solid beneath me, with my family circled around and listening.

"Why, that's very good," they say to me afterwards. And I grin in reply.

Narration as Knowledge

Why do I begin with a small story from my past? Because my experience is what I know. And it's this little experience plus many others—some not so happy—that have shaped my attitudes, beliefs, and skills in the area of writing. In other words, what I truly *know* about writing and the world results from what I've experienced, either directly (through immediate experiences) or indirectly (through reading and other vicarious means). Put simply, our stories enable us to tell what we know.

The notion of writing "from the inside out"—remembering key experiences and reflecting on their significance—provides the focus for Chapter 1. This simple, basic strategy works in all content area classrooms, as students are invited to recall past events that have shaped their attitudes, beliefs, and skills in an area of study. For example, what are their key memories in math and music, science and social studies, or health and humanities? Some experiences will be positive or exciting, others just the opposite. But all of them teach. The point isn't to fixate on the past but to learn from it. And writing is just the tool, regardless of content area, for accomplishing this aim.

It is so important to understand where your attitudes, beliefs, and skills come from because knowledge is power. Understanding your learning history helps you realize that you're involved in a lifelong learning adventure and that you have the means—because of your self-knowledge—to create positive experiences for yourself. For example, the next time your old habit of procrastination rears its ugly head, it may be possible, using self-knowledge and self-discipline as your twin swords, to send this many-headed beast howling back to his lair.

Asking secondary students to recall stories of significant learning almost always leads to insights. For example, when Michael writes about "being put on the spot and made fun of," you better understand his scowling red face and crossed arms as you try to involve him in a history discussion. When Heather tells of her dad's celebration of her math award, you understand the dynamics of her nose-to-the-grindstone motivation. When Maria praises last year's teacher "who helping to better my English speaking," you're reminded of why you became a teacher in the first place.

Should stories about past learning be graded? I recommend simply "checking" the papers and savoring the insights they provide. In reading them quickly, it's helpful to have a packet of sticky notes handy. For each student, jot down a comment or two like the following:

- "Mark, your computer camp story hooked me! Tell me more!"
- "Ali, I hear your concerns. This year is a fresh start in math—let's talk!"
- "Emily, I look forward to knowing you better. Career goals?"

Brief personal comments like these communicate your interest in individuals and your desire to get them involved in content learning. Later, as students study in class or work on assignments, you can roam the room, doing on-the-spot mini-conferences—or you can invite students to your desk, with writing in hand. Your comments will set the direction for dialogue, but you can also use general prompts like this one to refresh your memory: "Now, Tony, remind me of your story."

For most students, having a teacher *solicit* and *value* their personal learning story will be a totally new experience. Expect some students to be a bit wary or tongue-tied, while others might try to share lots of background information and detail. To manage both situations, announce to students your aims for the mini-conference—to know them as individuals, not to evaluate them—and explain that you'll have an egg timer (or some such device) to limit the length of conferences. Of course, for some students, a quick flip of the egg timer will provide the extra bit of attention they need.

The point of writing and conferring isn't simply for students to share cute little stories but instead to reflect on their significance. As a responder to writing, or as a listener in a mini-conference, your key questions will be ones like these:

- "So what do you think this experience *taught* you?"
- "How did this experience help *shape* who you are today?"
- "How does this experience relate to *other* stories in your learning history?"

Inviting students to consider such questions in advance of a mini-conference not only focuses instruction but also encourages in-depth insights, the kind not often seen in some secondary classrooms. Such assessment activities pay long-term dividends in terms of motivation, goal-setting, and willingness to engage in content learning.

Sharing Our Stories

Just for a moment, picture yourself at a family celebration—Thanksgiving, say, or maybe a Fourth of July get-together. You're among family and friends, and there's lots of food, while everyone gets reacquainted. Uncle Jake asks, "So how's it going?" And Aunt Marge gives you a big hug and says, "Now tell me everything you've been doing."

Stories frame our lives. Thus, we shouldn't be too surprised that primitive stories like "Milk spill!" are among the first things we learn to say and that more complicated summative tales, called obituaries, are our exit stories. Of course, in between our childhood stories and our obituaries, we are continually telling stories to Uncle Jake and Aunt Marge and anyone who feigns even the slightest interest. As psychologist Roger Schank puts it, "Communication consists of selecting the stories that we know and telling them to others at the right time" (1990, p. 12).

Take this one. Not long after writing the those words, I was driving through the rugged Utah mountains during a no-nonsense snowstorm, the kind we often get in February. I was fifteen miles from the nearest town when I saw the hitchhiker, a lean, slump-shouldered man in his late thirties or early forties—collar up against his beard, thumb out. How had he gotten there? This was an open stretch of blizzard-swept road just below jagged peaks. I hesitated for a moment, thinking about newspaper accounts of hitchhikers and foul play, then slowed my car and pulled over.

As it turned out, there was a resort area about a mile off the road, where the man worked. His sister lived in a nearby town, but he didn't want her driving the treacherous canyon road in bad weather. Generally, his winters were spent building furniture in his Idaho shop, but this one had been different. He'd taken four months off to be with his father—they'd traveled to Texas, California, and other places—because his dad was dying. For years, his father had taught physical education and coached high school kids. And over the past weekend, the family had buried his father.

I'm giving you the broad outline of the hitchhiker narrative, without the rich details and anecdotes that tumbled forward over our half-hour together. Roger Schank defines stories as "a set of interesting things that one has already thought up and stored, ready to say when necessary." "To get human beings to be intelligent," Schank adds, "means getting them to have stories to tell and having them hear and perhaps use the stories of others" (1990, p. 34). Of course, Schank is using the term "stories" in the broadest possible sense, to include whatever we know about the world, both directly (through personal experience) and more indirectly (through mediated and second-hand experience) in all content areas of the curriculum.

I regard the hitchhiker's tale as interesting—or intelligent, as Schank puts it—not only because it was so skillfully rendered but also because of its relevance to my story. You see, when I picked up the hitchhiker, my father was living in a handicap-accessible apartment attached to our home, one that I'd built for him a few years back. The hitchhiker's father was in a wheelchair, and so was mine. Like the hitchhiker, I too had made long-distance pilgrimages to places my father had known and loved. Driving through whirling snow, I explained how lucky I felt to have cared for my dad for nearly four years—giving him a quality of life he'd never get in a dreary care facility.

Little did I know, in uttering these words, that in the wee hours of the morning just a month later I'd find my own father dead on the bedroom floor—or that I'd soon carry his ashes back to Oregon for a memorial service with family and friends.

The point is that as our lives intersect through shared stories, we seek insights to illuminate our own situation. "You know, I can relate to that," we say. And then we tell *our* story, the one that helps us make sense of our experience.

Prompting Narrative

Telling a story to an interested listener—one who sometimes asks thoughtful questions—encourages the storyteller to revisit and reflect on experience, to see it in larger contexts. An active listener, like any active learner, wants to know more than the bare outline of a story. Interactive talk provides a very powerful rehearsal for narrative writing—including the memories of past content area learning.

You can make the processes of active listening explicit through in-class **modeling.** For example, as you tell a learning story tied to your content area, students can ask questions that serve as scaffolding for the details you provide. Your story might describe the disaster of your own middle school science project, or powerful feelings of your summer visit to Gettysburg, or your current struggles with statistics in a graduate class. Such explicit modeling can be followed with a "think-pair-share" activity so that all students can practice story-telling and question-asking about learning, first in pairs and then in small groups. Of course, because students have already practiced their stories—and because they have internalized some of their listeners' questions—they'll write more fluently about past learning events. Remember that a well-developed story provides the basis for reflective *insight*, a form of higher-order thinking.

Another useful prompt, also based on student-to-student talk, centers on **personal artifacts.** As kindergarten teachers discovered long ago, valued objects stimulate story-telling and reflection. What school-related artifacts do your students still keep in their dresser drawers, closets, or attics? Do they possess achievement ribbons, report cards, photos, old notebooks, yearbooks, athletic trophies, term papers, or other memorabilia? What vivid memories of learning are aroused by these artifacts? Again, through teacher modeling, students can be introduced to "time travel" via artifacts; and through think-pair-share activities, they can revisit earlier learning experiences in preparation for writing. Encourage students to reflect on the significance of past learning events—as well as their present-day relevance.

A third kind of prompt to stimulate memory writing involves the brainstorming technique of **clustering** (Rico, 1983, 1997) or free association "mapping." The process begins with a focus word or phrase in the center of a page. Basically, you allow your creative mind to follow its own path of random links and associations, however quirky they might seem to your more logical, task-oriented side. You quickly generate a series of words that radiate outward from your central focus and then use these to generate other links or connections. Don't dwell on the associations—just keep them coming as you enjoy the free-wheeling process of memory search. Inevitably, you'll feel or "see" what you want to write about—just as I did for the following cluster. Looking over my cluster in Figure 1-1, you'll recognize some key words for the brief story that opens this chapter.

Literacy Autobiographies

In my work with preservice and inservice teachers, I've read hundreds of literacy stories, and I always find them interesting. Each story has its own insights, and each provides a window into a life. Of course, the narratives I value most are those that reflect genuine inquiry into specific personal experiences, not those that lightly skim the surface. It always interests me, too, that as I reread well-told stories years later, I can often picture the individual authors in my mind's eye. Stories have staying power.

Here, for example, is an excerpt from a narrative written by Chris Gooch, a physical science teacher. This paper went through initial drafting, peer response, a reading by me, and final revision. Chris has strong memories of penmanship instruction, which influence his definition of "writing."

> Mr. S. worked hard to help us develop our cursive writing. Over the first few months of fifth grade, I became a student Mr. S. felt comfortable joking around with, even in front of other students. I was turning in an assignment by hand, and I knew full well that I risked the dreaded on-the-spot paper grading. Sure enough, my number was up and he checked my handwriting while I was still standing in front of him. "Chris," he said, "this looks just like chicken scratch."
>
> What he said was true. It did look like a chicken had convulsed on the paper. But that was not why the comment impacted me. The whole class knew that the teacher did not approve of my handwriting. I had always been looked at as an average, or slightly above average, student by my peers in both the academic and athletic spheres. Now, I was being publicly told my handwriting was below average! I handled the situation in a very casual fashion. I did not let on that I had taken a blow.
>
> I turned in countless more assignments on that brown recycled paper. I remember the wide rows divided by dashed lines. I remember using the dashed lines to practice proportion for upper- and lowercase letters. I remember the sound of my pencil on that paper and it still gives me goose bumps, similar to fingernails on a chalkboard. I do not remember, however, getting a positive comment from Mr. S. about my handwriting, especially not one the whole class heard. While my confidence was partially shaken, my stubbornness was just beginning. I decided I was no longer going to care how my teachers felt about my handwriting as long as they could read my work and the work itself was adequate. If it weren't for the next event I will talk about, I would still have that same attitude.

FIGURE 1-1   A Writing Memories Cluster

Do you find yourself drawn into the story that Chris has written—wanting to read more? Of course! You're curious about what happens next, and you're wondering how Chris has used his experience to inform his own work as a teacher. Remember, it is the reporting of experience, plus the reflection about it, that actually creates narrative knowledge. You'll see such reflection in the next sample text.

Music teacher Jennifer Fackrell had a very different sort of literacy narrative, one that centered on being able to cruise through high school with little engagement. As I read and commented on her draft, I tried to be encouraging but also to challenge her exploration of academic fears. The revision process, in Jennifer's words, was "an amazing thing" because "suddenly I was writing to myself." A short excerpt from her courageous final paper—much different from the original—is shown here.

> I was able to scrape by with the bare minimum in length and content that was full of "fluff." I knew how to play the system. The teachers were just so grateful to get a readable paper that they didn't really care what was inside. I learned the tricks to a good essay: use five paragraphs, make sure you have an introduction and conclusion, write a good thesis, and support your thesis. This formula did very well for me because it made all of my papers look good. However, I never really learned to write. I remember really struggling with the creative side. I never realized how much this would affect me until I got to college.
>
> My teachers now look for what is inside the paper as well. This has been an eye-opening experience for me. In some ways I feel like I am learning to write all over again. It has been good for me, though. I have been forced to move outside my protective bubble as I share my innermost thoughts with people I barely know. This is something I thought would never be possible, but I think I have finally discovered how to own my own writing and leave my protective bubble behind. It is a great feeling to know that I am capable of writing something with substance. I wish I had discovered this years ago.
>
> I think I have finally discovered the value of writing assignments. If done with proper guidance from a teacher, they can be liberating. As a future teacher, I hope to give all students the opportunity to discover the joys of writing. I think one very important element in all of this is helping them learn to love reading, too. It took me a long time to make the connection between what I read and what I write. I used reading as my protective bubble and feared writing because it forced me to leave that bubble. However, the two are intimately connected. The only way to truly understand what you read is to become connected to it. Writing helps you do that. I don't know why it took me until my last year of college to figure that out, but it will remain with me for the rest of my life. I just hope I can help my students see this while they are still in the public education system.

Finally, consider an excerpt written by ESL and language arts teacher Joyce McMullin, who shared her middle school fears in a very compelling way. Joyce recalled that because she wasn't "talented, smart, funny, popular, or cute," she had to be careful "not to do anything too stupid" that would push her into the "nerd" category. She then painted a scary picture of peer feedback—and illustrated why it's so important for teachers to monitor process writing tasks, providing training on appropriate methods of response. Her piece might well have been titled "When Bad Things Happen to Good Ideas":

> Now it was time to share our narrations and get feedback before completing our final draft. I sat across the desk from Heather, a pretty, semi-popular girl who

sometimes snickered at the socially backward things I did in school. I stared nervously at the mint-green plaster walls behind her, not wanting to catch her eye. My stomach tied up in knots as her pencil moved across my feeble paper, crossing out, adding on, and filling the paper with corrections. My status as a social outcast grew with every mark of Heather's pencil. I looked down at her paper, which I in turn was supposed to critique. I meekly scratched down a few worthless positive comments: "Good job—I can't see anything wrong." As she handed my paper back, I was completely embarrassed but also terrified, for I now had to conference with Mr. A. himself.

Mr. A. was a perfectly harmless guy. He was funny and friendly to everyone, and most kids liked being in his class. But when you are an insignificant social outcast in the seventh grade, everyone terrifies you, especially teachers. I hoped he wouldn't ream me too hard, since he could see Heather had already set me straight. Sitting across the cluttered piles of paper that camouflaged his desk, I tried to find somewhere to rest my hands, feet, and eyes. He had a sort of confused scowl as his eyes moved back and forth across the scribbled out words. My heart sunk.

Finally he looked at me and I shrank about six sizes into my chair. With the same confused scowl, he asked, "Why did you change this?" I went down another couple of sizes as I blubbered out some answer about how I had written it wrong but Heather had edited it in peer groups. "Change it back," he said.

A few weeks later, after all the papers were written and graded, Mr. A. sat in the center of our semicircle of desks and calmly announced that he was going to read anonymously one example that had scored a perfect five. My stomach dropped and my face went red as I heard the first sentence of my own writing. I put my head down and smiled. No one ever knew it was mine; but I did. For two minutes my writing was in the center spotlight. I had written a paper that my teacher considered a perfect five.

That was probably the most significant writing experience of my life because once I believed I *could* write my desire *to* write was rekindled. I went on to like writing all through high school.

Joyce's story has a happy ending because of her teacher's intervention. Mr. A. respected her writing aims, shielded her from wrong-headed advice, and acknowledged the high quality of her work. Given his professionalism, I'm confident he made sure to address the issue of overzealous peer response before his next assignment, perhaps using some of the training strategies presented in Chapter 7. As always, good teachers make a difference.

Reflecting on Narrative

In their landmark book *How Writing Shapes Thinking*, Judith Langer and Arthur Applebee (1987) report on a series of case studies extending across more than three years, and focused on instructional uses of writing in secondary schools. Langer and Applebee found that although writing took many different forms in content classrooms, it centered on three learning functions:

- Drawing on relevant knowledge and experience in preparation for new activities
- Consolidating and reviewing new information and experiences
- Reformulating and extending knowledge

(p. 41)

As we've considered narrative so far, its clear aim has been to "draw upon relevant knowledge and experience in preparation for new activities." But what about the other two learning functions? Can narrative writing also "consolidate and review new information" or "reformulate and extend knowledge"?

The answer, I believe, is yes. For example, as students keep ongoing **learning logs,** using activities described in chapters to follow, they construct a personal record of their own learning—perhaps about quadratic equations, or photosynthesis, or romantic poetry, or the Great Depression of the 1930s, or some other topic. The ongoing "story line" of a learning log consists of information, but it also reflects their doubts, questions, and insights. Because a well-kept learning log offers a first-person account of learning, it makes a great study tool for exams or for the writing of more traditional essays.

To facilitate and organize such daily writing, some teachers provide weekly single-page sheets, sectioned off by day, so that student understanding grows with each day's learning log work. Typically, students keep their log sheets in a personal three-ring binder or in a **working portfolio,** which houses the academic work for a term. Other teachers prefer spiral-bound notebooks for learning logs. Writing in the log may occur before a lesson (prediction), during it (questions and response), or afterwards (summarizing). But regardless of format, logs are integrated into the lesson as students share and swap entries or as they volunteer to read aloud.

The key point is that learning logs personalize learning. So why not have students tell the story of reducing their fast-food intake? Or share their process of researching local history? Or take field notes to document a series of animal behavior observations? Or narrate their personal solution to a math problem? Or do a write-up of make-believe stock market investments over a semester? These aren't school reports in the usual sense—they're imaginative and fun. And they're all story-based.

Moreover, as students prepare **learning portfolios,** they almost inevitably "reformulate and extend knowledge." The idea of portfolios is that students showcase selected examples of quality work, including a cover letter that explains the portfolio's artifacts. To construct a portfolio, students sequence and evaluate the artifacts, but in their cover letter they must also "tell the story" of their learning, reflecting on their growth over a defined period. As students explain how they came to select certain artifacts—and what each represents—the narrative unfolds "from the inside out." You'll learn more about portfolios in Chapter 8.

In Mike Rose's *Possible Lives: The Promise of Public Education in America* (1995), math and science teacher Michael Johnson makes a compelling case for using the students' own language to teach for insight.

I have students write narratives in math because it leads to deeper understanding. I'll ask them to explain to me what a decimal is. They'll say, "I'll show you." And I'll say, "No, don't show me. *Explain* to me what a decimal is, what it does." They know that when a certain thing happens, you move the decimal two places to the right. But they don't know why. Getting students to speak. To talk about concepts. One thing we do here is rely on study groups. Each student is linked to a buddy, and those buddies are linked to study groups. We'll take a concept—let's say reproduction in humans—and the students in the study groups cannot move on until everyone understands the concept. The students are teaching other students and are responsible for each other. You'll see a lot of talking going on.

(p. 219)

Like Johnson, I believe that talk and writing can motivate and involve students, hooking them into content area instruction. I'm aware, of course, that some students resort to story-telling as a default strategy on exams and high-stakes assessments because they haven't yet mastered analytic modes of thought. However, with good teaching, narrative provides a foundation for informational forms of writing, just as this chapter builds upon my fourth-grade story.

In other words, narrative is a *necessary* but not *sufficient* condition for effective instruction. "Writing assists learning," as Langer and Applebee put it—but different activities produce different effects (1987, p. 135). For example, short-answer prompts generally enhance "short-term recall of a good deal of specific information" but lead to little rethinking of the material, whereas longer analytic tasks often require students to focus on smaller amounts of information in more complex ways, resulting in less information retention in the short run but more in the long run (p. 135).

For balanced learning, students need a rich array of writing activities.

Content Area Examples

"But wait," you may be whispering to yourself. "What would a 'rich array of writing activities' mean in *my* content area?"

Here's a small collection of ideas for expressive writing. Many use narrative, but some draw upon other kinds of thinking skills. Do you see possibilities for your own class here, or assignments you might adapt? Take a moment to browse.

Heath and Physical Education
1. Write a biographical sketch of a favorite athlete—or adopt that athlete's voice.
2. Write in letter form, explaining how to play a game or perform a particular feat to someone who doesn't know how.
3. Write to convince a friend or family member to become physically fit.
4. Keep a journal of your calorie intake, exercise regimen, or athletic training.
5. Make up new games, and write descriptions of them, giving strategies and rules.

6. Analyze and critique a gymnastics event, basketball game, or other sporting event.
7. Write self-assessments of your performance from watching video playback.
8. Compare another team's performance, style, or strategy with your own.
9. Write about a sports event on TV as a referee or umpire.
10. Analyze the social class appeals of various games in our culture.

Consumer and Family Studies
1. Create recipes and write them for others after sharing cooked samples.
2. Write paragraphs deciding what should be added or omitted from the recipe.
3. Collect recipes and file them. Write short paragraphs, similar in style to the "Food" section of a newspaper, explaining the appeal of the recipes.
4. Work with others to create handbooks on good grooming, choosing a wardrobe, proper foods for good health, and so on.
5. Make annotated bibliographies for use in specific areas such as child care, or foods from other cultures.
6. Evaluate products and publish findings of those that do what they claim to do and those that do not.
7. Write newsletters about ideas for budget management or comparative shopping.
8. Write letters about consumer issues such as pricing, quality, unfair or unethical business practices.
9. Take notes and write up observations in child care classes; expand these into papers on child behavior or human growth and development.
10. Write and deliver consumer announcements for radio and TV spots.

Fine Arts
1. In music, write lyrics that may be set to music or read with accompaniment.
2. Write assessments of performances or artifacts.
3. Write descriptions of art done by students or established artists.
4. Analyze music with regard to tone, mood, expression, or other elements.
5. Analyze art with regard to color, form, balance, or other elements.
6. Write a letter to a music/art committee describing your preferences for future events.
7. Write a critique of your own artistic performance.
8. Compile a list of music or art for a public showing; then critique the evening for different audiences (PTA newsletter, school newspaper, etc.).
9. Explain your motivation for performing or creating a particular work.
10. Write imaginatively from an artist's or composer's point of view.

Mathematics
1. Explain the steps involved in solving a problem to someone else.
2. Write story problems like those in the text or given out as models; swap.
3. Write a description of your own strengths and weaknesses in math and offer suggestions for improvement.

4. Write about how a math skill just studied relates to the one now under study.
5. Create real-life sequences in which math is used to solve a problem.
6. Describe areas of math that you have questions about.
7. Explain math terms in your own words to someone who doesn't understand.
8. Keep a math journal of your insights and frustrations.
9. Study a numerical graph and translate its meaning into sentences.
10. Write weekly letters to parents explaining what you have learned in math.

English and Drama
1. Create character biographies and summaries.
2. Distill and/or analyze the central message in a literary work.
3. Write from the point of view of a literary character.
4. Write up observations of actors or contrasting presentations of a work.
5. Write about sensory experiences that parallel those in literature.
6. Write book reviews that persuade a person to buy a book.
7. Create works in the same form as those under study.
8. Write diaries (from author's point of view) about intention.
9. Compare a book version with its dramatic rendition on film.
10. Transform fiction or poetry into other literary forms.

Science
1. Keep journals of lab experiments.
2. Write imaginative diaries related to scientific achievements.
3. Write imaginative accounts from inside organisms.
4. Explain a scientific principle to someone who is deaf.
5. Write opinion papers related to pollution, ecology, nuclear energy, or other topics.
6. Describe on paper your process of thinking about an application problem.
7. Write a letter home explaining what you learned this week.
8. Interview a scientist about his/her research and prepare a report.
9. Make predictions about the future based on present trends or data.
10. Compare alternate theoretical explanations for an event.

Social Sciences
1. Write about a single event from different points of view.
2. Explain what two or more events have in common historically.
3. Create a "You Are There" scenario.
4. Conduct field research (interviews and polling) and write up the results.
5. Become an historical figure and create a diary.
6. Explain an event to someone from another planet.
7. Keep a journal recording news references to a particular topic.
8. Extrapolate into the future from present social trends.
9. Create a case study illustrating a psychological principle.
10. Persuade the public through a letter to the editor expressing your views.

Narrative Insights

So let's summarize: To write for insight is to make sense to oneself, first and foremost. At the same time, writing is also a principal means of communicating with others. Narrative writing helps students discover meanings in their own experience and connect those meanings to curriculum content through reflection. Shaping one's story for others requires a leap of imagination—keeping one's readers in mind, asking what they will need from the text, and then finding the right words.

Narrative is powerful because it invites students to revisit experience and learn from it. Moreover, as students share learning stories in their real voices—and as those stories are validated by others through applause and discussion and shared laughter—a genuine classroom community is created. Marginalized learners begin to understand, for example, that they're not the only ones who struggle with basic algebra concepts or with symbolism in literature. And the well-articulated insights of key students can serve as scaffolding for the entire class, raising the intellectual bar for inquiry.

Diana Mitchell sums up the case for such writing activities succinctly: "These autobiographies inform teachers where their students are in relation to their subject by giving them information about students' attitudes, achievements, and shortcomings in their subject area" (1996, p. 93).

As you recall the Four Writing Domains framework in the Introduction, you'll realize that learning autobiographies probably fall in the "expressive/writing-to-learn" domain. Such stories clarify the meanings of unique human experience in a particular content area such as history, science, mathematics, or music.

But narrative also provides the backbone for daily writing in learning logs—the expressive work so fundamental to active learning. The preceding section's array of prompts suggests that logs are limited only by our own imaginations. It's through them that students construct ongoing stories of what they understand. Information thus gets transformed into personal knowledge, which can be showcased in learning portfolios.

The rationale for narrative knowledge is neatly articulated by Roger Schank (1990), an expert in human memory and artificial intelligence research. Pay close attention to Schank's bottom-line assertion about human learning:

> Our knowledge of the world is more or less equivalent to the set of experiences that we have had, but our communication is limited by the number of stories we know to tell. In other words, all we have are experiences, but all we can effectively tell are stories. Oddly enough, we come to rely upon our stories so much that it seems that all we can tell ourselves are stories as well. Communication consists of selecting the stories that we know and telling them to others at the right time. *Learning from one's own experiences depends upon being able to communicate our experiences as stories to others.* (italics added)
>
> (p. 12)

The final sentence of the preceding paragraph—so simple, yet so profound—has deep implications for effective teaching. It links to the head note of this chapter by Anaïs Nin—that "we write to taste life twice, in the moment, and in retrospection." I invite you to *reflect* on these ideas as you brainstorm literacy memories from your past, ones that might become part of your autobiography. True stories lead to personal insights.

WRITE FOR INSIGHT ACTIVITY

As a literate person, you're able to write. Your beliefs about your skills, your attitudes toward writing, your present behaviors as a writer—all have been shaped by past experiences. So what memorable experiences have made you who you are today? Our aim is to explore this important question.

First make a quick list of school-related writing memories—elementary school, secondary school, and college. Then jot down other memories, such as keeping a diary, writing notes or love letters, and creating imaginative stories or poems for your own pleasure. Look over your lists. Which memories are particularly strong or vivid? Why do you think these memories have stuck with you?

Create a memory snapshot. In your learning log, put yourself in the time and place of your memory and tell the story of what happened. Then comment on what you see as the significance of this particular memory. Your memory of this experience is evidence that it was meaningful to you. So, looking back as an adult, what is the personal learning you now attach to this event?

Share your snapshot with colleagues, hear what they have written, and hand in a photocopy of your log entry to your instructor. Then turn to Appendix A for details of the literacy autobiography case study and the assignment's rubric.

2 Challenging the Hidden Curriculum

First we shape our institutions, and then they shape us.

—Winston Churchill

Teacher as Writer

It's just before class, with my teacher education students shuffling toward their desks, when Kim corners me. Her voice has a nervous edge as she asks whether last week's "literacy autobiographies" have been corrected.

"Well, yes and no," I reply. "The essays are coming back today, but no, I don't think I've been correcting them."

"Isn't that your job?"

I shrug. "I try to respond to what you've said and how you've said it because I see honest response as part of good teaching. But merely correcting a paper you won't revise is a little like manicuring a corpse. What's the point?"

Kim looks perplexed. "So what did I get?"

"What do you mean?"

"You know, like grade-wise."

"Well, that depends."

"On what?" Kim asks.

"On whether you decide to work on your paper some more. That's up to you. We're writing to learn, but also writing to communicate. So you decide whether you've written what you intended as effectively as you can." I pause to lighten things up. "Of course, there's no extra charge if you'd like to talk it over."

Kim shifts her weight and doesn't smile. "But I thought I was done."

I pull up my Paul Valery quote: "Writing is never finished, only abandoned."

"Hmmm." She knits her brows.

"You know, with luck, some of your students will use revision to explore and develop their ideas. For others, getting by will be the goal."

"Look, all I want is a good grade out of this class."

"I understand that. But you can also learn in the process."

"I don't get it," Kim says.

"Okay, first read my responses and then ask yourself whether you agree with my ideas—and whether my suggestions might help your text. Fair enough?"

"In other words, I have to do more work on it."

"That's really up to you—seriously."

"What's the point?"

"My job is to make sure you assess your own writing and get your money's worth for your hard-earned tuition."

"Uh-huh, sure."

"The idea is to write for insight."

"I really don't get it," she says again.

Resistance to Writing

Kim may seem like an extreme example of the new teacher who doesn't "get it" in lots of ways. But she (or he) does inhabit preservice and inservice classes, including those that use writing as a learning tool—a means of making knowledge personal, connected, and accessible to self.

From Chapter 1, you understand that my literacy autobiography assignment aimed to prompt reflection. However, Kim didn't like the idea that writing could make her an open book, one that others might read. She resisted writing-to-learn activities and had plenty of questions as we began drafting and sharing: How long does it have to be? Why write about your past experience? Do spelling and punctuation count? Why waste time in response groups?

I read her paper with interest. Aside from its technical flaws, the writing was detached and cool, describing with smugness how she'd eased through secondary schools without writing a single essay. Her strategy was to trade math skills for the writing talents of others. She'd dictate a few key points to friends, who'd do "the dirty work" that she'd recopy or download. When it came to reports and term papers, the issue for Kim was not so much ethics as efficacy—a division of labor.

Through cunning, Kim suggested, it was easy to beat the system. Fakery made sense because it reduced the workload.

"So who wrote *this* paper?" I asked in the margin, forcing a smile.

To veteran teachers, it will probably come as no surprise that Kim was also the archetypal sycophant who mouthed platitudes to deflect attention from her limited grasp of the current topics. On the other hand, she viewed all teachers (me included) as faceless functionaries in a long, weary line of grade dispensers. She saw schooling as a game, the main goal being to outwit those in positions of authority. Left unanswered was the question of why she'd even want to teach, given her cynical beliefs about the fraudulent nature of the enterprise—or how she'd treat learners in her own classroom.

Despite my best efforts, Kim saw personal meaning-making as "bogus." She regarded writing-to-learn activities as ways to keep kids in line, a kind of no-nonsense behavior management tool. She viewed grades as "the whole point of school, the only reason students show up." As she voiced these ideas in our conferences, her ideas about teacher and student roles also became clear. The teacher's task was simply to assign, correct, and grade writing; and the student's job was to "psyche out" the teacher and write to specifications. Kim wanted me to lead in certain traditional ways so that she could follow in others.

Reviewing my comments and suggestions, it amazed and unsettled her that a grade might be open-ended, with opportunities for revision extended over time, or that I might raise questions or discuss alternatives but not tell her what to do. Most of all, being asked to use the "I" pronoun and think on her own prompted anxiety. Her coping strategy was to ask repeatedly, "Is this good enough? So what do you want?"

The Hidden Curriculum of Writing

As I now work in schools, I'm forced to conclude that students like Kim are products of a hidden curriculum—"school experiences that result in unintended, unplanned, even unsuspected and undesired student learning" (Shaver & Strong, 1982, p. 1). The hidden curriculum of writing certainly isn't found in national standards, in state frameworks, or in colorful scope and sequence charts. Rather, it exists in messages that students read "between the lines," as we use (or abuse) writing in middle schools and high schools. Ask yourself whether any of these statements ring perversely true.

1. Writing in school is something you do to get a grade, and school is something you do to get a diploma or certificate.
2. The main purpose of writing in school is to tell the teacher what the teacher already knows, not to explore a topic or idea.
3. A second main purpose of school writing is to provide diversionary busy-work (or "time filler") so that the class is occupied.
4. A third main purpose of school writing is to serve as a management threat to students or as actual punishment for misbehavior.
5. The central intellectual activity in school writing is to guess what the teacher wants, not to figure out what's worth saying or how to say it most effectively.
6. Information about required length is essential in school writing in order for you to pad appropriately or to minimize the possibility of doing extra work.
7. Successful school writing takes no chances with ideas, thereby avoiding the risk of saying something interesting, important, or thought-provoking.
8. Good school writing uses a stilted, objective, and artificial voice—preferably heavy with ponderous words and vague abstractions.
9. The best school writing uses a safe, conventional approach (short sentences, formulaic paragraphs, and mindless banalities) so that errors are minimized.
10. Any type of personal writing (or writing on which one claims to have worked hard) automatically deserves a high grade, regardless of its other features.
11. Features of writing such as intelligence, quality of development, clarity, and logical support are merely the subjective opinions of the teacher.
12. Feedback from the teacher (responses, suggestions, and questions) are really corrections in disguise, and their purpose is to justify the grade.

Of course, our official goals for writing are quite different from those listed. Indeed, we use jargon like "assessing comprehension" and "developing critical thinking" to justify writing instruction. But despite our noble aims, the hidden curriculum of writing often gets taught in subtle, powerful ways—for example, when students are routinely assigned low-level worksheets, when objective exams are the assessments of choice, and when misbehaving students are given written reports as punishment.

Roots of the Hidden Curriculum

Let me be clear that my purpose in describing Kim isn't to blame the victim, as so often happens in discussions of classroom practice. Instead, I use this real case to ask why so many secondary teachers continue to view writing mainly as a tool for assessment and class control rather than as a means of learning.

Consider testing practices. Today, many teachers use tests instrumentally—that is, as tools to motivate reading or to prompt the learning of skills and content. And many of us (though we rarely admit it publically) continue to use quizzes, tests, and other academic work to control or manage student behavior. For example, when students act out or become unruly, they might get extra homework or busywork (such as preparing a five-hundred-word report). So imagine my reaction when one of my student teachers shared this journal entry involving Scott, her cooperating teacher:

> I did the listening quiz at the very beginning, and I should've waited until later. It didn't calm them down any, though. We didn't get much done. Fortunately, Scott was in the room working on something else, so afterwards he gave me some discipline pointers that he would have done in my place. So, next time I'll have some ideas. Mostly he told me when to throw the book at them. He told me that halfway through the period he'd have given up and given them an essay test due at the end of class. Next time I'll try that.
>
> (Anonymous, personal communication, 2003)

By coupling an aversive aspect of schooling with the threat of a low grade, we force misbehaving kids to "shape up." But after such lessons, should we be surprised that kids develop bad attitudes toward our content area and toward writing? Learners aren't stupid, and our punishing activities are ones they long remember.

The idea that *all* writing gets a grade—and that students write mainly to get a grade—is embedded in the hidden curriculum. Of course, real learning requires risk, and risk leads to mistakes, and mistakes can result in low grades. So students learn, quite naturally, to play it safe. The grades that follow writing bring elation or anguish, relief or resentment, indifference or confusion. But these emotions are incidental to their learning, which occurs—if it occurs at all—during writing.

Stated simply, grades often interfere with our efforts to use writing as a tool for learning. Learners focus on "psyching out the teacher" and "writing to specifications," as Kim put it, and teachers focus on grading stacks of student work instead of merely sampling the texts for evidence of learning—and providing the feedback that might inform tomorrow's instruction.

Thus, traditional ideas about grading deliver a double whammy to writing-to-learn activities. If the teacher is the sole audience, and if students view writing only in terms of grades, they usually adopt strategies of pleasing the teacher and playing it safe, rather than strategies of exploring ideas, raising questions, and making personal connections. And if content teachers think they have to grade all the miserable scraps of writing produced by all their classes, they don't assign any writing-to-learn activities. So here is Strong's First Law: *If the amount kids write is limited by what teachers have time to grade, there's no way they'll write enough to learn curriculum content.*

Clearly, the hidden curriculum of writing needs an overhaul. For Kim, it led to a single-minded fixation on grades and an unwillingness (or inability) to think on her own. Because she had never used a learning log to think about subject matter, her reasoning skills were weak; and because she'd never written for purposes other than a grade, her strategies for gaining insight were impoverished. Closed and fearful—and crippled by writing anxiety and a traditional view of teacher and student roles—Kim seemed disadvantaged as both a learner and future teacher.

As my poster child for fakery, Kim personifies the insidious effects of writing's hidden curriculum. At the root of such pathology, I believe, are adversarial roles for teacher and student. School is a game, and the score is kept with grades. Fakery is valued, and personal insight devalued. But it doesn't have to be that way.

Writing without Grades

I'm now certain that Kim had too few teachers like my friend Bob Tierney, a legendary biology teacher and coach from the San Francisco Bay Area who was a front-line fighter in the guerilla war against the hidden curriculum. "When you get a teaching certificate," Bob liked to say, "you get an unlimited supply of [grading] points."

Writing to learn was a continual, ongoing activity in Bob's classes. Kids used drawing and writing to put biology concepts into terms that made personal sense, then shared these notes during small group discussions and labs—in effect, teaching one another through high-engagement activities. Most of them loved learning in this way. They got points for participation; but Bob wasn't buried under an avalanche of grading work.

Bob's aim, in a nutshell, was to make learning a discovery experience. As his students made daily discoveries about biology, he made discoveries about how to assist their learning. For example, he pulled questions from their learning logs to focus his follow-up teaching. This dialogue generated additional writing.

Simply put, Bob outsmarted his students. Their overarching goal, he knew, was to get him to do all the intellectual work while they doodled in their notebooks. One tried-and-true way to accommodate the student agenda was to first assign biology homework and then, when they didn't do it, tell them what they should have learned. So Bob took a different approach. He let the students interrogate him. And just for the fun of it, he sometimes gave wrong answers.

"That isn't right!" his students would say, scrambling for their books.

"What do you know," Bob would have to concede. "I stand corrected again."

Bob also used writing-to-learn in all kinds of ways—to open class, to explore concepts during class, to summarize learning at the end of class, and to anticipate reading for tomorrow's class. Students often swapped papers and responded in dialogue fashion to each other's ideas. All of this written work was ungraded, but points did provide an incentive for staying on task. Each check mark in his grade book was worth a set amount, but Bob would sometimes offer double points for special learning log activities—or even, on rare occasions, triple points.

"No kidding?" Bob's students would ask. "Triple points?"

"This is important material," Bob would reply.

"Wow—triple points!"

As a management strategy, Bob had students keep their spiral-bound learning logs in the classroom, using separate color-coded boxes for each class. At the end of a period, kids didn't close their notebooks but instead left them folded open to the current day's work and deposited them in the box. Each log entry had the date and the student's name at the top. Of course, having the logs already open saved Bob time. He could check a stack in minutes. And he could use sticky notes to flag entries of special interest, ones he wanted to use as a bridge to follow-up teaching. The logs offered Bob a window onto each student's learning.

As you might already have guessed, the brighter kids in Bob's classes were the first to see that points mattered little when everybody had amassed roughly the same total number, all earned through active participation. But by then it was too late, because they had already been hooked on the fun of writing to learn. What they had learned about biology truly felt good—and this was apparent in end-of-semester assessments. Generally speaking, writing-to-learn activities enabled students to better understand concepts, and this understanding made the material more memorable.

In other words, Bob felt that learning, not grades, represented the true mortar of Western civilization, not to mention our best hope for the future.

Note-Taking and Note-Making

One of Bob Tierney's key strategies for active learning involved a two-column framework called the *double-entry journal*. Students began by making a simple T-chart in their notebooks or by folding worksheets lengthwise ("hotdog-style"). The left column was for taking notes, the right column for making notes. To keep this activity from becoming drudgery or busywork, students had opportunities to share and compare notes with friends, and to use notes on certain assessments.

Note-taking involved pulling key ideas and facts from written text or a lecture, whereas note-making involved thinking about the ideas and facts—for example, making judgments, giving personal examples, or asking questions. The note-taking column recorded information in "nugget" form, with big ideas set to the left and subordinate ideas indented. In contrast, the note-making column gave personal meaning to the information. Thus, the right column might include a drawing, an angry retort, or a memory triggered by information in the left column.

Figure 2-1 shows the note-taking and note-making work on "The Cell" done by one of Bob's general science students (personal communication, 2004).

Always interested in innovation, Bob also developed an imaginative and effective variation on two-column notes; he asked his basic, or remedial, students

Protozoa

Note-Taking	Note-Making
"Unicellular" supposedly one cell, but there may be a question	How big can they get?
They are divided into classes by how they move. 1. cilia – hair-like structures 2. flagella – whip-like structures 3. pseudopods – means false foot, it just flows 4. flotation – they go with the flow like amoeba or white blood cells	Flagella look the fastest. This is fun.
Protoza 1. Take in O_2 by diffusion 2. Respiration by Kreb's cycle 3. Aerobic 4. Take in food by oral groove or just engulfing it	We learned that diffusion and respiration stuff in chapter 4. It's starting to make sense.
Reproduction asexual – splitting, mitosis sexual – exchange DNA, more variety	When paramecia just split in half, is that the cloning? Is cloning asexual?

FIGURE 2-1 Note-Taking/Note-Making
Source: Copyright © 2004 National Science Teachers Association.

to keep notes in the four-part framework shown here. Bob found that this structure invited an interplay of thinking, with the drawing serving to clarify concepts and the "So What?" paragraph leading to reflection and insight.

Note-Taking	Note-Making
Drawing	"So What?" Paragraph

Still another Tierney innovation was the **Neuron Note** (Tierney, 2002, p. 15). With it, Bob asked general science students to summarize, in homework writing, what they thought they understood, but without the support of their textbooks or notes. He emphasized that it was okay if they didn't understand, but they needed to realize this fact. Students got full credit if they wrote a Neuron Note, but no credit if they didn't. Of course, Bob used insights from Neuron Notes to assess whether students were ready for upcoming tests. Here's a typical Neuron Note written by one of his basic writers:

> Osmosis is to do with water and cells. Osmosis is the absorbing of water by cells, or pass through. I don't know what it does exactly when it's inside. Osmosis is not the only way, but the one that is used the most is diffusion. I would like to know where they got a name like osmosis for it? Osmosis is different from any other form, but still gets the job done. When it occurs water actually passes through a somewhat membrane so as to equalize the amount on both sides of the cell or whatever kind of membrane it is.
>
> (Tierney, 2002, pp. 15–16)

Although Bob had plenty of compelling evidence in the form of Neuron Notes, he also wanted proof that writing had positive effects on student learning. Therefore, in an action research study with matched groups of learners, he tested the writing-to-learn method against traditional methods of instruction and found that as a group, students who wrote regularly learned every bit as much as their control group counterparts—and in addition, *retained* what they had learned in delayed post-tests of biology content.

The Wotring and Tierney research (1981) helped many skeptics see the instructional potential of writing. Today, in his new methods monograph, *How to Write to Learn Science* (Tierney and Dorroh, 2004), Bob reminds us of the root sense of the word *education*—"drawing out" student understanding—in contrast with the hidden curriculum's emphasis on "stuffing in" information.

Resisting the Hidden Curriculum

With the image of Bob Tierney's class in mind, let's now consider some practical writing-to-learn exercises—brief, functional, and usually ungraded. These may occur in students' response journals or learning logs, but they may also occur as stand-alone activities. Many teachers use writing-to-learn to prompt large-group discussion, with students first sharing their writing with a partner or small group, or as a springboard into more formal writing tasks. But anonymous writing can also work.

One such activity is the **admit slip** (Gere, 1985, p. 222). These are short, anonymous writings, often one-half page or less, that students use to gain admission during the first few minutes of a class. Typically, the writings are collected and the teacher reads a few of them aloud. Of course, the strategy can be sharply focused if students are asked to respond to reading with summaries, questions, or personal connections. Here are samples of what Barbara Page (1987) received from her students after they had read "An Occurrence at Owl Creek Bridge," by Ambrose Bierce, outside of class:

- I admit that I really did not understand while I was reading the story that Peyton was really dying and hallucinating images that he wished would come true. I thought that he actually fell into the water and found his way home to his wife and died there. I read the story twice more before I realized what the meaning was.
- I couldn't make any sense of the story. Was all that happened to him a dream?
- I admit I haven't read the story yet.

(p. 49)

Brief statements like those above offer natural openings for class discussion, especially as students give voice to their own readings. But equally effective is the **exit slip** strategy (Gere, 1985, p. 224). Instead of letting students shut down mentally during the last ten minutes of class, challenge them to summarize what they've learned, ask an unresolved question, or think about personal connections to the lesson. Then stand by the door and collect the exit slips. More often than not, these brief writings provide a bridge to the next day's lesson.

Writing-to-learn exercises personalize learning by inviting active knowledge construction. For example, if kids assume the persona of "Dear Abby" or "Dr. Phil" to offer advice on solving a story problem in math, they are usually eager to share their chatty texts with one another. Or if students write a letter from one literary character's viewpoint—say, Jim on Huckleberry Finn's raft—that character is certain to come alive. Or if students assume the role of a historical figure—such as Harry Truman deciding whether to use atomic bombs in 1945—a moral dilemma will be viscerally experienced.

Imaginative formats can make writing-to-learn fun. For example, students might keep the diary of a character as they read a novel or play. They might craft a book jacket for their "Healthy Lifestyle Guide." They might script an imagined interview with the author of their marketing text. They might write a scene (or alternative ending) for a political event. They might also create cartoons, prophecies, horoscopes, telegrams, obituaries and epitaphs, rap lyrics, posters, collages, mobiles, editorials, newspaper stories, email interchanges, business memos, or historical "you-are-there" scenes.

Here, for example, is a neat little assignment designed by math teacher Brandon Nelson (personal communication, 2004) to help students appreciate "The Wonderful World of Numbers."

> Imagine you are an element in one of the sets of numbers we have discussed in class. To refresh your memory, the sets are Reals, Rationals, Irrationals, Whole Numbers, Integers, and Complex Numbers. Each set has its own special quality that separates it from the other sets.
>
> Write a letter to a friend who also belongs to your set. Some points you may consider including are these: How do you feel belonging to your set? How do you feel about the other sets? What makes you similar to, or different from, the elements of other sets? Relate a story that occurred involving an element (or elements) from a different set and you. Be creative!

But while these alternative writing-to-learn formats might motivate learning, they also need to be linked to real educational aims. What mental processes do we hope to stimulate and develop? Following are some basic thinking processes worth attending to, as well as a few content area illustrations. Of course, the processes can be adapted across all subject matter areas as students work in learning logs.

Assessing.   Find out what students already know (or don't know) about a topic, theme, or issue. For example, "Tomorrow we start a new unit called 'The Holocaust.' Write what you already know about this topic."

Predicting.   Encourage students to consider what might happen next. For example, "Now that you've seen the lab demonstration of what happens under condition X, write about what you predict will happen under condition Y."

Recording.   Ask students to jot down their observations and reactions. For example, "Using notes from the debate, what are your impressions of the styles of the two speakers? Write about each speaker's strengths."

Questioning.   Have students take active questioning roles. For example, "Write down three questions you would like to ask the author of this text. What are you unsure about in your reading? What would you like to know more about?"

Responding.   Invite students to make journal entries about in-class or out-of-class reading. For example, "What do you imagine the Palestinian leaders will do in response to this emerging situation? Give reasons for your views."

Personalizing.   Ask students to make personal connections to a text or issue. For example, "Type II diabetes among U.S. children is now front-page news. In writing, express what you see as the main causes of this problem."

Defining.   Have students create definitions based upon their discussion, reading, or inquiry. For example, "Now that responses to your questionnaire are sorted, how would you define 'Good English'? Create a definition."

Applying.   Invite students to apply what they have learned. For example, "Now that you've participated in today's activity, take ten minutes to jot down the key points you need to remember for tomorrow's quiz and next week's project."

Summarizing.   Ask students to paraphrase, translate, or summarize a text or discussion. For example, "Write a letter to a good friend who was not in class today that sums up the key points of the lesson on osmosis."

Analyzing.   Direct students to think about a text or their own writing analytically. For example, "Now that you've read the policy statements of the candidates, create a Venn diagram that shows points of agreement and disagreement."

Evaluating.   Encourage students to make judgments about the worth or beauty of a text or event. For example, "Having heard the two composers, write about the one you regard as the better example of nineteenth century romanticism."

Finally, it's worth remembering that ungraded writing-to-learn activities help students develop fluency in written expression. A central tenet of writing process instruction is that learners make progress in the skills of writing to the extent that they use language functionally and purposefully. In other words, to get better at writing, students need to write a great deal—far more than they now do in many schools.

Writing-to-Learn Samples

From the previous discussion, it's clear that writing-to-learn activities take many forms—and that a variety of formats, purposes, and audiences can help to keep such work from becoming routine.

For example, here is an in-class learning log response to the phrase "Great Depression" in the context of U.S. history. To prepare for the upcoming unit, the teacher wanted to assess what students already knew about this historical period and what questions they had.

> I think the Great Depression is about the stock market crash. Like when the stocks went down, people got really depressed because there money was wiped out. A lot of people lost there jobs, and that was depressing too. The thing I wonder is, what caused it and how they got over it.

Clearly, there's a foundation of background knowledge here—the stock market crash of 1929—but the student's understanding of the word "depression" needs to be expanded to include its economic meaning. The questions provide a hook for teaching.

And here's a brief writing-to-learn entry from a typical student in middle school mathematics when asked to find the volume of an irregular three-dimensional figure in a "problem of the week" activity. The teacher's directions were to copy a geometric figure onto another sheet of paper, show math calculations in solving the problem, and then explain (in writing) the method used. The student's writing follows:

> I split the figure into three sections A, B, and C. Then I calculated the volume for section A by using the volume formula (length × width × height). Again, I found the volume for section B, then C. Afterwards, I added up all the volumes of sections A, B, and C. My answer is 26 cm.

Although students can easily fake their math calculations by copying, written accounts like this one provide a window into their real thinking and reasoning process.

A different type of writing-to-learn entry occurred in a general science class, where students chose from an array of natural objects including—among others—a sperm whale tooth, sheep jawbone, obsidian, sugar pine cone, insect gall, topaz crystals, gypsum, fossilized coral, chestnut, beard lichen, and bog peat. Capitalizing on the students' curiosity, the teacher asked students to make a series of "close scientific observations" on a single object, carefully describing its texture, composition, colors, patterns, or special characteristics. Here's one such entry:

> The abalone shell is about five inches long and sort of oval shaped. Its gleaming inner part is called mother of pearl. It's surface has colors like silvery white, green, gray, pink, blue and lavender, they are all blended together. Mother of pearl feels smooth and hard, like enamel paint. Little holes are found along the shell's outer rim.

The teacher then had students think about converting the literal description of science into the "language of wonder." After students thought about their object in its natural habitat, they read a few model poems and transformed their log entries into similarly styled free verse. An example follows.

Dreaming of
milk-white surf

an abalone shell
on a brown desktop

its smooth curve
gleams with
ocean pastels
blended by
lavender light

mother of pearl
from our mother
the sea

Finally, in a high school psychology class, students learned about brain waves linked to various psychological states. They watched a video concerning laboratory work with brain waves and discussed meditation techniques used to induce alpha waves. To help the class consider the pros and cons of biofeedback technology, the teacher asked student groups to create an advertisement for a biofeedback machine. Here's one example:

Model XR 2100

The Ultimate in Biofeedback

Color feedback and digital audio! Ten screens for biofeedback entertaining and family fun! Plus all the dependability you've come to expect from Psychotek, the leader in meditation aids!

The XR2100 helps you reach deeper into inner space than you ever thought possible! Our patented Bio-Hold Tuner tracks your optimal alpha, beta, or theta frequencies. And all our machines include a bedroom Med-i-Sleep hookup for oceans of deep, relaxing sleep!

Don't be satisfied with old-fashioned biofeedback. You and your loved ones deserve the Ultimate Quality Experience from Psychotek.

As these examples suggest, expressive writing connects students with the content under study. An imagined dialogue differs from a letter to the editor, which in turn differs from a summary of key points—but all have writing-to-learn potential. Such tasks are limited only by our creative thinking.

Thinking Outside the Box

This chapter's headnote—"First we shape our institutions, and then they shape us"—suggests that traditions have great momentum. In education, most of us tend to teach as we have been taught. Thinking outside the box is rare; and rarer still is taking action outside the box.

Put another way: The basic structures of schools resist change. Although we now have whiteboards rather than chalkboards, hand-held calculators as opposed to slide rules, and movable desks instead of desks with wooden runners, such changes are cosmetic. The desks often remain in rows, just as they did in yesteryear. And today's drill-and-practice software packages, though delivered on sleek high-tech computers, are much like the workbooks used by earlier generations.

The same holds true for grades and tests. Of course, some academic writing *is* a test, and tests matter. The stakes are high for students, teachers, and administrators in today's tense environment of performance standards. Recognizing that students need to be savvy about essay exams, many of us teach to the test, advising students to use five-paragraph formats. However, if we restrict writing to such mindless scaffolds, and insist that students always "keep it simple," we might also communicate a darker message: that form matters more than content and that the highest aim of school writing is merely to prove to some dim-witted reader that one can make three perfunctory points framed by an introduction and conclusion.

In this chapter, we've considered the insidious effects of the hidden curriculum. If we're honest, we'll probably confess that we too have been schooled in its lessons, just like Kim. As learners, haven't we all asked the "what-do-you-want" question? Yes, our geography report may have been copied from a musty encyclopedia rather than downloaded, but was this activity meaningful? And how about the essay exam we wrote without doing the required reading? Or the patchwork of quotations we submitted when a college research paper came due? Indeed, Kim's story may remind us of ourselves not so long ago—reluctant to confront our ignorance, uncertain about our skills. Although discovering ideas may be exciting, it can also be intimidating.

As we've seen, it's also easy to think of grades as a "given condition," a little like the air we breathe. Because of the pull of tradition, it seems only natural that all writing deserves a grade. Like Kim, we may even believe that grades are "the whole point of school, the only reason students show up." Some of us rationalize that ungraded writing may lead to mistakes and that we don't want our students practicing mistakes; others of us worry, based on past experience, that students will ignore our ungraded tasks. The possible loss of control may make us shudder.

But schools are the way they are because we make them that way. If the desks are in rows rather than a student-friendly U-shape, it may be because we doubt our own powers to shape the environment for productive dialogue. And if we refuse to consider ungraded writing-to-learn activities like the ones in this chapter, it may be because we're reluctant to question our own practice or muster the energy for forward-thinking ideas. After all, it takes courage to teach—the kind voiced by math teacher Amy Jensen (personal communication, 2003) in a learning log *about* learning logs:

> As an educator, it is important to remember that students understand and remember more when they are required to talk or write about the material. I think having students explain algorithms, etc. to one another, having them bring it to a verbal level, will increase their learning. When you teach someone else, you must clearly understand it first. . . . After students are involved in this way, they will achieve higher levels of learning.

My hope is that as we forego *some* of our grading in favor of the kind of learning described by Amy—using frequent writing-to-learn activities—we'll discover a powerful antidote to the mind-numbing effects of writing's hidden curriculum. Chapter 3 extends this outside-the-box thinking.

WRITE FOR INSIGHT ACTIVITY

Imagine yourself in the faculty lounge at the school where you teach. When a colleague asks what you've been up to lately, you mention *Write for Insight*, the little methods book you've been reading. Your colleague rolls his eyes.

"You've got to be kidding."

"Just finished Chapter 2."

"Let me guess," your colleague says. "Now we get to circle all the spelling and punctuation mistakes besides teaching our subject."

"Well, not exactly. It's really about a different approach—ungraded writing."

"Come again?"

"You know, having kids write to learn, sharing with each other—"

"And you believe in the Tooth Fairy, right?"

"Let's say it just got me thinking."

"About what?"

Team up with a partner to role-play this scenario. Use it as a springboard to improvise an oral dialogue about the ideas in Chapter 2. Try to keep it going for five minutes or so—and then switch roles. Develop a second oral dialogue, working to clarify your understanding of the chapter and raise questions about it. (Your instructor may call upon you to share your improvisation with the class.) Afterwards, write an email message to an imagined colleague, expressing your insights. For example, are there specific points of the hidden curriculum that resonate for you personally? Are there specific points you want to challenge? Share this learning log text with your instructor.

CHAPTER

3 Exploring Expressive Writing

How do I know what I think until I see what I say?
—E. M. Forster

A Mostly True Story

Long before you were born, in a land far, far away, I worried about the idea of **automaticity** (or fluency) in reading—more specifically, how to introduce this idea in an article without putting teachers to sleep. As you may know, education articles often have a tranquilizing effect on the central nervous system.

Working on the article, I felt my own eyelids grow heavy until they finally drooped shut. But my eyeballs inside remained restless and jittery, and it occurred to me how unnatural it was to have them captured by academic boredom. And this thought led me to open my article with playful, expressive writing.

Hungry Eyeballs

Your eyes slide
Left to right,
Rapacious,
Flicking-quick,
Consuming
Everything in sight.
Now am I right
Or wrong?
I'm right of course.
They need to read
To feed their brain.
They've got
An appetite
That's quite insane—
And are, in fact,
Well-trained for tracking
And attack on words.
Deep within
Their socket-cage

(Like vicious birds
That know no fear)
Your eyes can gauge
The shadow sounds
Of ink on white—
Can hear and
Hover near
A page of poem
Or tattered book
And hardly blink
A sideways look.
But then,
Without apparent cause,
They'll simply pause
As if to poise
Their will to kill.
They'll flit
From side to side—
A kind of glide—

And then   Of sprinting print
Without a bit   And eat
Of noise,   Their fill.
Leap down a page

And so the article, "Assessing Student Reading Skills," did indeed get published (Strong, 1976), and some teachers liked the poem enough to put it up on their bulletin boards. And the effect of the article was to halt the precipitous decline of SAT scores nationally, and the teachers got huge raises and the undying thanks of grateful parents, and we all lived happily ever after.

The Importance of Play

Did I have fun with my "hungry eyeballs" introduction? Absolutely.

And did I engage you as a reader? That's for you to decide.

Whatever your answer, this chapter makes the case that **play** is vital to learning. Of course, small children spare no effort in playfully exploring their environment—by dropping things, mouthing things, and asking many questions. Later, they pretend to be animals, dolls, space invaders, and grownups who can read and use cell phones. Still later, as jaded adolescents, they contend that "fun" classes make school "interesting." In other words, being playful and being mentally awake seem to go hand in hand.

It's old news that school structures tend to suppress—or sometimes crush—the playful, imaginative impulses of childhood. Teachers are hardly pernicious, but the day-to-day reality of managing large groups of high-activity learners means that order and conformity get heavy emphasis. Thus, in the course of learning to sit still and listen quietly and follow directions, many children also learn to shut down their curiosity and imagination. Such lessons continue in secondary schools. As drill-and-practice and quiz-show discussions conspire against genuine inquiry, far too many students voice the groaning question of adolescence: "Do we *have* to?"

In this chapter, my aim is to sample the richness of writing-to-learn assignments across the content areas—and then to explore a few expressive writing strategies in more depth. Like the activities introduced in Chapter 2, these have potential for playfully engaging the imagination; and while they aren't foolproof, they do serve as wake-up calls to many somnambulant students. Also, these ideas are easy to manage—as long as you're comfortable with a little laughter and lively interchange before a discussion, lecture, or lab activity.

Some teachers manage expressive work by having students number their entries in a learning log and then linking total entries to a percentage of the semester's letter grade. Other teachers ask students to flag their three best entries for spot-checks. Still others use a weekly "check mark" system to keep students honest with daily writing. Students earn a check mark for good-faith participation or a "check plus" whenever they do especially well—and these marks can easily be converted to points.

Will some students try to sabotage expressive writing? Perhaps. But over time, most will succumb to the appeal of prompts focused on discovery, particularly if you set them up well. Let me reiterate the important point that most writing-to-learn activities are *ungraded* in the traditional sense. Their real aim is to hook students into content area thinking, not to accumulate marks in a grade book.

Opening Expressive Windows

Writing to learn can become part of a class routine; basic to its culture. As Mike Rose has shrewdly observed, "Students will float to the mark you set" (1989, p. 26). Figure 3-1 lists some of the writing formats (or genre) in which students can exercise playful impulses beyond the constraints of the five-paragraph theme. Of course, these formats can also become the basis for more involved process writing activities, which are described in Chapters 6 and 9.

With the theme of play in mind, let's briefly draw from the work of Diana Mitchell (1996), who recommends many different formats for expressive writing across the content areas. Some ideas generate quick-writes, whereas others may

FIGURE 3-1   Formats for Writing

Advertisements	Eulogies	Posters
Advice letters	Feature articles	Prescriptions
Advocacy letters	Flyers (all kinds)	Press releases
Anecdotes	Game directions	Profiles
Announcements	Greeting cards	Prophecies
Applications	Historical fiction	Protest letters
Autobiographies	How-to manuals	Recipes
Awards	Information forms	Recommendations
Ballads/Songs	Interviews	Requests
Biographies	Journals (real, imagined)	Research reports
Bookmarks	Lab reports	Responses/Rebuttals
Brochures	Laws/Regulations	Resumes
Cartoon strips	Letters (all kinds)	Reviews (books, etc.)
Case studies	Memoirs	Science fiction texts
Certificates (birth, death)	Memos (business)	Scripts (plays, movies)
Children's books	Monographs	Sermons
Collages/Mobiles	Monologues	Stories (all kinds)
Complaint letters	Mottos/Slogans	Song lyrics
Concert notes	Multimedia scripts	Sports reports
Cover letters (portfolios)	Newsletters	Summaries
Current event reports	News reports	Survey results
Debates	Obituaries	Tall tales
Demonstrations	Observation notes	Technical reports
Dialogues	Op-ed pieces	Telegram
Diary entries	Oral histories	"Top Ten" listings
Dictionary entries	Pamphlets	Tributes
Editorials	Parodies/Satires	TV commercials
Essays (all kinds)	Poems (all kinds)	Utopias
Eyewitness accounts	Police reports	

invite more development. The point here is to open the window of writing possibilities.

What If . . . ?

This activity encourages hypothetical thinking about "absences" in a content area. As higher-order thinking is prompted by good "What If" questions, students may want to explore new writing formats.

> What if George had not killed Lennie in *Of Mice and Men?*
>
> What if there had been no Abe Lincoln?
>
> What if people didn't sweat during and after exercise?
>
> What would music sound like if there were no major modes?
>
> (Mitchell, 1996, p. 94)

Three Words

In this activity, students first choose three words that best describe some content topic—for example, a character, historical era, or chapter assignment. Then students write about why their three words capture the essence of what was read or studied.

> What three words describe the problems in the American diet?
>
> What three words best describe the Bill of Rights?
>
> What three words best describe the mossy stage of a climax community?
>
> (Mitchell, 1996, p. 95)

Take a Stand

As the name suggests, students can't sit on the fence with this activity. They debate issues relevant to a content area, taking positions for or against a proposition. Writing may either precede discussion or follow it.

> Gerrymandering other than by geographic location should be prohibited.
>
> Genetic testing should be required of all potential parents.
>
> Predictions of the earth being overpopulated by 2020 are/are not supported by mathematical projections.
>
> (Mitchell, 1996, p. 95)

Letters

The activity of letter writing seems to have broad appeal across the content areas. By its very nature, letter writing invites playful impulses, even among older students. Of course, letters can be personal (apology, congratulations, love, sympathy, thanks) or related to business (application, complaint, inquiry, permission) or pub-lic (advice letter, letter to editor, public letter).

> Write a letter from Mozart to you at the time he is writing his final Mass.
>
> Write a letter explaining to next year's students what they can expect from this class.
>
> (Mitchell, 1996, p. 96)

"You Are There" Scenes

This activity offers a practical alternative to traditional reports. Students inhabit a scene as reporters, eyewitnesses, or interviewers. As we'll see later, students can get imaginatively as well as cognitively involved.

> You are there when the existence of black holes is confirmed. Describe who was there, how they determined what a black hole was, how others reacted.
>
> You are there in Piccaso's studio when he is in his "blue" period. Describe what is happening.
>
> (Mitchell, 1996, p. 96)

Now let's further explore four easy-to-use strategies to enhance content learning: **guided imagery, dramatic scenarios, role-playing,** and **dialogues.** As we examine these approaches, remember that expressive writing can also prompt talk about serious or controversial topics that arouse powerful emotions and deep insights.

Guided Imagery

The technique of guided mental imagery asks students to imagine a scene or situa-tion and to *use* that involvement in discussion and writing-to-learn activities. Done well, a guided imagery exercise can be emotionally powerful, intellectually pro-ductive, and even physiologically rewarding.

That's why coaches and sports psychologists routinely train Olympic com-petitors and professional athletes to use imagery as part of their workout routines. The effects of such training are well documented. "Not only can mental imagery improve specific motor skills," writes Annie Plessinger, "but it also seems to enhance motivation, mental toughness, and confidence, all of which will help ele-vate the level of play"(2004, p. 5).

Basically, guided imagery is a story that you narrate to students, a kind of "mind journey." Students close their eyes to focus their mental attention. To set the activity for the first time, Richardson (1982) recommends an introduction like this one:

> We are going to do something a little different today to apply the concepts we have learned about [topic]. I'd like you to imagine in your minds as clearly as you can the scenes I will describe to you. There will be a time where I will have you complete the scene or story, and I will allow plenty of time for that. I'd like you to see in your mind's eye the things around you. Imagine the sounds you would hear, the smells you would smell, and perhaps the feel of the things you touch. If there are emotions that would arise from this experience, let yourself feel those emotions.
>
> (p. 23)

Often, the preceding directions will suffice. But for some groups—ones that veteran teachers can readily picture—another nudge may be needed. Richardson likes to extend a challenge, saying that guided imagery has been used mostly by college students and it's unclear whether younger students are mature enough to use it. "We will try it to see if you have the power to concentrate on what I say and ignore everything else in the room," he adds. "It is difficult, but I think you can do it" (p. 24).

Shown next is an activity developed by teacher Tom Watson (1985) as part of a unit on the Pacific Northwest, one that integrated readings from geology, geography, and history. After seeing the film *Hoh Rain Forest* without sound, students took an imagined hike through the forest, one prompted by Watson's guided imagery narrative, with appropriate pauses along the way:

> Describe what you are thinking about, what the river looks like, what the trail is like, and make other general observations about what you see. The sun has come out, yet it is still cool. . . . Why? Something brushes against your face. . . . What is it? Time for a rest stop. You look around and find an ideal spot. Describe it. Then you begin to speculate how it got there and why it was there. Hiking along, you observe some animals off in a clearing. Describe them. Later, along the trail, you crouch low to look at something. What is it? Midafternoon, you set up camp. What are you going to do with the rest of the day? After dinner, as the sun is setting, you listen quietly to the sounds of the rain forest. Describe them. Describe the weather the next morning.
>
> (pp. 143–144)

In Watson's words, follow-up writing forced students to "recall information; interpret what they have seen, heard, and read; and apply that information appropriately" (p. 144). This rationale suggests that guided imagery grows out of curriculum content but also can lead back into it. Here's what one student wrote:

A Hike through the Rain Forest
We're starting on the bark-covered trail into the wild wonder of the Rain Forest. There's moss growing over the trail so you can barely tell there's bark underneath it. I can tell they haven't covered it with bark in a long while. The river is moving rather rapidly, dodging the rocks and fallen trees and branches. The sun is coming out and shining rather bright. The forest is still cold though. It's like there's a giant

reflector over the forest reflecting the heat so it will stay cold. We're taking a break to rest a bit. There's an old nursing log with some trees and rocks by and on it. We like this place because there's a good place to sit and rest. There's a lot of action going on here. Some birds are in the trees above us. We're back on the trail now some moss hanging from a tree brushed my face. It's fascinating how it just hangs from this tree. . . .

(p. 144)

So if you're a history teacher, why not use guided imagery to transport students back to the Revolutionary War setting of the novel *Johnny Tremain* or the Battle of the Little Big Horn or some other event? If you're a biology teacher, why not take students on a "fantastic voyage" through the life cycle of king salmon (Richardson, 1982, pp. 41–43). If you're a health teacher dealing with the risks of cigarette smoking, why not use an activity like "Cancer Sticks":

I want you to be able to visualize smoke going into your lungs. Assume that on an experimental basis you elected to take one draw on a cigarette. There is a machine that is hooked up to your chest; it looks like an x-ray machine, but instead it projects a magnified picture of your respiratory system on a large screen. Visualize taking a large puff on the cigarette and holding it in. (pause) On the screen you can see the smoke rush down the trachea; the smoke appears dark gray on the screen; you can see the cilia in the trachea get covered with smoke, and their movements slow down. Imagine smoke pouring down the lung. You can see little black spots being deposited along the side of the brachioles; you know that is tar. As the smoke arrives at the alveoli, the screen magnifies the smoke and analyzes it. On the side of the screen you see a list of different poisons within the smoke. (pause) Examine the oxygen exchange. You can see at the pulmonary capillaries the carbon dioxide coming off the red blood cells, and instead of oxygen grabbing onto the sites of the red blood cells, the carbon monoxide poison attaches. (pause) Imagine now expelling the smoke, leaving behind some grayish color.

(Richardson, 1982, p. 116)

As an English teacher, I often used guided imagery to set the scene for poems, stories, and plays. For example, in advance of reading Archibald MacLeish's "Lines for an Interment" aloud, my students mentally visited a graveyard in Belgium, where MacLeish speaks to his brother, killed 15 years earlier. In advance of Matthew Arnold's "Dover Beach," my students took a night journey to the white cliffs of Dover, where I wove in the philosophical debate of religion versus evolutionary theory in the mid-nineteenth century.

When linked with brief writing prompts, guided imagery can make curriculum content unforgettable. For example, here are two interesting prompts—one in math, one in science—that could easily follow a guided imagery activity.

Imagine that your whole family has been turned into geometric shapes: write a story explaining what shape each person is and now that works to his/her disadvantage as they interact with other family members.

Create a story in which you pretend you are an atom of hydrogen in a water molecule. Describe in detail how you would feel and what would happen to you if you went through two different types of changes—physical and chemical.

(Mitchell, 1996, p. 94)

Guided imagery feels *different* from regular school routines. And that's why this easy-to-use writing strategy is worth a try, especially as a prereading activity.

Dramatic Scenarios (Cases)

Closely linked to guided imagery is the technique of dramatic scenarios or "cases"—an imaginative prompt that puts students in an unresolved situation. Often the scenario presents a problem or conflict related to skills or knowledge currently being studied. In order to solve the problem or resolve the conflict, students must discuss or write or engage in other productive activities.

When some teachers first hear about scenarios, they dismiss the idea as educational "fluff." Real education, they say, is all about getting students to knuckle down and do their reading. So why is it, one might ask, that Harvard University has long used case-based teaching (extended dramatic scenarios) to train the nation's top business executives, administrators, and lawyers? After all, Harvard is hardly a place where professors cut corners when it comes to intellectual rigor. And why have many medical schools and engineering programs also adopted case-based teaching?

The answer, of course, is that the method works. The case (or scenario) gives learners a context in which to apply what they are learning. Moreover, the dramatic scenario forces students to think through the competing claims and issues embedded in the problem—which is what they must do in the real world. In other words, they must *actively* bring knowledge to bear on the given problem and *actively* organize their responses into coherent language that reveals their thinking.

Of course, to be fun and engaging, scenarios don't really have to be as elaborate and detailed as those used at Harvard or elsewhere. For example, psychology teacher Bruce Beaman used a dramatic scenario to hook the interest of high school students on the very first day of class. He was handed a bulletin that he read aloud.

The Edmonds School Board met last night at the administration center and passed the following rule effective immediately. All seniors, in order to graduate, must take a new course entitled, "consumer and community living." In case you cannot fit this into your current schedule before graduation, this class will be offered at night.

(1985, p. 64)

As Beaman puts it, "the uproar that followed was lively and animated" (p. 64). After the shock subsided and Beaman confessed that he was kidding, he asked students to put down all their physical and emotional reactions in journals. A typical response follows.

> I was shocked. I have just enough credits to graduate and my heart doubled in speed. I felt sweaty and nervous and horrified that this added pressure was put upon me. I couldn't believe what I was hearing but believed it and felt panicked like I'll never graduate on time.
>
> (p. 64)

Journal entries like this provided a link to the lesson's goal—a working definition of "psychology" to begin the semester's study. According to Beaman, "No student left that class period without understanding the definition" (p. 64).

Here's an example of a compelling little scenario that might spark lively discussion in a government or history class. Of course, to respond to this case, students must review the historical context and the facts:

> You are on the jury of the Sacco and Vanzetti case in the 1920s trial. Of the 12 jurors, you are the only one who thinks they are innocent. Write a letter convincing the other 11 of their innocence.
>
> (Mitchell, 1996, p. 95)

A more detailed scenario was developed by physics teacher F. D. Lee (Bean, Drenk, and Lee, 1982) as part of an imaginative series of "quandary-posing" cases involving velocity, acceleration, and other physics concepts. In these exercises, Lee restricted student writing to a microtheme format of a single 5 × 8 card. Of course, this constraint forced students to get to the point, using clear, specific language.

> Suppose that you are Dr. Science, the question-and-answer person for a popular magazine called *Practical Science.* Readers of your magazine are invited to submit letters to Dr. Science, who answers them in "Dear Abby" style in a special section of the magazine. One day you receive the following letter:
>
> Dear Dr. Science:
>
> You've got to help me settle this argument I am having with my girlfriend. We were watching a baseball game several weeks ago when this guy hit a pop-up straight over the catcher's head. When it finally came down, the catcher caught it standing on home plate. Well, my girlfriend told me that when the ball stopped in midair just before it started back down, its velocity was zero, but acceleration was not zero. I said she was stupid. If something isn't moving at all, how could it have any acceleration? Ever since then she has been making a big deal out of this and won't let me kiss her. I love her, but I don't think we can get back together until we settle this argument. We checked some physics books, but they weren't very clear. We agreed that I would write to you and let you settle the argument. But, Dr. Science, don't just tell us the answer. You've got to explain it so we both understand, because my girlfriend is really dogmatic. She said she wouldn't even trust Einstein unless he could explain himself clearly.
>
> Sincerely,
>
> Baseball Blues

Can This Relationship Be Saved? Your task is to write an answer to Baseball Blues. Because space in your magazine is limited, restrict your answer to what you can put on a single 5 × 8 card. Don't confuse Baseball and his girlfriend by using any special physics terms unless you clearly explain what they mean. If you think diagrams would help, include them on a separate sheet.

(p. 35)

If you're interested in the case method as applied to science and mathematics, check out two important web sites. The award-winning National Center for Case Study Teaching in Science (**ublib.buffalo.edu/libraries/projects/cases/case.html**) has developed wonderful material for both science and math. Also, the Far West Educational Laboratory (**www.wested.org**) has an extensive collection of cases for math education. High-quality materials like these have great potential as discussion and writing springboards.

Role-Playing

Any teacher faced with classroom chatter knows how much kids love to talk. We'll examine next an approach that invites students to give voice, literally, to their imaginations. Role-playing sometimes offers a welcome break from the traditional routines of read, recite, and review—and harnesses energy toward productive ends.

The idea of role-playing is to have students *imagine* their way into content area situations. To accomplish this end, role-playing asks students to talk and write from an imagined perspective, adopting the voice of someone other than themselves. Eventually, of course, the talk leads to writing.

For example, in a government class, they might study a problem scenario—for instance, the issue of how to handle national security while also protecting civil rights—and write from the viewpoint of a presidential advisor. In industrial arts, they might adopt the role of shop foreman and explain a welding process to apprentices. In literature, they might write a diary entry from a character's viewpoint, like Esperanza in *The House on Mango Street* by Sandra Cisneros. In a marketing class, they might take on the role of an advertising firm, planning a campaign to create awareness of a new product.

Also, you can have students imagine themselves as members of an organization and then write from an institutional viewpoint. Here are three prompts posed by Mitchell (1996) for biology, literature, the arts:

What would People for Ethical Treatment of Animals say about pig dissections?

What would the National Organization of Women say about the works of Ernest Hemingway?

What would members of the National Endowment for the Arts say to school board members who think that music and art are "frills"?

(p. 96)

In the context of American history, special education teacher Ray Marik (1985) believed that students needed "to interact with selected events without losing a sense of historical momentum" (p. 85). Toward this end, Marik devised "touchstone" tasks for his special education learners. One such assignment had students assume the role of a newspaper reporter covering the Boston Massacre during the Revolutionary War. Of course, such an assignment was preceded by reading and animated discussion, then followed by sharing. Here's the beginning of a long, richly expressive piece by Marie, a special education student:

> **Five Innocent People Get Killed!**
> It was March 24, 1770 the early evening about 6:00 p.m. When a special British Military force from Canada was sent to the Boston area. Solder's and colonists soon were involve in quarrels. A force of solders fired on crowded of people. There was five people killed out the crowded. . . .
>
> (p. 88)

The key to managing a role-playing exercise is to prepare the class carefully for the activity. Students need to understand why the activity is worth doing, what it requires of them, and how it's to be accomplished.

For example, in a speech or human relations class studying "conflicts with authority," you might introduce the idea of **oral negotiation,** a strategy involving good communication skills. The purpose of role-playing, you'd explain, is to help students test their skills of communicating respectfully (not arguing). You'd explain that each student is paired with a partner and that all pairs role-play simultaneously. Depending on the class, you might model your expectations or write directions on the board. After a few minutes of practice in small groups, you'd have selected pairs of students perform their role-play as a focus for large group discussion or follow-up writing.

Here is a simple set of role-playing situations.

Problem A

Characters: Teacher, student.

Scene: After school in a classroom.

Situation: The teacher needs to have the semester's grades in tomorrow. The student has not completed the class. Without the course credit, the student will be ineligible to participate in a special school event.

Problem B

Characters: parent, teenager.

Scene: Dinner on Friday evening.

Situation: The teenager wants to go to a dance on Saturday night but has not met the parent's curfew rules from the weekend before. The penalty for breaking the rules is being "grounded."

Problem C

Characters: Employer, employee.

Scene: The employer's office.

Situation: The employee wants a raise in pay from minimum wage. The employee has missed several days of work recently and sometimes seems rude to customers.

Problem D

Characters: Coach, basketball player.

Scene: Hallway near the gym.

Situation: The coach has demanded that all players have their hair trimmed to a "reasonable" length. The players want to wear longer hair.

While role-playing may seem like a class management nightmare, it can pay big dividends in student involvement. For example, science teacher Chris Gooch worked with eighth graders who were studying rock classifications and the rock cycle. Based on the three types of rock (igneous, sedimentary, and metamorphic), he divided his class into small groups and had them compose "group essays." Gooch told students that aliens from Mars were threatening to attack and that the aliens worshiped rocks. If the groups could convince the aliens that Earth had "cool rocks," the attack would be averted; but if not, Earth was doomed. Each group had to describe at least three rocks, discuss their classification, and say a little about their geologic history.

Gooch (personal communication, March 2003) was "pleasantly surprised at how engaged the students were." The groups presented their short essays to the class, and the class in turn played the role of aliens, voting on whether the earth was doomed based on each short essay. Of course, voting had nothing to do with each student's grade in the activity. Such exercises can easily lead to dialogue writing, our next topic.

Dialogue Writing

Like other activities in this chapter, dialogue writing involves imagination. That is, instead of taking quizzes or doing reports, students have to invent language that meets the dramatic constraints of given situations. Typically, such activities are regarded as "fun," because they're a break from routine and because they're mentally stimulating. Dialogues serve as a reminder, as if one were needed, that learning feels good.

Art teacher Priscilla Zimmerman (1985) experimented with dialogues in the context of her art appreciation course. Zimmerman believed that students need clear guidelines for writing and that the activity should enhance understanding of the artistic concepts being studied—namely, lines and shapes as well as principles of unity, contrast, and variation. To set up the activity, she had students list and describe the elements in a reproduced painting and then analyze how its principles worked. Then they wrote a dialogue that incorporated their analysis. After the initial drafting, she challenged students to revise their dialogues, focusing on clarity. Her writing prompt required students to use two voices—an art gallery owner and a visitor, who was a potential customer. She provided this opening line for student-created dialogues: "How on earth can this be worth $100,000?" (p. 38).

Here's one example of what students produced:

VISITOR: How on earth can this be worth $100,000?

OWNER: Now, sir, please don't be so irrational, note its extraordinary qualities.

VISITOR: What qualities? You mean a few multiple colored oil paints slapped on a piece of canvas?

OWNER: Sir, please note the artist's use of contrast, repetition, and variation.

VISITOR: What do you mean? What's contrast?

OWNER: Contrast is just one of the three principles of art I just mentioned. Contrast is defined as a strong difference, for example, dark versus light, or big versus small.

VISITOR: Okay, I see the darker colors of the painting are contrasting with the light ones as are the large triangles and squares to the smaller ones.

OWNER: That's right. Now you're catching on. Shapes can contrast as well as color and shades of value.

VISITOR: And what do those other two principles mean that you mentioned? Repetition and variation.

OWNER: Repetition means to repeat the same shape over and over, but the artist doesn't just stop there, he also uses variation in the shapes. Variation means a slight difference, a slight change from shape to shape. The two combined create unity. Otherwise the painting would be very dull.

VISITOR: I see, so without repetition and variation working together, the design would be missing something, right?

OWNER: Right, because unity brings together all the principles and elements of art to create a sense of oneness to make the perfect design.

VISITOR: Boy, without contrast, repetition, variation, and especially unity, art would be worthless. I can see now how designs are valued at such high prices.

OWNER: By Jove, I think you've got it. So would you like to purchase this particular painting?

VISITOR: Are you kidding me? A painting with such caliber as this is priceless, it should be put in a museum of fine art.

OWNER: Why I never!

VISITOR: Yeah, and you probably never will either, but thanks for the lecture.

OWNER: @#:!!%

(pp. 39–40)

What do you think? Did this student (and others in class) probably have fun in creating their witty dialogues and sharing them? Of course. But, equally important, did this student (and others) actively rehearse the target concepts of the art class, the ones in Zimmerman's unit plan? Yes again. And this is the point of good writing-to-learn activities. They invite active integration—active processing—of ideas.

Here are several more ideas, drawn from Mitchell (1996), for dialogue writing in other content areas:

Construct a food chain conversation between a mouse and a hawk.

Construct a conversation between a negative number and a positive number showing some similarities and differences.

Write a conversation between Booker T. Washington and W. E. B. DuBois.

Write a conversation between potential and chemical energy.

Write a conversation between the bench press and pectoral muscles.

Write a conversation between a musician and his/her instrument.

(p. 94)

Dialogue is psychologically interesting, because it enables the human mind to stimulate and teach itself. The tension between the two voices propels the dialogue forward. The technique is especially interesting when students "invent" the author of a text they're reading and begin a conversation. Can you imagine students interacting with Shakespeare or with the authors of their biology text? What would students have to say? What answers would the authors give?

Finally—and on a more personal note—can you imagine a dialogue between you as reader and me as writer?

A Reader/Writer Dialogue

Your eyebrows arch like twin question marks as you cross your arms. "Look, what I'm really worried about is the *workload*—all that grading."

"Maybe writing for insight doesn't always need a grade. It's just a thought."

You laugh. "A crazy one."

"Why is that?"

"Because teachers make writing assignments and then grade them."

"Maybe that's the crazy idea. Since when do athletic coaches or music teachers or drama coaches grade the practice efforts? Maybe practice doesn't *need* a grade."

You laugh again. "But kids *expect* grades."

I hesitate. "So they're running the show?"

Now you shrug. "Sometimes I'm not sure."

"Well, give it a try without grades. Let kids earn points for expressive writing and a zero if they don't write. Let the drawing and creative written work occasionally earn small prizes like penny candy. Let writing be the 'gateway' or 'ticket' to fun activities or follow-up discussion. Make writing—in all its forms—a way of participating."

"Okay, but the idea of 'insight' still puzzles me. How do I explain that?"

"Think about the punch line of a joke and that split-second of understanding when you can't help but laugh. When your circuits light up—*that's* insight. Or think about familiar childhood stories—say, 'The Ant and the Grasshopper' or 'Cinderella.' Each had a point—some insight—that you took away and thought about."

"Like seeing things from another viewpoint."

"Exactly," I reply. "Understanding doesn't happen in a vacuum. When you truly *know* something, it becomes part of you—and writing can tell your story."

"But sometimes I don't know what I know. It's just a muddle."

"Writing helps with that, too. You name what you don't understand. Just naming things sometimes helps you deal with them."

You smirk. "When I'm doing math problems, sometimes I make a drawing—or jot down key information. I'll talk to myself—make notes—"

"That's the tool function of writing. And when you solve it—how does that feel?"

"It's like—hey, no problem—what took me so long? It feels good."

"So put it all together."

You nail the thought. "The insights kids have—that's what they take away, what they *really* remember. Writing helps them track what they know and don't know."

"Okay, let's build on that. Let's say you're trying to understand something new—and reading your own words. What's that like?"

You pause, then shrug. "I *see* my own ideas—and sort of hear them."

"Think about that."

"So writing puts me in control. I can see my gaps in understanding—"

"And therefore?"

"I've got the power. I can build on what's there, change it, whatever."

"And what if you share your writing with others? And read what they've written?"

You hesitate. "Okay, I learn from them, and they learn from me."

"Right. Insights come from within but also from working with others." I pause. "If nothing else, you know where learners are, what they're thinking. That's pretty useful."

"Hmmm," you reply. "This sounds too good to be true."

WRITE FOR INSIGHT ACTIVITY

If you're a teacher at heart, you know why I used a dialogue between us. It was a device designed to surprise and entertain you—but also to clarify the concept of insight. The perils of such an approach are many, but I hoped to engage both your imagination and intellect.

Plato used the same approach over two thousand years ago in his famous Socratic dialogues. If we're lucky, you'll recall the issues in my reader/writer dialogue whenever you overhear spirited talk about writing in the teachers' lounge. Because vivid narratives and dialogues are easily remembered, religions the world over have long used them to teach. Stories engage us imaginatively.

Let's extend the reader/writer dialogue. *Give voice to your questions, and then try to answer those questions in my voice, the voice of this text.* Doing so, you'll discover what's on your mind—and perhaps what's on mine as well!

To get into the spirit of expressive writing, I suggest teaming up with a friendly colleague in oral role-playing. In the exercise, you pose an honest question to your partner, who will valiantly attempt to respond as the "author." For example, you might ask, "Okay, so how might I use dialogue writing in my health education class?"

Stick with oral role-playing for five minutes or so—at least long enough to get past the laughter and awkwardness of not knowing what to say. Then switch roles. Your partner will voice his or her questions, and you'll try to respond as the "author."

After this oral warm-up, you're ready to write. Put down your honest questions and generate what you see as my responses. Of course, don't pose softball questions or soft-headed answers! After you develop your dialogue, share a copy of it with your instructor. Then reflect (in writing, of course!) on what the dialogue exercise taught you about this chapter's focus—expressive, imaginative writing.

4 Helping Basic Writers Succeed

I never wrote a word I didn't hear as I read.
—Eudora Welty

A Bridge to Literacy

Let me call him Eddie.

Wearing glasses with thick plastic frames, he sat right in front and looked up at me with shy, questioning eyes. His arms were thin, even for a seventh grader, and he wore oversized hand-me-down knit shirts buttoned at the throat. He often doodled in a blue denim notebook, putting his face close to the page.

He really wasn't any trouble, this brown-skinned kid with close-cropped black hair, almost invisible among his Asian and Pacific Islander classmates in downtown Honolulu. He was congenial and compliant, even as others goofed around. Although he pretended to read, his main interest was the notebook, with sketches of fire-breathing dragons and ninja warriors.

At first I thought he was lazy. "Come on, Eddie," I'd say. "Let's get to it, okay?"

Later I thought motivation might be the problem. I told him how interesting he'd find the reading if he'd just get started—and I emphasized upcoming quizzes.

Only gradually did it dawn on me that Eddie's problem might go deeper than shyness or an aversion to academic work. As he ducked his head in discussions and handed in two-sentence papers, I wondered how much his non-English-speaking home background compromised his ability to understand written English. Eddie struggled in reading and writing—and I wasn't doing much to help develop his skills.

So one morning, while the class worked, I pulled him aside for a little talk, "a chance to know you better." I learned about his sketchbook and his mom, who cleaned hotel rooms. Eddie's extended family lived together not far from the school.

"So what's the hardest part about reading?" I asked.

Eddie wrinkled his nose, figuring this might be a trick question. "Uh, like to understand the words?" he replied.

Our special ed teacher had already told me that Eddie didn't qualify for pull-out reading instruction. His decoding ("word attack") skills were surprisingly good. But his English vocabulary and sentence structure abilities were weak. In short, his oral language skills didn't yet support the demands of seventh grade reading and writing.

Reaching into my desk drawer, I pulled out a ninja comic book. Eddie grinned from ear to ear. "Cool."

"Could you read a little of this aloud?"

His comic book reading was halting, but he managed to decode the simple text. After two or three minutes, I asked some basic questions, and he handled them without much trouble, glancing at the pictures as he talked.

"That's good reading," I said. "How about our textbook?"

Eddie glanced away and shrugged. "Hard words."

"The words are hard," I repeated.

"Yeah, for me."

"Okay," I said. "What if I preview the hard words for the class?"

Eddie hesitated. "What's *preview*?" he asked.

"Like looking ahead? Maybe you've seen video previews that get you excited about new ninja movies?"

Eddie grinned. "Yeah, cool."

"We could have word previews. What do you think?"

Still eyeing the comic book, Eddie was eager to get off the hook. My question went unanswered. "Tell you what," I said. "You're a smart kid, but we need to strengthen your word knowledge. That okay?"

Eddie shrugged again, maybe unsure of what I was suggesting.

"But if we're working together," I added, "I need your help."

"Like what?" he asked.

"Eddie, I can't preview all the hard words. So in your notebook, keep a list of them and discuss them with your study buddy each day."

"Copy them?"

"Right—copy the ones you can't figure out as you read. Do this all week, okay?"

Now he looked worried. "Do something wrong?"

"No," I said. "You haven't done anything wrong. You're helping me teach you. Keep that word list so you can get help learning them, okay?"

Eddie nodded assent.

"And one other thing about writing," I added. "Maybe you need help with spelling during writing time. Just raise your hand and I'll put words on the board for you."

"Like *preview*?" he asked.

"Exactly," I nodded. "Whatever word you need, just raise your hand."

We shook hands on the deal: I'd preview hard words before in-class reading, and he'd keep track of hard words to discuss with a study buddy; and when it came to writing, all he had to do was raise a hand to get help with spelling.

What I didn't tell Eddie was that other hands besides his would go up during in-class writing—or that the board would sometimes be *covered* with new words, ones he'd first hear and then find himself using. Nor did I mention that I'd ask able readers to do read-alouds in a small group that included him. I reasoned that hearing and seeing the text would help Eddie comprehend more as it developed his skills. My plan was to create solid footings for Eddie's literacy bridge.

He still eyed the comic book.

"At the end of the week, if you work hard, you get the comic book. Fair enough?"

"I'll draw you a picture," he replied.

"Cool," I said.

Back to Human Basics

Eddie's story is hardly unique. If you're a veteran teacher, you know basic writers like him—as well as others with sullen or indifferent expressions. These are the kids who don't experience much school success and often keep us awake at night. We can't fix their poverty, or give them magic language pills, or wish away a bleak academic history. All we can do is try to teach well.

Let me emphasize at the outset that basic writing isn't "bad writing" any more than walking is "bad running." Yes, basic writing is often marked by surface errors, but such missteps are hardly cause for gnashing of teeth in the faculty lounge. In the big picture of skill development, it's better to think of "basic writing" as "novice writing."

Imagining ourselves as basic writers and asking how we'd like to be treated can be a revealing exercise. We'd like to be respected, of course; we'd like to know *what* we're doing in class and *why*; and we'd like to feel we're learning every day.

These are daunting standards for a hard-working secondary teacher who is trying to share knowledge with 150 (or more) learners, some of whom telegraph their alienation in dress, language, and behavior.

> *Literacy Club*
> *Pants dey baggy, an' mouth be cruel;*
> *Our sneer hidin' hurt from dey ridicule.*
> *Caps flip back—we lookin' so bored—*
> *Ignorin' dey word 'cause we be ignored.*
> *Dey say we lazy, an' dey say we rude—*
> *But maybe we learnin' dey attitude.*
> (Strong, 2001, p. 10)

Will we find ways to equip this voice with strategies for academic success? Or will we consign it to the chilly margins of our classroom, where it can sleep unnoticed?

To teach basic skills effectively, we have to know what we're doing and why. Moreover, we have to know how to motivate discouraged students who are afraid to take risks—and how to sustain attention over the long haul of learning, especially for those who may bring troubled backgrounds or deficits in English language to school.

This chapter addresses the challenge of working with novice, low-performing writers in middle school and high school settings. To me, it makes little difference whether these are English as a Second Language (ESL) learners or mainstreamed, special education kids who need extra coaching to succeed. With common sense adaptations, what generally works with one kind of student often works with the other.

This chapter's strategies, like those in Chapters 2 and 3, emphasize expressive writing and the development of **fluency.** What's different is that these ideas provide plenty of support, or scaffolding, to help learners with special needs begin to approach (and then achieve) our academic expectations. Developing writing fluency among struggling writers is really a means to an end. But it's an essential first step in helping students learn subject matter on their own.

In this chapter, then, we'll see how to help students learn basic literacy skills, such as spelling and vocabulary as well as transcribing accuracy. We'll also see how to structure basic thinking tasks in writing—for example, summarizing and paraphrasing, so critical to school learning. And finally we'll see how skill-building work such as fact sheets and sentence combining can teach academic content.

Basics of Good Teaching

To begin this discussion, let me share three teaching premises borrowed from the work of Gerald Camp, an expert teacher of basic writers:

- In learning a skill, success is the most important motivation to continue.
- Success means knowing how to do something you didn't know how to do before, and *knowing* you know.
- Any reasonable assignment can be structured in such a way that *every* student in the class can succeed.

(1982, pp. 4–5)

This clear, brilliant formulation undergirds the ideas in this chapter. It's a principled vision to guide instruction, especially when we feel the urge to throw in the towel or to blame basic writers for their impoverished backgrounds.

Camp pretends that his struggling students are eager and able to learn, and he also gets them to behave as if they have such commitments. His management system, a weekly contract with a "Commitment" section and a follow-up "Performance" section, rewards students each day for making a good-faith learning effort. As part of his weekly contract, students understand that *no* put-downs or negative remarks are permitted, even in jest. Each insult or negative comment results in the loss of a point. Believing that basic writers need a safe, positive environment for learning, Camp would no doubt agree with the views of Kylene Beers:

> When children are belittled by their peers, something happens that is hurtful almost beyond repair. When it happens in front of an adult, an adult who is supposed to care, and the adult does nothing, then the damage is even greater. Let your

students know that in your classroom, belittling remarks—through written language, oral language, or body language—will not be tolerated.

(2003, p. 266)

Camp's management system, when coupled with clear, well-organized teaching and daily practice enables basic writers to transcend their identities as academic throwaways. Helping such students find daily success is critical because small, incremental steps motivate ongoing learning.

But what if your basic students resist the idea of writing in learning logs? Try a simple, but vivid, demonstration. After a well-taught content lesson, ask them to summarize its main idea into a single sentence, *which they hold silently in their heads.* Have them raise their hands to signal that they've got their sentence figured out, and they're ready to write. Then pull a surprise: *Have them switch pens or pencils to the opposite writing hand and transcribe the sentence.* After the groans and laughter subside, the single-sentence writing will take a minute or two.

Afterward, discuss the point that writing with the opposite hand makes us focus on handwriting rather than on the content of our thinking. It saps mental energy. And that's why it's so important to develop writing fluency with daily practice in learning logs. Fluency releases brain power, giving us access to the good ideas between our ears.

Another way to sell fluency development is to have students consider the skills they've *already* learned—for example, riding a bike, playing the guitar, skateboarding, shooting baskets, surfing the Internet, driving a car, and so on. Challenge them to think about the small steps—and practice—that moved them from novice learning to some level of proficiency. Learning to drive a car makes a vivid example because the task is so often nerve-racking at first, but becomes absolutely automatic with practice.

Finally, for doubters in your class, there's the story of George "Shotgun" Shuba, one of baseball's greatest home run hitters of all time. Shuba was legendary for his incredibly "natural swing," the utterly "fluid power" of his batting. But what no one knew was Shuba's evening routine from adolescence on. Every evening—day after day, week after week, year after year—he descended the basement stairs, picked up a heavy, weighted bat, and swung it 600 times. A fluid swing indeed!

Teaching Basics Strategically

In *Strategies for Struggling Writers,* James Collins lays out a four-step plan for teaching basic skills effectively:

- Identifying a strategy worth teaching
- Introducing the strategy by modeling it
- Helping the students try the strategy out with workshop-style teacher guidance
- Helping students work toward independent mastery of the strategy through repeated practice and reinforcement

(1998, p. 65)

With these steps as context, let's briefly consider the issue of spelling, one of the most vexing problems for skill-deficient students. We'll assume you're trying to help basic writers learn key vocabulary words in your content area.

Many basic writers have serious spelling problems because they don't read very much (spelling is a visual memory skill, mostly learned through reading) and because they have few strategies for learning to spell. So how do we approach spelling in a way that informs them about what will happen and why, invites involvement, and assures day-to-day progress?

First, we need to pull target words from content lessons and demonstrate how visual memory works. We begin by studying each word's shape and syllables, saying it slowly, and then tracing (or writing) it—first while looking at it, then while covering it up. I like to model large-scale "air writing" (visualizing the letters as they are whispered), but students can also close their eyes and do finger tracings on their arms. Some learners try tactile surfaces—silky fabric, fur, or sandpaper—to improve their memory of words. Kids can be amazingly inventive when they take on the challenge of learning to spell.

Next, we can model how learning logs can be used for personal word lists—not only of words students misspell but also of "words worth knowing and using." Many will be content-related words, but they can also be words of general interest. Personal lists provide the basis for spelling quizzes, with students paired up to quiz each other: You give me your list, and I'll give you mine. As for the misspelled words drawn from writing tasks, students should organize their target words into three columns: *Misspelling* (with the correction indicated); the *Corrected Word* in its proper form; and a *Reminder or Rule* generated by the student (Strong, 2001).

A third strategy is to give students targeted lists. Type "high-frequency words" into your web search page, and you should find Fry's list of the three hundred most common words, which "make up about 65 percent of all written material" (Fry, Kress, and Fountoukidis, 1993, p. 23). While you're at it, type "spelling demons" into your web search, and you'll find useful short lists of tricky words for students to master.

"Think about it," you say to your classes. "Learn these words, and you're two-thirds of the way to being a good speller!"

For practice, put basic writers in pairs and let them quiz each other, with one point for each correct spelling. Missed words go on each student's personal list.

And finally we can preview the key concept words in advance of our reading assignments. Putting new words in a list is useful, but it's often better to present them within a graphic organizer that shows their relationships to each other. For example, here's a simple three-part overview for the topic "Rocks" in a geology unit:

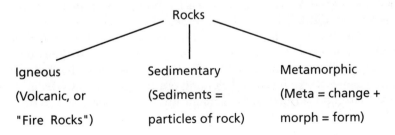

Rocks

Igneous
(Volcanic, or
"Fire Rocks")

Sedimentary
(Sediments =
particles of rock)

Metamorphic
(Meta = change +
morph = form)

As students copy the organizer into their notes, use think-aloud modeling to focus on synonyms, encourage guesses about meanings, and highlight structural clues. For example, the word "metamorphosis" is made up of two parts—*meta* (change) and *morph* (form)—which combine to mean a "change in form." For fun, students can visualize the metamorphosis of Spiderman or the Incredible Hulk as they break the word into two parts for easy spelling. Now, as other earth science words are added to the organizer, encourage students to use the visualizing strategy, sharing ideas aloud. Eventually, you can erase (or cover up) parts of the graphic organizer, asking students to visualize its missing elements.

Under "igneous rocks," for example, you might contrast intrusive cooling and extrusive cooling, inviting guesses about where such cooling occurs. You'd explain that the slow cooling of magma ("molten rock") beneath the earth's surface leads to large crystals in rock, whereas surface cooling leads to fine-grained rock. You'd have both kinds of rock for students to handle, and you'd add the two processes as well as the specific rock names to the graphic organizer. Working in this way, you'd build background for your reading assignment and for expressive writing follow-up.

All of these ideas encourage students to adopt an active, strategic approach to learning. No longer are they victims of past teaching or their own laziness. This move to engaged, attentive learning represents a real psychological shift for basic writers.

Developing Transcribing Skill

In this chapter's headnote, the legendary writer Eudora Welty confesses, "I never wrote a word I didn't hear as I read." And C. S. Lewis offers advice for anyone willing to pay attention, including basic writers and their teachers:

> Always write (and read) with the ear, not the eye. You should hear every sentence you write as if it was being read aloud or spoken.
>
> (in Murray, 1990, p. 134)

Unfortunately, many students don't understand that the ear is an organ to be trusted. Instead, they believe what they have been taught by well-intentioned but clueless teachers—that good writing results from following abstract grammar rules. As a result, novice writers shift their focus from making sense of their half-formed, inchoate thoughts to an anxious fixation on "writing correctly" or "doing the assignment right." They are blocked before they even begin.

Another issue for basic writers—and teachers as well—is their conception of writing. Students usually don't understand that easy reading (the kind that anticipates our needs and respects us) is *difficult* to write—and that hard reading (the kind that leaves us confused and shaking our heads) is *easy* to write. Basic writers believe that good writing arrives magically if a person has a writing "gift" or "talent." And because writing is so hard for them, they conclude (incorrectly) that they are "just dumb"—and they shrug and give up.

It's important to reprogram the thinking of basic writers, but it's equally important to provide practice that develops skills, step-by-step. You might begin by posting the C. S. Lewis admonition. Invite students to talk about it so they understand the need to *hear* written language; then explain why you want to conduct a series of brief in-class activities to develop the skill of **transcribing,** the most basic of basic skills.

Transcribing underlies "two-channel thinking" (Mellon, 1981), or the ability to put down words while others are being held in short-term memory or are arising in verbal consciousness. Without such thinking, it's impossible to write. Moreover, if students are focused on figuring out spelling and basic writing conventions, there's no way they can engage in **decentering** (Moffett, 1983), the activity of attending to the meaning of their words. The human brain is awesomely efficient, but it doesn't like overload.

Motivation matters—so students must know what they'll be doing and why. Such dialogue increases their willingness to work, as Gerry Camp (1982) has shown us. But students also need to understand that as they begin hearing (and holding) language in their heads in content-centered dictation practice, they should commit themselves to developing fluency through free-writing practice in their learning logs. Why? Because fluency helps make writing fun—or at least much less of a chore—and because it frees up their brains to consider *what* they're saying and *how* it might be revised.

The developmental sequence for basic writers is easy to articulate, but hard to implement: First we focus on fluency, then on form and content, then correctness. Help students understand that if they "keep the faith" and work *with* you, their writing skills and content learning will improve simultaneously.

Using Content-Based Dictation

Oral dictation exercises—two or three sentences at first—will help basic writers develop transcribing skill. Choose content-related material from your field, but make sure the vocabulary is accessible and the sentences not too long. I recommend two oral readings of the selection, "chunking" the phrases so students can hold them in short-term memory. With practice, students will hold increasingly long chunks of language in memory, and dictation can be speeded up. However, five or ten minutes of dictation practice each day is plenty.

For example, because my field is writing and I want students to understand that writing is hard for everybody, not just for them, I might use sentences by professional writers like Peter deVries, Margaret Atwood, and Robert Cormier:

- I love being a writer. What I can't stand is the paperwork.
- The fact is that blank pages inspire me with terror. What will I put on them? Will it be good enough? Will I have to throw it out?

• The blank page is there every day; that's what keeps you humble. That's what keeps your feet on the ground. No one can do it for you; and the page can be terrifyingly blank. As much joy as there is joy in writing, there's always the little bit of terror to keep you on edge, on your toes.

(in Murray, 1990, pp. 72, 187)

After oral dictation, put the source material on an overhead projector. You (or a student) should read it aloud again. Let students compare their versions to the originals, checking spelling, punctuation, and capital letters. Of course, repeated practice—like calisthenics—is what strengthens the connection between oral and written language. Simply paying attention helps students acquire skill in marking sentence boundaries.

In the material presented as an example, students should pay attention to contractions, question marks, and semicolons. In the dictation follow-up, you might point out that semicolons are "stronger" than commas for linking two closely related sentences.

"Oh," some students will say to themselves. "I get it."

After modeling dictation over several days, you can make the practice more student-centered in short skill-building drills. Pair students up and have one student read two or three key sentences from the textbook aloud to his or her partner, who takes down the dictation. Then the partners switch roles, and a second brief passage is read aloud. Finally, have students put their heads together over the textbook to check their transcribing accuracy. As partners, they are now ready to participate in your content-related discussion or other activity.

Having encouraged practice in transcribing, you can also use dictation as a response to content material—whether a brief lecture, video, or problem scenario. This activity can be done in pairs or small groups. It involves *oral* response to a stimulus, one that partners transcribe word for word. The speaker says one sentence and allows time for transcription. The speaker says another related sentence, and transcription continues. Finally, a third sentence is spoken to complete the dictation. Afterwards, the speaker and transcriber huddle over the text, which is read aloud as a paragraph. This content-focused interchange sounds simple, but it demands real focus for both the speaker and transcribers.

As noted previously, such activities helps basic students develop the capacity to write expressively in learning logs, as described in preceding chapters. Of course, writing skills develop slowly, and it's unreasonable to expect overnight miracles.

Summarizing and Paraphrasing

Let's pause here to consider the comprehension skills you're using as you read this book. If someone challenged you to summarize the preceding section, you'd probably say (or write) something like this:

The section explains how to set up and use brief oral dictations in content-based teaching. A teacher can use the textbook or other content material to give basic writers daily practice in holding sentences in short-term memory and then transcribing them. Afterwards, students check their transcribed sentences against the originals. Teacher modeling is followed by paired dictation practice and by oral (transcribed) responses to regular content lessons. The aim of these activities is to teach content and basic writing skills at the same time. Such skill development helps basic writers increase their writing fluency.

Our ability to summarize what we've read—to reconstruct its gist—is a skill we've acquired through academic practice. But although it's mostly automatic for us, it's often a mystery to our students. Therefore, we shouldn't be too surprised that low-performing students tend to ignore academic tasks focused on summarizing. It's tough to respond when no one shows you how.

One way to teach such skills is through "given language" exercises. Here's an activity prepared by special education teacher Dave Nielsen (Strong, 1986, p. 39) that helps students develop paraphrasing skills.

Planning an Essay Answer
1. You are taking an essay exam.
2. You should set aside a few moments.
3. You should plan your answer in advance.
4. You should make a list of key points.
5. You intend to cover them in your answer.
6. You can get distracted under pressure.
7. You may leave out important ideas.
8. You know the ideas well.
9. You will refer to your basic list.
10. You will often remember more details.
11. These details will give your essay depth.
12. They will also improve its organization.

The task is to put this information into fewer sentences. Doing so will force students to engage in mental activities basic to paraphrase. After showing what's expected on the first few sentences, turn students loose to work on the problem. Here's one outcome.

(1) If you are taking an essay exam, you should set aside a few moments and plan your answer in advance. (2) Make a list of key points that you intend to cover in your answer. (3) You can get distracted under pressure, leaving out important ideas that you know well. (4) As you refer to your list, you will often remember more details. (5) These details will give your essay depth and improve its organization.

(Strong, 1986, p. 39)

Notice that this activity not only teaches the skill of paraphrasing but also imparts useful information about writing.

A related activity is the fact sheet, drawn from content material. According to Nielsen, "fact sheets can be written in minutes and used in many ways—to introduce a topic, reinforce learning, or increase comprehension while helping to improve writing skill" (Strong, 1986, p. 39). A typical fact-generating scenario is a unit review, with students working in small groups, and teachers listing student ideas on an overhead transparency. Figure 4-1 shows a fact sheet on whales.

And how is such an activity used? As Nielsen puts it, "the student's first task is to select phrases that make sense together. Then the phrases are combined to form sentences. Finally, the sentences are arranged into a paragraph" (Strong, 1986, p. 39). The "levels" listed by Nielsen challenge students to stretch themselves. For

FIGURE 4-1   Fact Sheet: Whales

are among the most intelligent animals
have no ears
use sound signals to communicate
use sound signals to navigate
are the largest living creatures
strain plankton from the seawater
are mammals
can sometimes be found in fresh water
have voices
may become extinct
have teeth
eat fish
have fishlike bodies
have paddle-shaped flippers
range in size from the porpoise to the blue whale
can hold their breath up to two hours
are insulated by a layer of blubber, or fat
are aquatic animals
have lungs, not gills
have horizontal tail fins, unlike fish
are different from fish
have thick, smooth skin
can dive to depths of 4,800 feet
do not see very well
range from 4 feet to 100 feet in length
are social animals
may weigh as much as 150 tons
cannot smell
have nose openings, or blow holes, atop their heads
are hunted for oils in their bodies
live in all of the world's oceans

At level	Students are able to
A	use five facts in no more than four sentences
B	use ten facts in no more than six sentences
C	use fifteen facts in no more than eight sentences
D	use twenty facts in no more than ten sentences
E	use twenty-five facts in no more than twelve sentences

example, the following short paragraph uses five facts in no more than four sentences (level A), but students can then move up the ladder by writing more information.

> Whales are mammals. Ranging from 4 feet to 100 feet, they live in all of the world's oceans. These mammals are among the most intelligent animals. This social animal may become extinct.
>
> (Strong, 1986, p. 39)

Moving beyond such activities, we can have learners find the topic in sentences, paragraphs, and sections of content area material. Of course, "topic" refers to what the material is about. Teacher-led demos should be followed by paired student practice, first in sentence contexts, then in short paragraphs. Practice material comes directly from the content area—usually the textbook or class handouts—so students learn key ideas and skills simultaneously.

After students have developed skill in finding topics, they can write one-sentence summaries (called "headlines" by some teachers) for paragraph-length content material. Again, this process needs to be modeled, so learners know what they're doing and why. When modeling, put a content paragraph on the overhead projector and show how one must first find a topic and then draw from the paragraph's ideas to say something about it. Do a think-aloud so students can hear the process of your thinking. Verbalize your one-sentence summary aloud, transcribing it (and tinkering with it) on a transparency before the class.

Afterwards, use another content paragraph and repeat the process, inviting students to help develop a one-sentence summary. Ask them to find the main topic and to volunteer ideas that say something about the topic. Prompt them to pair up and generate ideas. Pass around acetate sheets and water-soluble pens, so student teams can transcribe one-sentence summaries. Then project the transparencies, inviting discussion. Finally, provide several content paragraphs for individual or paired practice.

Such a teaching sequence shows kids *how* to do what you expect them to do. It's later, of course, that you use the same process of modeling and paired practice to help students summarize multiple-paragraph selections in their own words, a much more challenging task. The point is to build skills, step by step. Once skills are learned, you can use graphic organizers to assist student note-taking.

Nine types of graphic organizers in Appendix B provide useful frameworks for summarizing and note-taking. Like the Venn diagram that invites comparison/contrast thinking and the double-entry journal format discussed in Chapter 2, these organizers serve as content area scaffolds. The visual cues offered by such organizers are helpful for all students—and especially so for basic writers.

Sentence-Combining Basics

Transcribing practice, coupled with practice in summarizing, will help develop skills that support writing fluency. But how do we further enhance skills? How can we help basic writers pay attention to language, reducing the frequency of garbled sentences or serious errors?

Enter **sentence combining**—or SC, for short. SC exercises are made up of short, "kernel" sentences—the simple, unmodified units of meaning that seem to underlie more complex constructions. Short sentences, all focused on the same topic, are organized into clusters, and each cluster represents a potential new sentence. Thus, each cluster presents its own sentence-combining challenge—and sometimes multiple challenges.

As students work with these activities, they draw upon their existing knowledge of language and also discover new ways of solving the SC problems. Typically, the combined, or transformed, sentences result in a coherent paragraph or short essay. Of course, such exercises can serve as springboards for independent writing and lead to follow-up work on basic skills.

To help you understand what a typical SC exercise looks like—and how it can promote skill development while also imparting curriculum content—consider the following history-related activity:

Name Game

How important is a name to a person's identity? Do you agree with Shakespeare that a rose is still a rose by any other name?

1.1   Bill Clinton was elected U.S. President.

1.2   Most Americans welcomed Hillary Clinton.

1.3   A majority did not welcome her preferred name.

1.4   The name is Hillary Rodham Clinton.

2.1   Debate on women's surnames goes back to 1855.

2.2   Lucy Stone was a passionate voice.

2.3   The voice opposed slavery.

2.4   The voice spoke out for women's rights.

3.1   Stone organized a first national convention.

3.2   The convention was on women's rights.

3.3   She also published *Women's Journal.*

3.4   It was an influential periodical of the day.

4.1   She rejected marriage offers for years.

4.2   She eventually agreed to marry Harry Blackwell.

4.3   Blackwell shared her belief in equal rights.

5.1 Stone and Blackwell were married in 1855.

5.2 They formally protested the marriage laws.

5.3 The laws gave power and property to men.

5.4 They argued for marriage as a partnership.

5.5 The partnership was permanent and legal.

6.1 Their protest created a storm of controversy.

6.2 Many people were angered by Stone's decision.

6.3 The decision was to keep her own name.

6.4 It symbolized individuality.

7.1 Stone won the right to the name of Stone.

7.2 She was later refused the right to vote.

7.3 The local registrar refused to recognize it.

8.1 Hillary Clinton's experience suggests this.

8.2 Attitudes toward women's roles die hard.

8.3 Attitudes toward women's surnames die hard.

8.4 The attitudes are traditional.

Invitation   Use "Name Game" as a springboard for expressing your own views about women's surnames following marriage vows.

Source: Strong, W. (1994). *Sentence combining: A composing book* (third ed.). New York: McGraw-Hill. © 1994 The McGraw-Hill Companies, Inc.

Notice that the exercise has eight clusters of kernel (and near-kernel) sentences. In modeling expectations, I emphasize that each cluster has multiple right answers rather than a single "correct" solution. I also say that the goal isn't to make long sentences but instead to make good ones. I tell students that it's okay to occasionally leave a cluster uncombined—or to break up a cluster into two shorter sentences.

What's important is that students hear different ways of solving the combining problems—and then choose the best-sounding sentences. I pair students so they can read sentences aloud, figure out good transformations of meaning, and transcribe their solutions independently. But sometimes I have pairs (or small groups) use water-soluble pens to put combined sentences onto acetate transparencies. I can then project these to the class, and we can discuss what students are doing well.

Here's one way to combine the given sentences—but there are also other ways.

Name Game

When Bill Clinton was elected U.S. President, most Americans welcomed Hillary Clinton, but a majority did not welcome her preferred name—Hillary Rodham Clinton. Debate on women's surnames goes back to 1855 when Lucy Stone's passionate voice opposed slavery and spoke out for women's rights. Stone not only organized the first national convention on women's rights, but she also published *Women's Journal,* an influential periodical. After rejecting marriage offers for years, she eventually agreed to marry Harry Blackwell, who shared her belief in equal rights. When Stone and Blackwell were married in 1855, they formally protested the marriage laws, which gave power and property to men. They argued for marriage as permanent, legal partnership. Their protest created a storm of controversy, with many people angered by Stone's decision to keep her own name—a symbol of her individuality. Although Stone won the right to the name of Stone, she was later refused the right to vote because the local registrar refused to recognize it. Hillary Clinton's experience suggests that traditional attitudes toward women's roles and surnames die hard.

This exercise may be too hard for some basic writers, especially ESL learners. But this SC exercise—or any other—can be adjusted in difficulty, simply by changing its vocabulary and shortening the clusters for combining. Moreover, this exercise—or any other—can be made more accessible by adding "closure clues." I put such clues on transparencies and project them to the class. The closure clues provide keywords to assist learners in making a target sentence. Students "fill in the blanks" mentally as they transcribe sentences on their own or work with partners.

For example, here's a closure clue for cluster 1 in "Name Game," a clue that introduces the semicolon as a mark of punctuation.

> When _____,
> most _____;
> however, _____ ,
> which _____.

Sentence-combining practice invites students to solve basic problems of written expression in a positive, nonthreatening way—and without resorting to grammar terms. Students work together, bringing their oral language to the table and strengthening their transcribing skills. Also, the exercises can introduce, expand, or reinforce key ideas from a content area. And finally they can set the stage for in-class workshops that reduce the frequency of errors.

Workshop-Style Teaching

Let's say you've divided writers in your history class into eight groups, with each group assigned to tackle one of the "Name Game" clusters without the help of closure clues. You've told students that you want them to do their best at combining, but that it's okay to make mistakes. And you've also reminded them that no one can make fun of another person's effort—and no points are lost for errors. "Our aim," you emphasize, "is to *learn* from mistakes!"

Each of the eight groups puts its sentence-combining solution on a transparency, which is projected to the class. Within the set of transparencies is this sentence, written by a small group of struggling writers in response to cluster 3 of "Name Game":

> # 3. Stone organized a first national convention, it was on womans rights and publish Womans Journal, it was a influential period of the day.

A sentence like this shows a lot about your students' developmental levels. You see the missing endings on words—and missing words. You see the misspellings, the absence of apostrophes, and the comma splices. But you also see what students *can* do—for example, use capital letters at the opening of the sentence and on proper nouns, and use end punctuation. So is the glass half-full or half-empty?

"What's *good* about this sentence?" you ask.

"Capital letters," Jason responds.

"It's got all the information," Tonya adds.

"Commas," says Carlos. "It's got them, plus a period."

You nod at Carlos. "Yes, we're going to talk about the commas. So does anybody spot a problem, something we can learn from?"

And so it goes. As the collective intelligence of the class focuses on careless errors such as dropped endings, missing words, and misspellings, students learn how to proofread their own writing, and you show how to fix errors. And if students don't see the sentence boundary errors, you have the perfect opportunity to teach what kids need to learn—in context, on the spot. And you then move on.

Teaching skills in workshop minilessons works for three reasons: First, students are not defensive about the content of their writing (the content is provided); second, the class setup emphasizes what students are doing well in addition to what they need to learn; and third, there's absolutely no risk (or penalty) for making mistakes.

And what about source material for SC exercises? My textbooks, listed in this book's references, contain many exercises for use in secondary content areas. Here are a few titles from *Sentence Combining: A Composing Book* (Strong, 1994) and the relevant disciplines in which they might be used:

Exercise Title	Content Area
Value Judgment	English/Language Arts
Hispanic Movement	Government
Bait and Switch	Economics/Personal Living
Hurricane Behavior	Earth Science
Gambling Fever	Social Studies
Alcohol Facts	Health Education
Nuclear Waste	Environmental Science
Karate Explained	Physical Education
Black Music	Music Education
Hypnotic Trance	Psychology
Genetic Counseling	Biology
World Population	Mathematics
Black Death	World History
First Settlers	U.S. History
The Potter	Art Education
Black Holes	Physics

In addition to commercially prepared SC exercises, don't overlook the idea of teaming up with other teachers to develop short, interesting activities for your classes. Focus on a curriculum topic—say, the Civil War—and team up with your U.S. history colleagues to create (and swap) good materials. The exercises are fun to create and often provide a welcome diversion from routine in-class activities.

Finally, you may wonder whether SC exercises really help students write better. On this point, I'm pleased to report the results of George Hillocks's meta-analysis of empirical studies in writing instruction. As one of the nation's top writing researchers, Hillocks carefully examined the best studies, pooled the data statistically, and computed "effect sizes" for various teaching methods. His conclusions follow:

> The practice of building more complex sentences from simpler ones has been shown to be effective in a large number of experimental studies. This research shows sentence combining, on the average, to be more than twice as effective as free writing as a means of enhancing the quality of student writing.

(1986, p. 249)

Clearly, such exercises offer a research-proven teaching tool, one that gives students hands-on and risk-free practice in putting phrases, clauses, and sentences together in meaningful ways.

And, yes, Eddie liked them.

WRITE FOR INSIGHT ACTIVITY

Look back at Gerald Camp's three-point philosophy of instruction for basic writers found earlier in the chapter. Now think about a key concept in your field that you want to teach. How might activities in this chapter help you teach this concept to basic writers? For example, can you visualize how this concept might be taught through dictation work, through summarizing or paraphrasing activities, or through sentence-combining? Develop a brief lesson plan that identifies a content area concept and includes one or more basic writing strategies. As you do so, reflect on your personal philosophy of working with skill-deficient or unmotivated learners. In your opinion, what attitudes must you project to be successful? What moves do you need to make to help most students most of the time? Be ready to share your discipline-specific application and your personal reflection with colleagues and instructor.

5 Tapping the Power of Metaphor

Creativity is continual surprise.
—Ray Bradbury

Valentine's Day

Outside my office window, snow falls in dreamlike blossoms. I'm working on two small poems for the Saturday afternoon mail: one to a son in Seattle, the other to a daughter in San Jose. Each will be accompanied by a fading photograph from a beach trip many years ago, then slipped into a simple frame. In one photo, my seven-year-old son sprawls on his beach towel, arms and legs akimbo, like a young John Travolta practicing a disco move. In the other, my ten-year-old daughter lies on her stomach in an orange two-piece suit, with droplets of water glistening on her skin, grinning up at me. My Valentine's Day deadline is near.

The twelve lines of "Chestnuts" will go to my son.

> As a boy, years ago,
> You brought chestnuts to my desk,
> Each one burnished brown,
> A smooth perfection in your hands.
> Your gesture said it all,
> You with chestnut eyes.
>
> Words get in the way sometimes.
> Love, perhaps, is like a chestnut,
> Whose eloquence is known by touch—
> Polished, buttery, warmed by sun.
> Time will return the favor,
> Wordless as chestnuts.

And the twelve lines of "Stones" will go to my daughter.

> The winter ice is gone.
> You shiver in the turquoise glare,
> Lapis lapping ankles and calves,
> Sun warming your goosebumps.

You are bony shoulders, skinned knees,
Toes burrowing the sandy gravel.

The flat round stones you find
Are poems flung from the summer heart,
Leaping like love across the lake—
Skitter, bounce, and splash.
We follow their wild, wordless arc,
Know the moments of in between.

So what prompts an aging dad to fuss with Valentines? Surely, a greeting card would accomplish the same goal—namely, to remind adult children of the ties that bind. Yet I'm trying hard to please a reader within, one who often whispers, "Try again."

Maybe my motivation lies in the fact that chestnuts and stones are **metaphors** to express matters of the human heart. Metaphor helps me connect one thing (like parental love) to another (like chestnuts or stones). Thus, metaphorical thinking is an attentive state of mind.

So far, we've considered narrative as a tool for knowledge construction, explored learning logs, discussed expressive and imaginative writing, and examined ways to help basic writers develop fluency. Let's now tap the power of metaphorical thinking.

The Power of Metaphor

Metaphorical thinking draws upon our *image-making* ability as human beings. It's thinking characterized by the exhilaration of personal discovery as we see things in surprising new ways. In fact, metaphor is absolutely essential to good teaching—and writing—because it helps us understand and explain big ideas.

Am I arguing that evocative "poetic" language should replace the no-nonsense language that gets the world's work done? Am I discounting the need for clear, logical language in academic work or in communication generally? Of course not. All I'm saying is that metaphor *also* plays a vital role—and that logical language, for all its virtues, is sometimes too crude an instrument for expressing subtle, complicated ideas. Metaphor helps get the job done, for teachers and writers.

For example, suppose you're a science teacher, and today's topic is the atom. In order to help students visualize the atom and have some basis for understanding, you're almost forced to resort to metaphor. Notice how Deepak Chopra uses just such visual language in the explanation that follows:

An atom has a little nucleus with a large cloud of electrons around it. To visualize this, imagine a peanut in the middle of a football stadium. The peanut represents the nucleus, and the stadium represents the size of the electron cloud around the nucleus. When we touch an object, we perceive solidity when the clouds of electrons meet.

(2003, p. 40)

Or suppose you're a U.S. history teacher whose class is studying the Civil War. You focus on the "house-divided-against-itself" metaphor used by Lincoln in June, 1858, in accepting the nomination for U.S. Senate. Then, too, there's the Underground Railroad metaphor, an informal network of halfway houses used by Frederick Douglass and other fugitive slaves to escape bondage. And what about the metaphorical description of Harriet Tubman as "the Moses of her people" (Blockson, 1987, p. 1)? In describing the war's political context, you might even use the metaphors of eminent historian Bruce Catton:

> Slavery poisoned the whole situation. It was the issue that could not be compromised. It put a cutting edge on all arguments. It was not the only cause of the Civil War, but it was unquestionably the one cause without which the war would not have taken place.
>
> (1996, p. 7)

Or suppose you're a physical education teacher who likes W. Timothy Gallwey's idea that "Every game is composed of two parts, an outer game and an inner game" (1997, p. xix). It resonates with you, his inner game metaphor; it "takes place in the mind of the player . . . against such obstacles as lapses in concentration, nervousness, self-doubt and self condemnation" (p. xix). So you create a poster showing how Self 1 (the "teller") and Self 2 (the "doer") conflict until one learns the inner game.

> The player of the inner game comes to value the art of relaxed concentration above all skills; he discovers the true basis for self-confidence; and he learns that the secret to winning any game lies in not trying too hard. He aims at the kind of spontaneous performance which only occurs when the mind is calm and seems at one with the body, which finds its own surprising ways to surpass its own limits again and again. Moreover, while overcoming hang-ups of competition, the player of the inner game uncovers a will to win which unlocks all his energy and which is never discouraged by losing.
>
> (Gallwey, 1997, p. xix).

Or suppose you're a business education or economics teacher who wants students to understand that all economic policies involve political decisions. To do so, you might use an extended metaphor of two award-winning economists, Robert Heilbroner and Lester Thurow:

> [The] engine of an economy is different from the engine of a car in one vital respect: Its parts are people. A mechanic may be able to fix a badly working engine by disconnecting or reconnecting things or by discarding worn-out parts for new ones. But when you fix an economic engine, you are disconnecting or reconnecting *people*—to work, money, opportunity. When you throw old parts of the engine aside and put in new ones, you are consigning industries, regions, cities, to hardship or good fortune. Thus an economist can never fix an economy the way a mechanic may fix a car. No matter whether he assures you that economy will run faster and farther and more smoothly after his repairs than before, there are always human

costs as well as human benefits involved. Changes in the economic machinery never lift everyone evenly, like boats on an incoming tide.

(1981, p. x)

In a final example—this one from my own experience—I still remember trying to teach the concept of transcendentalism in American literature to a class of high school juniors. We had read Emerson's words, "Every heart vibrates to that iron string," but students had glazed looks, especially as I tried to explain the idea of the "oversoul." It was just before the next class that I had the idea of borrowing tuning forks from the physics lab to show how striking one fork could cause others of the same frequency to vibrate and emit a musical note. So the tuning fork metaphor illuminated Emerson's abstractions.

Which brings me back to the poems. In "Chestnuts," when I describe my son's gift as a "smooth perfection in your hands," I acknowledge, imaginatively, the love they signify. When I refer to "you with chestnut eyes," I hint at more than eye color. In "Stones," when I refer to "poems flung from the summer heart," I am emphasizing, imaginatively, the larger significance of skipping rocks at the lake. When I describe stones as "leaping like love" in a "wild, wordless arc," I suggest, without saying so, that some memories transcend language. Clearly, metaphorical thinking has its own special power.

Exercising Metaphor

Let's turn now to practical issues. This chapter offers a rich array of ideas for helping middle school and high school students get imaginatively engaged in content learning. In this section and following ones, we'll consider ways to stimulate metaphorical thinking and writing.

To get started, we return to the teaching of Bob Tierney, whose work with learning logs was discussed in preceding chapters. Understanding that biology students can drown in technical terms and abstractions, Bob decided to make the ideas of his discipline both visual and dramatic with stimulating assignments. He created a list of "Trigger Concepts" (see Appendix C) that could be used repeatedly to stimulate metaphorical thinking.

When studying cell energy, for example, one group of students might be asked to think about the cell as an electric guitar, another group to consider it as a lightning bolt, and so on. Of course, metaphors "work" when then are internally consistent—that is, when parts of the central image relate meaningfully to the concept or process being visualized. In small groups, students worked to *transform* their understandings of the cell into drawings of an electric guitar or a lightning bolt—or whatever metaphor they chose or were assigned. Drawings were posted on the bulletin board and became props for oral presentations and follow-up writing about cell energy. As students constructed their own meanings—and came to understand the drawings of other groups—they developed vivid core concepts in biology.

Shown in Figure 5-1, for example, is a typical student drawing that depicts plant photosynthesis. Using a factory metaphor, the drawing shows how plant

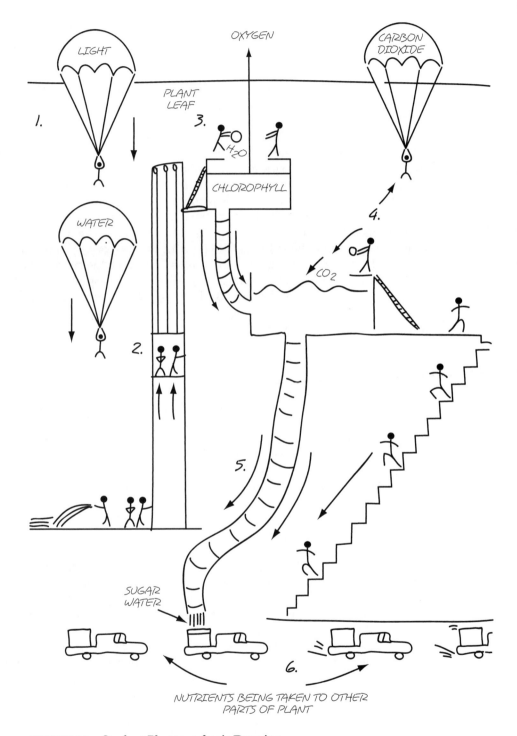

FIGURE 5-1   Student Photosynthesis Drawing

leaves receive light and water, and how the cells convert these into chlorophyll, which in turn mixes with carbon dioxide from the atmosphere to produce sugar water, a nutrient that is taken to other parts of the plant to sustain life. Notice, too, how photosynthesis also releases oxygen back into the atmosphere as a nice by-product. Since "a picture is worth a thousand words," you should now better appreciate the power of metaphor.

But to further your understanding, let me offer a brief demonstration, focusing not on biology but on *writing*, the subject of this book. My demonstration begins as I turn to Appendix C, close my eyes, and let my index finger fall randomly on one of the "Trigger Concept" words. As it turns out, fate has selected the word "army" as my writing focus. So let's see what I can do in just five minutes of nonstop **freewriting,** without any preliminary thinking. The idea of freewriting is to keep moving. So here goes:

> The writing process is like an army because writing works from the top down. Just as an army must have a commanding general, a person to plot strategy and give directions, a writer has to have a controlling idea. Also, just as an army is well organized, with different jobs for different people, so writing has different "jobs" for its different paragraphs. Some paragraphs are like the bold soldiers who establish a position, or thesis; other paragraphs follow to provide support and develop the campaign; and finally come the paragraphs that secure the position and protect the flank from counterattack. The secret to success in any army is discipline, organization, and a battle plan; the same is true for writing.

Looking back at my "army" paragraph, I feel okay about it. It won't win a Pulitzer Prize, but I'm pleasantly surprised with my sentence about the commanding general, which is linked to the notion of "controlling idea." I discovered this small insight in the process of writing—and I'll probably use it the next time I teach this topic to beginning writers.

In fact, I'm so encouraged by my army paragraph that I've again turned back to Appendix C to see if I can make lightning strike twice. The randomly selected word is "wedge." So how is writing like a wedge? Good question!

> Writing is like a wedge because it enables me to analyze, or "split," ideas. Right now, for example, I am splitting the broad idea of writing into parts though the wedge of analysis. There is writer and audience, content and form, message and style—a series of splits. But the writing process can also be split into behaviors, or stages. We can think of a generating stage, a drafting stage, a rewriting stage, and a publication stage. Each of these stages can, in turn, be split into different parts. In rewriting, for example, there is revision (reworking content) and editing (reworking form). Using writing as a wedge, I can better understand the complexity of ideas that I encounter. This analytic function of writing seems essential for rational thought. Thus, writing is like a wedge.

For some reason, I'm less enthusiastic as I reread my "wedge" paragraph. It's logical, I suppose, but the insights here don't interest me as much. On the other hand, the wedge metaphor is vivid in my mind as I glance back at the paragraph. I like to picture a writer splitting ideas cleanly apart, like white pine logs on cold winter day. And the wedge metaphor also reminds me that I need to reread Robert Pirsig's *Zen and the Art of Motorcycle Maintenance* (1974), a brilliant exploration of rationality and its limits.

Working with trigger concepts is easy and fun. This expressive activity is easily adaptable to all content areas as students focus on key concepts of a discipline—and then share their metaphoric insights in pairs and small groups.

More about Metaphor

"Wait a minute," you may be thinking. "What if my students resist metaphorical thinking? Or what if they don't have a clue about metaphor?"

The following lesson sequence, adapted from *Bridging: A Teacher's Guide to Metaphorical Thinking* (Pugh, Hicks, Davis, and Venstra, 1992), offers a flexible, creative plan for introducing metaphor in a hands-on way to secondary students. For this lesson, you'll need a box of familiar items—American flag, lightbulb, candle, valentine, photograph, mirror, key, scissors, hammer, paper clip, eyeglasses, package of seeds, measuring tape, banana, sponge, cup, diskette, rubber band. Whatever's handy will work fine. Just make sure you have enough items for each of your students, plus extra items for demonstration purposes. Of course, if you can get students to contribute junk drawer items to the "metaphor box," so much the better.

To begin the lesson, choose an item with familiar metaphorical comparisons—a valentine or an American flag, or perhaps a lightbulb or candle. The idea is to for students to think about the "associations" such objects have—the valentine with *love,* the flag with *freedom,* the lightbulb with *bright idea,* the candle with *life.* The lesson gets interesting as you invite the class to discuss comparisons between a single object and concept—for example, between a sponge and the mind/brain:

Sponge	*Mind/brain*
absorbs liquid	absorbs knowledge
holds liquid	holds knowledge
can be rinsed	can be washed (brainwashed)
dries up when not used	dries up when not used

(Pugh et al., 1992, p. 6)

Once students understand the general idea of metaphor, try displaying the objects and then announcing a target concept such as "human memory." Students then begin to examine the objects for their metaphoric properties. For example, one student might point to a diskette as a metaphor for human memory—but another student might suggest a photograph. The fun comes in exploring comparisons.

Diskette	*Human Memory*
holds information	holds information
can be searched	can be retrieved
can be written over	can be changed
can be damaged	can be damaged
must have input	must have experience

Photograph	*Human Memory*
contains an image	contains images
captures experience	captures experience
can fade over time	can fade over time
conversation starter	conversation starter

With just a little hands-on practice, students can begin to appreciate the subtlety and power of metaphor. Suppose, for example, that your target concept is "knowledge." Many students will gravitate to familiar metaphors—the key or candle, for example—but with a discussion, they can be encouraged to stretch their thinking.

> For example, a student might decide that knowledge is pair of scissors because it can cut through confusion. The context for this metaphor would be the student's knowledge of how scissors work. The salient feature would be the common idea of cutting edges; the relationships might be the progressive cutting action and the notion of individual control of this action. The connection would be in the physical feel of having the right knowledge with which to address a problem.
>
> (Pugh et al., p. 6)

A follow-up activity, for either individuals or small groups, is to provide a list of several concepts, ask students to choose one, and then have them select an object for doing the metaphorical comparison that was modeled previously. An even more engaging activity is to prepare a list of "metaphor starters" on slips of paper that students draw, sight unseen, to go with their chosen object. (For a typical class, you'd want to have each metaphor starter on three slips of paper so that students can form small groups.) Metaphor starters like these will work well.

Hope is a _____.	Joy is a _____.
Friendship is a _____.	Beauty is a _____.
Learning is a _____.	Authority is a _____.
Procrastination is a _____.	Illness is a _____.
Loneliness is a _____.	Uncertainty is a _____.
Inspiration is a _____.	Excellence is a _____.

After students individually list the ways that their object is like—and unlike—a given concept, they join with others who have drawn the same concept. Their task, as a group, is to decide which metaphors they like best and share these with the class. Interesting comparisons are put on the board in the large-group sharing process.

Finally, of course, students can be asked to *apply* metaphorical thinking by finding their own objects, selecting a new concept, and creating extended metaphors to be shared (in writing) with the class. Of course, it's the background of scaffolded teaching that prepares students to use metaphors in content area writing.

Using Semantic Charts

Now that you've got students producing metaphors, consider using a semantic chart to solidify their understanding. Using a broad concept like those listed earlier, you could ask students to help you generate a list of metaphorical words and phrases. Or you could follow the lead of Pugh et al. (1992, p. 75) and use "school" as the concept word as shown here. Your students will have lots to say about this topic!

School is. . . .

a joke	a social club
a factory to prepare you for life	a war zone
a game or contest	a prison
a way out of the ghetto	a warehouse for kids
a construction site for learning	a fantasy island

In the next step of the process, have students choose two or three metaphors as the focus for brainstorming. The idea is to develop a list of random characteristics.

School is. . . .

Game or Contest	**Prison**
competition to get grades	teachers like wardens
recognition for winning	students forced to be there
students against teachers	highly regimented
teachers like coaches	students sometimes riot
cheating frowned upon	punishment for misbehavior
self-discipline matters	forced labor
teamwork helps	students get released sometimes

Having given students a *method* for generating extended metaphors, it now makes sense to turn to some of the key concepts of your discipline. What are some of those "big ideas" that make up your content area? As students are encouraged to transform these ideas into meaningful and coherent metaphors, their comprehension is constructed from the inside out.

Using Pattern Poems

Now let's look at some practical ideas for using metaphors, focusing on simple pattern poems that help students rehearse curriculum content or respond to their in-class reading.

A pattern poem used by social studies teacher Brendan Smith is the **cinquain** (Topping and McManus, 2002, p. 113). Smith asked middle school students to use key words from their unit on westward expansion—words such as *steel, plow, reaper, national road, Erie Canal, steamboat* and *steam locomotive*—to compose poems in the cinquain format, with numbers referring to lines.

1. One noun (or noun phrase)
2. Two adjectives describing the noun
3. Three words that describe action
4. Four words that express feeling
5. A synonym for the noun in the first line

Of course, the point of such expressive writing isn't to produce deathless poetry, but instead to awaken and motivate students. Here's a nice student example:

> *Reaper*
> *Large, sharp*
> *Moves, slashes, throws*
> *Scary, threatening, ominous, replacement*
> *Machine*
> (Topping and McManus, 2002, p. 114)

Another easy format for students is the **diamante** (or "diamond-shaped" poem). Interestingly, as Topping and McManus point out, this form helps students use terms or concepts that have opposite meanings (2002, p. 114). The first half of the diamante deals with one concept while the second half deals with its opposite. Here is the diamante formula.

1. One noun (subject)
2. Two adjectives that describe line 1
3. Three verbs ending in *-ing* or *-ed* that describe line 1
4. Four nouns (first two relate to line 1; next two relate to line 7)
5. Three verbs ending in *-ing* or *-ed* that describe line 7

6. Two adjectives that describe line 7
7. One noun (subject, opposite of line 1)

Here's a diamante example that deals with the water cycle opposites of *condensation* and *evaporation*. In order to process such concepts poetically, students have to think about them, not just memorize textbook definitions. It's in this process that they can construct personal insights about major concepts.

> *Condensation*
> *Unpleasant, soggy*
> *Dropped, pelted, soaked*
> *Rain, snow, sunshine, heat*
> *Dried, aired, disappeared*
> *Pleasant, welcome*
> *Evaporation*

(Topping and McManus, 2002, p. 114)

In the same vein, biology teacher Patricia Johnston (1985) reasoned that "unless the student can explain the concept or experiment clearly to someone else, he or she does not, in fact, understand the concept or the research project very well" (p. 95). She therefore had students compose simple **biocrostic poems** early in the year, either as unit summaries or as a break from regular routines, stipulating that each line "must begin with the first letter of sequence in the spelled animal's name" (p. 93). To do this task, students had to understand content and work within constraints. Points were given for correct use of vocabulary words.

Here are two samples of student writing from Johnston's classes, both of which are small gems of adolescent imagination:

Mollusks (CLAM)
C alcium PROTECTS the average BIVALVE
L ike a HATCHET a foot gives the movement they have
A ll people think the SIPHON'S the neck
M uscles close the shell quick to save them by heck!

Phylum Mollusca SQUIDS
S hells are VESTICLE and we call them a "pen"
Q uick is the movement that caves them again
U nder their suckers is a toothed horny nail
I nk sacs protect them by making "smoke screen"
D eep sea kinds are LUMINOUSLY seen
S trong vicious jaw make them not like a snail.

(p. 93)

Another type of pattern poem used for self-expressive writing—or for the imagined diary entry of a literary or historical figure—is the widely used **"I Am" formula:**

I Am
I am (two special characteristics you have)
I wonder (something you are actually curious about)
I hear (an imaginary sound)
I see (an imaginary sight)
I want (an actual desire)
I am (the first line of the poem repeated)

I pretend (something you actually pretend to do)
I feel (a feeling about something imaginary)
I touch (an imaginary touch)
I worry (something that makes you worry)
I cry (something that makes you very sad)
I am (the first line of the poem repeated)

I understand (something you know is true)
I say (something you believe in)
I dream (something you actually dream about)
I try (something you really make an effort about)
I hope (something you actually hope for)
I am (the first line of the poem repeated)

A related format is the popular **biopoem** (Gere, 1985). This pattern can also be used to write about a literary character, historical figure, celebrity in the news, or oneself. As Gere points out, "Biopoems enable students to synthesize learning because they must select precise language to fit into this form" (1985, p. 222).

Biopoem
Line 1   First name
Line 2   Four traits that describe character
Line 3   Relative ("brother," "sister," "daughter," etc.) of _____
Line 4   Lover of _____ (list three things or people)
Line 5   Who feels _____ (three items)
Line 6   Who needs _____ (three items)
Line 7   Who fears _____ (three items)
Line 8   Who gives _____ (three items)
Line 9   Who would like to see _____ (three items)
Line 10   Resident of _____
Line 11   Last name

(p. 222)

Teacher Jessie Yoshida adapted the biopoem to help students better understand the character of the Grand Inquisitor in Dostoyevski's *The Brothers Karamazov*. She noted that while many students analyze character in literal terms, one student achieved more through his use of metaphor and imagery. By painting "an unflinchingly cold portrait" of the Grand Inquisitor, to use Yoshida's words, the student "takes the thinking process a step higher and fuses it with imagination."

Inquisitor,
Cynical, bold, all knowing, and fearless.
Friend of no one, peer of few.
Lover of self, wisdom, and unconquerable knowledge.
Who feels neither pity nor compassion nor the love of God.
Who needs no man, save for himself.
Who fears the kiss that warms the heart.
And the coming tide that will not retreat.
Who radiates cold shafts of broken glass
And who fits all mankind with collar and chain.
Who would like to see the deceivers burned
And Christ to be humbled before him.
Resident of ages past.
The Grand Inquisitor.

(1985, p. 124)

After reading such student work, you better understand what "writing with metaphorical power"—the focus for this chapter—is all about. It's writing that amplifies the voice of students, reminding us that good solid teaching is still worth the effort.

Extended Metaphors in Prose

While the previous examples emphasize metaphors in poetry, note that metaphors also occur in prose, and that these metaphors can be developed, or extended, through analogies or other means. John Bean (1996) gives these examples that might serve as writing starters in music, world history, and psychology:

- Baroque music is like _____, but romantic music is like _____.
- Napoleon is to the French Revolution as _____ is to _____.
- How does the weather change as you go from Freud's view of the personality to B. F. Skinner's?

(p. 111)

A special type of extended metaphor is **personification.** Using personification, students "become" an object and write expressively from that frame of reference. Here are several prompts for personification in different content areas (Mitchell, 1996):

- I am a muscle, and I'll tell you what I like and don't like about my life.
- I am a decimal point. Here's what my life is like.
- I am an electron. Come with me as I describe my journey through the GM cranking circuit all the way back to the battery.
- I am an irregular verb. I will explain the advantage to being this kind of verb.

(p. 95)

Encouraging students to develop extended metaphors can help you assess their understanding of key ideas. For example, in my teacher education course, focused on content area reading and writing, I ask students to personalize—and visualize— what they've learned and then share these in papers and projects. What matters, I emphasize, is what makes sense to them personally, the knowledge they construct.

Of course, not everyone welcomes such invitations. Schooling is easier, some say, if expectations and activities are laid out step-by-step. I point out the possible confusion between "schooling" (what one does to earn credits and get a grade) and "learning" (what one truly takes away in terms of insights, changes in attitude, or new behaviors). I am all for clear goals and scaffolded expectations, but I also believe there's plenty of room to personalize learning.

"Surprise me," I sometimes urge. "Have some fun with this assignment."

So imagine it's late in the semester, and you're reading the take-home section of exams. You've challenged students to create some way of visualizing (and organizing) whatever they've learned. And then you come to a paper written by agriculture education teacher Melanie Peterson (personal communication, 2003):

Lint and Language: Using Words to Learn

I pull out the metal lint screen in the dryer. Then I peel the strip of bluish-colored velvet off the screen, pondering the idea that is lint. Lint is a fluffy smorgasbord of bits of thread and ravelings from yarn or cloth. Lint does not just come from one source. Lint comes from blue jeans, white t-shirts, and even the red hat your grandmother knitted you for Christmas. The lint from each of these items is sucked into the dryer screen to make one continuous lint sheet that you pull out and discard after each cycle. Lint, clothes, and dryer remind me of language and this course.

I think of the individual methods I've learned in this course like lint, the categories I place each of these methods in as items of clothing, and the way in which I organize them all together in my mind like the lint sheet. How do the pieces of information (lint) get arranged in your head in the nice lint sheet? Let me explain. In order to get to the lint strip, you need a mechanism, which in this case is a dryer. Likewise, in order to arrange information (each of the pieces of "lint") in your head, you need some kind of mechanism. This course has taught me that the mechanism for organizing information, and creating a lint strip in your head, is language.

Language can be used to create the lint sheet in students' heads and help them to learn from five big ideas. In this course Prereading, Talking, Writing, Graphic Representations, and Study Skills are the big ideas that help students to learn from language. Each of these ideas has its own methods.

As Melanie's teacher, did I want to read on? Of course! Drawing upon her real-world laundry experience, Melanie had created a compelling personal metaphor for sharing her insights. Her three-page essay went on to identify some of the methods that she regarded as interesting and useful, thus satisfying my goals for the assessment.

By encouraging extended metaphors like this one, I believe that we shift the dynamics of traditional instruction. The students become our teachers, if only for a few moments. As I enjoyed Melanie's paper, I scrawled a note in the margin about being "forever changed by your analogy"—and I think I spoke the truth.

Extended Metaphors of Teaching

Finally, I want to clarify the concept of extended metaphor by offering examples from the world of teaching to make the point that metaphor is really an important everyday event, not an esoteric or "poetic" one.

Take, for example, the many "construction" metaphors used in this book. It's no accident that I've characterized writing as a learning *tool,* or expressive writing as a *foundation* for tasks in the *upper domains,* or *scaffolded instruction* as the means for students to *build* knowledge. Clearly, all of these related metaphors grow out of my "constructivist" philosophy of instruction, one that regards individual students as active *meaning-makers* and their teachers as engaged *on-site facilitators.*

Other examples of educational metaphor will be familiar to you. You've no doubt heard teachers use "photography" as a metaphor, explaining how they *focus* attention, *expose* learners to ideas, and *develop* appreciation of the *big picture.* Or perhaps you've heard colleagues use "medical" metaphors to describe how they *diagnose* problems in order to *remediate, correct,* or *prescribe therapy* for the learning *deficits* of students. Or perhaps you've heard "gardening" metaphors that involve *enriching* the environment, *planting seeds* for the future, and *nurturing growth,* as students engage in *a field of study.* Or perhaps you've heard policymakers use "factory" metaphors to urge greater *accountability* for a *world-class product* through *frequent testing, outcomes-based planning,* and *time on task.*

While all of these metaphors are common currency, the most pervasive one, as Frank Smith points out, is the "military" metaphor for schooling:

> We talk of the *deployment* of resources, the *recruitment* of teachers and students, *advancing* or *withdrawing* students, *promotion* to higher grades, *drills* for learners, *strategies* for teachers, *batteries* of tests, word *attack* skills, attainment *targets, reinforcement, cohorts, campaigns* for achievement in mathematics and *wars* against illiteracy. The fact that this language seems natural to us, that we have become so accustomed to it, perfectly illustrates the insidious infiltration of militaristic thinking in education.
>
> (1998, p. 47)

Adding to Smith's points, I'll simply observe that popular methods of *discipline* include *proximity control* and *divide-and-conquer*—and that teachers who complain of *being on the front lines* or *in the trenches* often suffer symptoms of *battle fatigue* and *burnout.*

How important are such metaphors in defining our teaching outlook or approach? Perhaps more important than we think. In *Metaphors We Live By,* Lakoff and Johnson have this to say: "If we are right in suggesting that our conceptual systems are largely metaphorical, then the way we think, what we experience, and what we do everyday is very much a matter of metaphor" (1980, p. 3).

So the bottom line is this: Having students use extended metaphors to write about curriculum content encourages them to process that information both visually and cognitively. And when *that* happens, something called learning occurs.

WRITE FOR INSIGHT ACTIVITY

In this chapter you saw how **freewriting** could lead to unexpected results with Bob Tierney's "trigger words" in Appendix C. The idea was to write fast so the process itself pushed metaphorical thinking. As your students practice freewriting, you'll discover increases in idea fluency and sentence fluency. Try upbeat music in the background.

Let's review how the process works. First, you let serendipity choose one of the trigger concepts. Then you challenge yourself to keep the writing going for five minutes or so, remembering that less fluent writers will probably take more time to get rolling. It's very effective to model freewriting on an overhead projector, because most students are fascinated with the unfolding language. Some teachers like to say the words as they write in a kind of "think aloud" modeling. If you make mistakes or misspell words, so much the better. Simply emphasize that freewriting is about fluency, not correctness! Editing can come later.

Of course, the concepts you'll use relate to the key ideas of your course. If you're a biologist, the concept might be "photosynthesis"; if you're a history teacher, it might be "tariffs"; if you're a mathematician, it might be "prime numbers"; and if you're an English teacher, the concept might be "writing." Here's one more brief example, written in a five-minute learning log exercise.

> Writing is like a cauldron. Sometimes words just boil up unexpectedly from the heated ideas bubbling in my brain. It's terrific because I don't have to worry about how to write—it's just there, cooking away, and I can dip into the cauldron, ladling the material into paragraphs that fill up right before my eyes, hot and steaming, just the way I like them. Later, after the writing has cooled, I'll go back and work the surface of the warm material, smoothing its form.

The follow-up strategy, if you're courageous, is to have a partner select a "golden line," a phrase or sentence that really works, from your freewriting. As the writer, you then use that golden line as the starting point for *focused freewriting*, which presses you to make further discoveries. Some students groan, but bright ones often love the challenge of this double-barreled activity, because they surprise themselves with new insights.

Your write-for-insight activity has five simple parts. First, find a familiar concept in your content area and use the "serendipity method" to select a trigger word in Appendix C. Second, do a freewrite for a full five minutes (ten is better), pushing yourself to discover new ideas. Third, get a partner to read your paragraph and have that person select a favorite golden line, one that's especially interesting, cleverly expressed, or simply insightful. Fourth, as an option, do a focused freewrite for another five minutes, using the golden line as your launching pad. Fifth, reflect on the process: Was it fun? Was it interesting or surprising? Would it work with students?

Share this written work with others and with your instructor.

CHAPTER 6

Designing Assignments and Rubrics

The ultimate confrontation is with that blank sheet of paper.
—John McPhee

Darth Vader in Action

Let's imagine a *Star Wars*–themed movie script—one that features Darth Vader, that helmeted and heavy-breathing figure of sinister intent, the archetypal villain we love to hate. Vader's purpose is *mind control*. So our themes are dramatic, large-scale ones, like darkness versus light and ignorance versus insight.

And Vader's method? That's the scary part. You see, the setting isn't the remote regions of intergalactic space but instead the middle school and high school classrooms of our nation. Imagine if you will that the powers of the Evil Empire have gained control of what goes on in the name of writing instruction.

In an opening shot, we see an ordered scene of middle school kids at computer terminals, hard at work. At the back of the room, a camera monitors time-on-task for the school's nine-step Assessment Support System ("ASS-in-Nine," for short). Each young face is bright-eyed, well-scrubbed, eager-to-please. Then we hear Darth Vader's evil, chilling voice in an ominous voice-over, speaking directly to us.

"Observe," he whispers. "Process writing in the nation's schools."

The camera zooms in, focusing on a computer-monitored worksheet. A girl chooses words from a multiple-choice list that names the writing process steps but requires no writing. She completes her drill on terminology, then moves on to matching items that deal with outlining.

"Busywork," Vader murmurs. "We make sure students avoid any writing about curriculum content."

A boy looks up, his brow furrowed, as Vader continues. "Fear is such a *useful* tool. By making students *fearful* of errors, both real and imagined, we reduce motivation. Over time, our lessons become a belief system. And that's really the secret to our success—undermining the child's early beliefs that writing is power. We teach just the opposite."

As the camera picks up off-task behavior, an Instructional Manager swoops into action, her voice rising sharply. Two students head for the principal's office, but not before they're assigned to write a theme for punishment.

Vader's raspy voice is tremulous with enthusiasm. "Using writing to discipline students is a *wonderful* approach," he intones. "Coupling punishment with fear, we can virtually *guarantee* non-writers later on!"

Abruptly, the camera shifts to a ninth grade classroom, where students take objective exams—true/false and multiple guess questions—then glance restlessly at the clock. Is this science, math, social studies, health, business, or another content area? It's hard to tell. Now, the students seem less bright-eyed, well-scrubbed, eager-to please.

"Writing *must* be removed from content teaching," Vader continues. "Essay exams only promote thinking. Instead, we ask for single-word answers, a phrase at most. Our aim is to constrict thinking, not expand it."

The students have finished their tests. The camera swings to an assignment on the board: *Class research reports due Friday.*

"How long?" one student asks.

"How many sources?" another wonders aloud.

"How much is it worth?" comes the classroom chorus.

The Instructional Manager hands out assigned topics, and students groan, then march sullenly toward the Media Center.

Again we hear Vader's throaty whisper. "We assign reports for the sake of appearances. But we don't allow choice or coach students in research. By keeping expectations murky, we help them see plagiarism as a smart approach to busy-work."

A boy leafs aimlessly though reference books. At a computer terminal, a girl downloads material, pastes it into a document, and types her name at the top. When two students propose collaboration, the Instructional Manager kills the idea.

Vader hisses with dark enthusiasm. "Working together is dangerous—because that's how work in the real world gets done. We have students work alone to prevent them from sharing any interest in what they've learned."

The scene shifts a third and final time. High school seniors are slumped in their desks, and the Instructional Manager looks weary. Once again, the discussion has fallen flat. The students' eyes are opaque, their faces slack.

The Manager glances at the clock where forty minutes remain. "Take out a sheet of paper," he barks.

A topic is scrawled across the board. Some students write a line or two, then gossip with friends, while others stare at their desktops, waiting for release.

"Well done," Vader says. "A topic is snatched from thin air, and writing becomes a time-filler. Students have no interest in their assignment, or skill for accomplishing it—and teachers see their role as correcting the pathetic, scribbled lines ripped from spiral-bound notebooks."

Suddenly and dramatically, Vader's blank, black gaze fills the screen. "What is writing?" he hisses, letting the question hang. "Writing is a *laser*—a tool for thinking and learning. By disarming future citizens of the searing laser light called writing, the conquest of darkness is *inevitable*. Wouldn't *you* agree?"

Assignments by Design

Lest you think I'm exaggerating in my scenario, let's turn to typical assignments documented by Arthur Applebee (1981) in his landmark study of secondary school writing. Although Darth Vader would no doubt give his approval to these assignments, imagine yourself as a ninth-grader taking courses in mathematics, science, and social studies, and ask whether you'd be motivated by these tasks:

- Write a paragraph on solving quadratic equations.
- Write a one-page report on one of the following topics. Please be neat with your work. Check for spelling and sentence structure.
  1. the diesel engine
  2. the gas engine
  3. supersonic flight
  4. sound
  5. what can I do to conserve fuel?
- Western Europe on the eve of the Reformation was a civilization going through great changes. In a well-written essay, describe the political, economic, social, and cultural changes Europe was going through at the time of the Reformation (25 points)

(1981, pp. 74–75)

Having raised the issue of writing motivation, I must now confess, with embarrassment, that I've made assignments every bit as mind-numbing as those. It's all too easy to pull dreadful assignments out of thin air and then blame students for lackluster prose.

So what makes a good writing assignment? That's the basic question we'll consider in this chapter, which builds on earlier ideas about exploratory writing. In general, we'll consider process writing tasks that invite students to discuss a substantive content area topic or issue. As such, these assignments often invite students to write in the three upper domains of literary, informative, and persuasive writing outlined in the Introduction (Figure I-1, p. 9). Of course, the activity that engages one class may inspire yawns from another. On the other hand, certain principles of assignment design are worth reviewing as we think about content area writing prompts in more than trial-and-error fashion.

To get started, let's contrast the next assignment with the previous ones. Again, try to read from a student's perspective, focusing on motivation or intellectual involvement. This particular math writing task is drawn from the work of John Bean:

In class yesterday, 80 percent of you agreed with this statement: "The maximum speed of sailboat occurs when the boat is sailing in the same direction as the wind." However, that intuitive answer is wrong. Sailboats can actually go much faster when they sail across the wind. How so? Using what you have been learning in vector algebra, explain why sailboats can sail faster when the wind blows sideways to their direction rather than from directly behind them. Make your explanation clear enough for the general public to understand. You can use diagrams if that helps.

(1996, p. 27)

This assignment works for three reasons. First, it creates cognitive dissonance as students are situated in a problem they helped create. Second, the task asks them to *use* recently acquired knowledge to resolve the dilemma that has been posed. Third, the assignment specifies an audience and invites drawing to support the writing.

Unlike a traditional assignment—where the main problem is to guess what is expected and then "please" the teacher—the sailboat assignment encourages students to think critically about an issue, apply their math skills, and communicate their results within certain constraints.

Here's another example of an engaging assignment, again drawn from the work of Bean, but this time in the area of psychology:

> In the morning, when Professor Catlove opens a new can of cat food, his cats run into the kitchen purring and meowing and rubbing their backs against his legs. What examples, if any, of classical conditioning, operant conditioning, and social learning are at work in this brief scene? Note that both the cats and professor might be exhibiting conditioned behavior here.
>
> (1996, p. 80)

The follow-up directions define a study-group situation in which "you are convinced that the other members of the group are confused about the concepts" and then asks students to write a "one- to two-page essay that sets them straight" (p. 80). Again, we see a situational problem, a focus on application of key concepts, and directions that specify a purpose and audience beyond the teacher.

Finally, here's a culminating assignment I developed for Ray Bradbury's *Fahrenheit 451*, a perennial choice in high school literature classes because of its high-quality writing and relevance to contemporary life. The novel depicts a future world where reading is censored—indeed, the job of firemen is to burn books—and where big-screen reality TV occupies society's center stage.

> The editor of our local newspaper is planning a special issue focused on "School Life." She has invited selected community leaders and students to develop interesting feature articles dealing with topics of their choice. Her suggested topics include, but are not limited to, the following:
>
> - Television and School Life Today
> - Censorship versus the Student's Right to Read
> - How Democracy Depends on Books
>
> If you have a better topic for your article, feel free to use it. Of course, make sure to use *Farenheit 451* as support for whatever points you choose to make. Also, remember to title your newspaper article and to develop a "lead" that will hook busy adult readers (and other students) in our community.

Notice that this writing-about-literature assignment provides a *context* for writing, a *role* for the student writer, an *audience* beyond the teacher, a feature article *format*, and a choice of *topics*. There are real academic expectations here, but there's also room for students to exercise creativity in their responses.

In my opinion, such tasks help us dismantle the hidden curriculum discussed in Chapter 2. So let's consider the basic principles of assignment design in more detail.

Ten Design Principles

Although the following principles are separated for ease of reading, they really depend on each other. Think of them as a set of interrelated recommendations.

1. Create topics that invite *inventive* thinking; conversely, avoid topics that invite clichés or a straight listing of factual information. Since the usual purpose of a process writing assignment is to stimulate an integration of content knowledge, keep the assignment focused. A vague assignment with confusing directions invites dull, vacuous responses.

2. Select topics that have a *purpose*. Ask yourself, "What kind of writing do I really want my students to do? Would *I* be interested in doing this assignment if I were one of my students?" The more purposeful the assignment in your students' eyes, the more likely you are to accomplish your teaching aims. In other words, have a reason for your assignment and communicate it.

3. Make sure your topics are *meaningful* within your students' experience. Design topics that allow students to draw upon their own experience, or your teaching during the semester, for examples and support. Skilled teachers often build in specific prewriting activities that help students explore personal connections to the topic or writing task.

4. Design topics to elicit *specific, immediate responses* from your students, not vague, abstract ones. Notice the difference between "discuss freedom" as an assignment and the following task: "List the freedoms you enjoy and freedoms you are denied. What is the reason for the denials? To what extent do you accept the reasons? Write an essay on the subject."

5. If you use a *hypothetical situation*, make sure it's within your students' grasp. Such problems may ask students to use voices other than their own, to work in forms other than the traditional essay, and to use their imaginations to solve problems. Such forms of writing can demand thinking skills that range from basic reports to high-level analysis and persuasion.

6. Use *specific terms* (such as define, illustrate, persuade, compare, contrast, analyze, evaluate, or invent) as precise indicators of your thinking and writing expectations. Talk to students about what these terms mean. Specify the steps you want students to follow in an assignment—particularly the prewriting steps such as discussing, interviewing, listing, clustering, and so on.

7. Use *creative formats* for at least some of your assignments. Why not a letter from Mendel to a colleague explaining certain genetic principles? Why not an editorial arguing for (or against) a piece of legislation in our nation's past? Why not a response to a "Dear Abby" math problem? Why not a report on nutrition written by a Martian visitor? Such formats can be fun for students.

8. Think of *CRAFT* when designing your assignments. That is, does the task specify a Context for the writer? a Role? an Audience? a Format? a Topic? By using CRAFT as a mental checklist, you can dramatically improve lackluster writing tasks. Of course, not all assignments need to contain all the CRAFT elements. The acronym is a useful guide, not a straitjacket.

9. Whenever possible, give students a *choice* of writing assignments. It's hardly news that most students like choice—and that a chosen topic is usually more motivating than a forced topic. Offering students a choice of topics isn't always possible, but sometimes it's the best way to accommodate the enormous range of abilities you face in your content area classroom.

10. Define the *criteria* you'll use to evaluate student writing. The more explicit and public your criteria, the more likely it is that students will meet your writing expectations. Explicit criteria can actually free students to be thoughtful and creative. Most students appreciate knowing what's expected, so why not share (and thoroughly discuss) these criteria in advance?

Context + RAFT = CRAFT

As noted earlier, CRAFT is a useful acronym for assignment design. Good teachers have long used the basic RAFT formula with success, helping their students visualize a *role* for themselves, an *audience* for the writing, a text *format*, and a writing *topic*. (For a quick review of genre for assignments, see Figure 3-1, p. 46,) Table 6-1 shows a layout of diverse RAFT assignments across secondary content areas. Notice how even the informational tasks invite creativity.

To the RAFT layout in Table 6-1, I suggest adding "context" to situate a writing prompt dramatically. The majority of middle school and high school students *hunger* for context.

For example, in middle school geometry, Sarah Gale (personal communication, 2003) developed a prompt from the RAFT formula. Students were asked to take on the role of rectangle and to imagine the Council of Parallelograms as their audience. The specified writing format was a letter, and the topic involved proving that the rectangle should be included in the set of all parallelograms. With the basics in place, Sarah then added context—namely, the rectangle's desire to "gain admission" to the Council of Parallelograms, an elite group.

Sarah encouraged students to be creative and have fun with the assignment. They were also directed to write a minimum of ten sentences in correct letter form and to include key definitions, pictures of themselves, and so on.

TABLE 6-1   Examples of RAFT Assignments

Role	Audience	Format	Topic
Stem cell researcher	Aldous Huxley	Letter	Response to *Brave New World*
Vincent Van Gogh	Self	Diary	Painting of "Starry, Starry Night"
Sojourner Truth	Abolitionists	Fund-raising solicitation	Needs of black volunteers in 1863
Tiger Woods	Weight Watchers	Motivational talk	Lifelong exercise
Editorial writer	General public	Newspaper editorial	Analysis of recent political trends
Archimedes	Hiero, king of Syracuse	Report of field test on gold crown	Law of buoyancy and law of the lever
Possessive apostrophe	Young writers	Complaint	How it's left out or misused
Willy Loman	Family members	Last will and testament	*Death of a Salesman* story
Sequoia tree	Sun	Poem	Photosynthesis
Bill Gates	Microsoft shareholders	Annual report	The future of computers
Grand Inquisitor	Galileo	Church edict for imprisonment	Grave suspicion of heresy
Square root	Whole number	Love letter	Explaining our relationship
Physician	Young newlyweds	Informational talk	Fetal Alcohol Syndrome
Osama bin Laden	Nations of the West	Public letter	Motivation for terrorist activity
Martha Stewart	Business executives	*Fortune* magazine article	Importance of personal integrity
Newspaper reporter	Readers in 1859	Obituary	Hanging of John Brown
Space alien	Intergalactic commander	Analysis of crowd psychology	Holiday shopping
Hermit	Self	Diary	Personal hygiene
Lungs	Tobacco products	Complaint	Effects of smoking
Lawyer	U.S. Supreme Court	Appeal speech	"Separate but equal" decision of 1892
Harry Truman	Dear Abby	Advice column	Decision to drop atomic bomb
Meriwether Lewis and William Clark	Sacajawea	Letter of appreciation	Service to the expedition
Emeril Lagasse	Gourmet cooks	Newsletter	Fun in the kitchen

(continues)

TABLE 6-1   Continued

Role	Audience	Format	Topic
Citizen	U.S. senator	Persuasive letter	Control of assault weapons
Mountain man	Self	Diary	Relationships with Native Americans
Ophelia	Hamlet	Personal letter	A woman's view of *Hamlet*
Newswriter	Public	News release	Global warming
Shop foreman	Welders	Safety poster	List of reminders for welding safety
Repeating decimal	Set of rational numbers	Petition	Proving you belong to the set
U.S. Department of Health	TV audience	Public service announcement	Vegetables in the diet
Black elk	White settlers	Meditation	The westward expansion
Potato chip	Other chips	Travel guide	Journey through digestive system
Adolf Hitler	Anne Frank	Letter	Response to *Diary of Anne Frank*
Brook trout	Self	Diary	Effects of acid rain

Taking on the role of "Rhonda Rhombus, Council President," Sarah did more than check spelling errors. She developed a clever form letter to respond to students whose writing didn't quite hit the mark. Notice Sarah's open-ended, invitational tone:

Dear Madam or Sir:

Thank you for your letter to the Council of Parallelograms. We have reviewed your case and decided, based on the information you have given us, that there is insufficient evidence to warrant a membership for you in our council. You did not specify one or more of the following:

• Opposite sides are parallel.
• Opposite sides are congruent.
• Opposite angles are congruent.
• Diagonals bisect each other.

Please feel free to contact us again.

Sincerely,

Rhonda Rhombus, Council President

Of course, upon receiving the student's "revised" application, the Council President immediately responded with a congratulatory letter—one that apologized "for any pain or grief we may have caused due to your previous exclusion from our group."

Fun? Absolutely. But it also served to motivate learning. In fact, Sarah had a two-word summary for her little writing prompt: "Extremely successful."

CASE STUDY OF AN ASSIGNMENT

Now that you've been introduced to the principles of assignment design, let's look at two illustrative tasks, related to earth science and, more specifically, to volcanos, a topic that fascinates many adolescents. Thanks to a *Nova* special on giant waves, called "tsunamis," I became interested in volcanos as a possible generator of such waves. What I found were amazing Internet resources on volcanos, and a story of a potential disaster looming in the future.

Of course, in the terrible aftermath of December 26, 2004—the catastrophic tsunami in southeast Asia that unleashed trillions of tons of sea water, taking hundreds of thousands of lives—the world better understands the power of such waves. No longer do we visualize such waves merely as the product of special effects, as in movies like *The Day After Tomorrow*. We've all watched videotape footage of houses, buses, and people being swept away by walls of water, and we've reeled from seeing images and statistics depicting the unprecedented magnitude of devastation to life and property.

My research focused on the island of La Palma, part of the Canary Islands off the coast of West Africa. On October 4, 2000, the BBC published an article titled "Giant wave could threaten U.S." (**news.bbc.co.uk/1/hi/sci/tech/956280.stm**). Then on August 29, 2001, the BBC published a second report, titled "Giant wave devastation feared" (**news.bbc.co.uk/1/hi/sci/tech/1513342.stm**), authored by Alex Kirby. Both reports referred to the instability of the Cumbre Vieja volcano on La Palma. While no-one was predicting an imminent collapse, the articles warned that the volcano's eruption could trigger a landslide of enormous magnitude—500 billion tons of earth—creating the biggest tidal wave in recorded history. In fact, "the energy released by the collapse would equal the entire U.S. electricity consumption for six months."

The BBC articles are based on papers developed by Dr. Steven Ward, University of California, and Dr. Simon Day, University College, London—papers that scientifically estimate the tsunami size and speed: "The dome of water it caused would be 900 metres (2,950 feet) high, and the resulting tsunami . . . would travel outwards, reaching speeds of 800 km an hour (500 mph)." According to Dr. Day, "It's entirely possible you'd see 50-metre [164 foot] waves coming ashore in Florida, New York, Boston, all the way up to Greenland, and in some cases reaching up to 10 kilometres [about 6 miles]."

Because the Internet resources related to La Palma are so remarkable—and because the story itself is so compelling, especially from a geology perspective—this topic seemed like an excellent springboard for a process writing assignment. To illustrate the CRAFT principles listed earlier, I developed two writing tasks. See what you think:

CRAFT Assignment 1   Recent geologic activity on the island of La Palma, off the west coast of Africa, has begun to raise fears along the eastern seaboard of the U.S. that the "unthinkable" might happen in the future. Imagine yourself as part of a team that will design and produce an information brochure as part of a campaign on disaster preparation. The brochure's purpose is to help the citizens develop their *own* advance plans for coping with a possible general evacuation from eastern cities and low-lying areas. However, it is very important not to spread panic about the prospect of a giant tidal wave. Also, you must use clear, direct language, because many citizens (up to 20% of adults) read at very basic levels. As a writer, you will need to understand giant tidal waves (tsunamis) and La Palma geology. Also, you will need to inform yourself about basic civil defense strategy by doing Internet research (e.g., FEMA, USGS, and other web sites). Finally, you will need to choose a city or region and study Internet maps to plan exit routes. National Civil Defense planners have established broad guidelines— for example, that almost all highways along the eastern seaboard will be converted to one-way traffic headed west. Work as a team to gather information, take notes, and report back to your team members; then work as a group to decide on the approach your brochure will take.

Context: Development of a Civil Defense booklet/brochure
Role: Researcher and writer of the booklet/brochure
Audience: General public
Format: Booklet/Brochure (with graphics)
Topic: Disaster preparation (mega-wave)

CRAFT Assignment 2   Imagine yourself as a real estate developer and resort property manager on the island of La Palma. Because of concerns about a giant wave at some unspecified point in the future, your business has fallen sharply in recent years, as have prices of the island's resort property. You are interested in developing an advertising brochure about the many attractions of La Palma that will entice people to plan vacations there and also to invest in resort property such as condos. From past experience in real estate sales and condo management, you know that wealthier and better-educated individuals represent your target audience. Some of these are young, upwardly mobile professionals; others are successful persons who have retired or who soon plan to retire. It will therefore be important to communicate in a way that appeals to them. What are the attractions of climate, geography, and lifestyle that make La Palma so desirable? What appeals will you make to help possible investors overcome their concerns about personal safety or the possibility of their investment sliding into the ocean? Learn all you can about giant waves caused by volcanos. Also, do Internet research on La Palma to learn more about its geography, geology, culture, and many attractions. Using information and graphics from such resources—but your own language—develop these into a booklet/brochure.

Context: Sales booklet/brochure
Role: Real estate developer/Property manager
Audience: Upscale, affluent audience
Format: Booklet/Brochure (with graphics)
Topic: Many natural attractions of La Palma

Of course, the brochures developed by students for such assignments will be quite different. One will be *informational/functional writing* (emergency preparation), the other *argumentative/persuasive writing* (marketing of real estate). Yet both will require content knowledge, research skills, collaboration with others, and thoughtful writing. I contend that such work holds far more instructional promise than a dreary multiple choice test drawn from a publisher's test manual.

As for evaluation rubrics—the checklists that students use when composing or meeting in response groups—I recommend keeping them simple. Here, for example, are five basic questions that could provide direction for students.

La Palma Brochure Checklist
- Is it *scientifically accurate* with respect to earth science?
- Is it clearly aimed at a *target audience?*
- Are *quotes and paraphrasing* used appropriately?
- Do *Internet graphics* support the message?
- Are *conventions* (spelling, usage, mechanics) correct?

Of course, a simple rating scale can be attached to these criteria for in-class use and for purposes of teacher evaluation. Providing such criteria to students, as shown here, helps clarify expectations. (Note that a five-point scale is used: 5 = excellent; 4 = strong; 3 = good; 2 = marginal; 1 = needs work.)

La Palma Brochure Grading Rubric

	1	2	3	4	5
Scientific Accuracy					
Audience Appeal					
Quotes and Paraphrasing					
Internet Graphics					
Grammar and Usage					

These criteria set broad parameters for the task but allow plenty of room for students to exercise creativity and imagination.

Content Area Writing Tasks

With the basic principles of assignment design in mind, let's now consider some other writing tasks that might appeal to middle school or high school students. What they have in common is the CRAFT approach. Several additional tasks featuring this approach are found in Appendix D.

Using a role-playing strategy, history teacher Natalie Burningham (personal communication, 2004) developed an assignment with built-in choice. Note that this prompt draws upon critical thinking (propaganda techniques) and that it includes Internet sites for student research.

Creating Propaganda

You are a newspaper columnist who works for one of the well-known papers in New England in 1775. You are new to the job, and your first assignment is to create a piece of propaganda either for or against a revolution from British rule. To spark the interest of colonial readers, you are to write your feature article in an obituary format, including a picture and caption to illustrate your statements. If you choose to be pro-war, you will write your obituary about the death of British values and rule. If you choose to be against the war, you will write your obituary about the death of the rising American independence and self-rule.

The first step in writing is to choose your side. Look in your textbook or on the Internet to research the situation if you are not sure which side to take. Here are a few Internet sites about America and Britain:

- **http://revolution.h-net.msu.edu**   The American Revolution
- **http://www.lib.jmu.edu/history/internet.html**   Research Guides: History
- **www.spartacus.schoolnet.co.uk/Britain.html**   British History Page

Make sure to research three or more British or American values and to include them in your obituary along with supporting details. We'll use the following rubric when we discuss writing quality for this assignment.

	Keep Trying (1 point)	Good Work (2 points)	Excellent Work (3 points)
Accurate historical facts			
Three values and supporting details			
Picture and caption with text			
Use of propaganda techniques			
Spelling and grammar			

Physical education teacher Clark Funk (personal communication, 2004) wanted to use persuasive writing to prompt higher-order thinking, so he outlined a hypothetical problem and developed items for students to think about as they discussed the assigned issue and then got ready to write.

Notice how this assignment "scaffolds" expectations. For example, as students are asked to compare the benefits of Ultimate Frisbee with other sports, they move beyond a simple description of the game to an analysis of it. Handling such a task will probably require at least some revision, which can lead to insight.

Ultimate Frisbee

Imagine that during the past year you and some friends have gotten very involved with Ultimate Frisbee. You've enjoyed playing "pick-up" games together but have had trouble finding places to play without being disturbed. In the last month, you've been kicked off fields over a dozen times. Some of your friends are getting discouraged, and their numbers are starting to dwindle. You and your friends decide that now is the time to take action and seek help from the principal. You want to convince the principal that starting an intramural program for Ultimate Frisbee would be a good idea.

In your letter, describe to him or her the game of Ultimate Frisbee and explain its rules. Express your concern for what is happening to your group and try to persuade the principal of the need for an intramural program for your sport. Compare the benefits (physical, social, emotional, etc.) of Ultimate Frisbee to the other school-sponsored sports and explain the need for a reserved place to play. Give the principal your ideas of how Ultimate Frisbee could complement the other sports programs. Finally, to convince the principal that there is enough interest in the sport to justify it being included in the school's intramural program, describe the success you've had with your Ultimate Frisbee group.

Persuasive Letter Criteria (1 = low; 5 = high)	1	2	3	4	5
Ideas are clear and focused, with support for claims.					
Text organization is logical and easy to follow.					
Voice is confident and convincing in making a request.					
Sentences are correctly and effectively written.					

A very different kind of persuasive prompt was prepared by home economics teacher Amy Crosbie (personal communication, 2003) for her culinary cooking class. However, Amy's assignment was anything but a "cookbook" approach to writing. Students were put in a situation of choosing an entrée to submit to the president of a restaurant chain and persuading that individual to include it on the restaurant's new national menu. Amy framed the writing task so that students had to consider nutritional value, balance of chosen foods, plate presentation, and appropriateness for their restaurant. In Amy's words, it gave students "a situation in which they must apply the content they have learned and use the skills they have perfected in the lab." Look for the CRAFT elements in Amy's assignment.

"Healthy Choice" Meal Proposal

The Situation   You are Chief Chef in a restaurant for one of the following large chains: El Torrito, Olive Garden, or Tony Roma's. The company president has sent a memo to all Chief Chefs inviting a proposal for a new entrée on next year's menu. The company seeks menu items that offer a healthy choice to customers. You have decided to submit a lunch or dinner entrée to be evaluated by the president, knowing that the winner will (1) receive a "meaty" bonus, (2) be featured in *Bon Appétit* magazine, and (3) have his/her entrée in the new menu.

Your Task
- Prepare a recipe, including a listing of all items (meat, starch, vegetable, etc.) that will be included in the meal. The recipe must be appropriate for the restaurant chosen and health-conscious.
- Submit a title and short, creative description of the meal to grab the customer's interest. Format it just as it would appear in the menu and include the number of fat grams for the meal. Also, design the logo that will indicate that the menu choice is health-conscious.
- Submit an analysis of the meal's nutritional value associated with the Food Guide Pyramid. Use the computer program "Computrition" in preparing your analysis.
- Write a two-page paper that proves why your entrée is an excellent healthy choice menu item. Include the analysis of the nutritional content and explain why it fits the existing menu, characteristics that will appeal to the customer, and balance of the meal in relation to taste, texture, aroma, color, and presentation. The goal is to persuade the president of the restaurant to choose your entrée; therefore, the proposal needs to be written in a confident and professional voice.
- Put items #1–4 in a packet and complete by adding a brief cover letter written to the president. In half a page, introduce yourself, the location of your restaurant, and briefly mention your meal selection and why it would be a healthy and appropriate addition to the existing menu. If this cover letter is not carefully written, the president will likely not waste time looking at the rest of your proposal. Leave him or her eager to learn more about the menu item you submitted.

Summary   This project is an opportunity to showcase the content information learned this semester related to nutrition, plate presentation, menu writing, and appropriate meal choices. Be confident and creative as you persuade the president to choose your entrée, yet professional in the presentation.

Assignment Criteria for "Healthy Choice" Meal Proposal	Points possible	Points earned
Recipe is functional and appropriate for restaurant.	10	
Nutritional content relates to Food Guide Pyramid.	10	
Meal title and description reflect care and creativity.	05	
The proposal includes all assignment elements.	30	
The cover letter is professional and effective.	30	
Overall appearance and correctness of materials.	15	
TOTAL	100	

Finally, let's examine a business education task designed by teacher Sara Johnson (personal communication, 2004). Sara's goal was to link technology skills (such as the ability to create a web site) with communication skills (such as the ability to develop and present a professional proposal). Interestingly, her assignment asked students to integrate many skills—research, technology, writing, and speaking—thus simulating real-world expectations. In the prompt that follows, notice how skillfully Sara weaves together the elements of context, role, audience, format, and topic.

Web Site Design Proposal

Context   Your group has been selected as a finalist for the designing the school's new web site. The web site must be functional and visually appealing. Students, parents, teachers, administrators, and district representatives will all be using this site in the future.

Role   You will want to approach this assignment with a professional voice. Imagine your group as a company presenting the web site report proposal to a prospective client.

Audience   The school board, administration, and student body officers each have a vote in selecting the winning web site proposal. Consider each group's needs, concerns, and desires when compiling your proposal.

Format and Process
- Begin by doing an Internet search for other high school web sites. Compile a list of strengths and weaknesses of the sites. Be sure to keep a log of URLs you visit for reference.

- Create a map of your proposed site. This map needs to show relationships between pages and the navigation options throughout the site (how a user can move from page to page or return to the home page).
- Create a professional report that details your group's vision of the new school web site. Include a clear rationale for your design by addressing the (1) purpose of the web site, (2) predicted users (who will be accessing the site), and (3) its technology.
- It is strongly recommended that you create an MS PowerPoint or other visual aid for your presentation to the selection committee. Revise your writing several times to ensure correct grammar and spelling.
- Finally, prepare a 10-minute oral presentation that summarizes key points about good high school web sites and shares your proposal.

Topic You must consider two topics in completing this assignment. First, the purposes of the web site are to provide current information on academic and extracurricular activities, to provide a directory of faculty and staff, and to display the school policy and procedures. The school board is open to your group's suggestions for additional features. Second, the purpose of your proposal is to thoroughly explain your web site to the selection committee and persuade them to select it as the new, official school web site. Remember, you do not have to create the web site at this point. However, you must have a clear image of the site's design and be able to answer questions about it.

Proposal Grading Rubric (1 = low; 4 = high)	1	2	3	4
The writing contains all necessary elements: research notes, site map, report, and visual aid.				
Report clearly describes the purpose of the web site, the predicted customers, and site technology.				
The ideas are creative, well organized, and structured in a professional, compelling manner.				
The report shows good word choice and sentence fluency, with no spelling or grammar errors.				

Darth Vader Revisited

This chapter began on a dark note, with Darth Vader threatening to extinguish *insight* with his diabolical plans for mind control. Vader pointed out, in his throatiest, blackest voice, that by disarming future citizens of the searing laser light called *writing,* the conquest of darkness was inevitable.

So what happens next? One possible scenario is quiet surrender. For example, we can continue to pretend that warehousing kids for standardized tests is the central goal of secondary education. On the other hand, we can marshal our collective wits against the Black Knight, adopting the guerilla tactics of good, hard-working teachers.

The camera zeros in on a classroom visited earlier—but now groups of students are brainstorming ideas for writing. Some set to work drawing maps, while others work on creative description and factual information for their travel brochures.

"I love teaching like this," the teacher says. "There's interest and energy—and the students exercise their creativity. They do lots of research, plus they put their ideas in a real-world format, one that others can read."

The scene shifts to another class, where students are reviewing learning logs and highlighting the material they plan to use on tomorrow's in-class exam. This will be an "open notes" essay for which the teacher has provided a study guide.

"Cool," they say. "We get to use our logs."

"To *think* with," their teacher adds. "We're raising the bar here."

"So we can study together?" they ask.

Finally, the scene shifts to a high school classroom where small groups edit their final drafts and check them against a rubric. Previous versions of a paper are stapled beneath the final copy to showcase each student's writing process. A quick glimpse at the drafts reveals changes in organization and mechanics. In this classroom, students earn one grade for active engagement in the process and another grade for the quality of the final product.

The teacher shrugs. "What can I say? It *works*. You give good prompts and a few student models and a little advice—and what do you know? They learn by doing. There's no way I'd go back to the old approach of stand-and-deliver teaching."

And so it goes. Now that you understand the theory and practice of assignment design, check out several more model assignments and rubrics in Appendix D. Then try your hand at developing an assignment in your own content area. My "Writing Assignment to Construct a Writing Assignment" is discussed in the next section.

WRITE FOR INSIGHT ACTIVITY

Let's imagine you're part of a Career Ladder Program focused on "Writing Across the Curriculum." This program asks teachers to design writing assignments to teach curriculum content and publishes the best tasks for other teachers. To be selected for publication means a library of paperback books for your classroom, plus leadership prestige!

Here are the criteria used by a teacher selection committee (chaired by your supervisor) for deciding upon top writing tasks. (Note that a five-point scale is used: 5 = excellent; 4 = strong; 3 = good; 2 = marginal; 1 = needs work.)

Committee Criteria for Process Writing Tasks					
1. Deals with a topic of *significant content value*.	1	2	3	4	5
2. Invites *imagination* and *problem-solving* skills.	1	2	3	4	5
3. Uses CRAFT to create a *context* for writing.	1	2	3	4	5
4. Provides clear *prewriting* guidelines or advice.	1	2	3	4	5
5. Outlines evaluation criteria in a rubric.	1	2	3	4	5
6. Uses correct language conventions.	1	2	3	4	5
7. Rationale for task is provided in memo.	1	2	3	4	5

According to the committee's guidelines, this assignment should be a "major take-home or in-class assignment developed in stages." Therefore, your goals are (1) to develop a writing task of high quality, and (2) to develop a memo that explains the rationale for your assignment to your supervisor and the selection committee.

To accomplish these aims, first review the "Assignments by Design" section of this chapter, paying special attention to the CRAFT suggestions. To begin, brainstorm the basic concepts or principles in your content area. Then consider using Internet resources to gather ideas for a writing task.

Your writing prompt will most likely consist of a task sheet (like this one) that offers instruction, step-by-step activities for students, and other kinds of guidance (e.g., a time line or resource reference). Of course, it's great if you can provide students with writing options so that they have some choice in writing tasks. After creating the writing assignment, create an accompanying grading rubric (like the previously shown one).

Then, write a clear professional memo to your supervisor—in this case, your course instructor—explaining your goals for the assignment, the intended grade level and context for writing, and teaching strategies that will support the task. Use a memo format and professional voice—and please make sure to use your spell checker!

Finally, share the writing task and memo with your instructor so that you can participate in follow-up discussion with your content area colleagues.

7 Managing the Writing Process

It's like driving a car at night. You never see further than your headlights, but you can make the whole trip that way.

—E. L. Doctorow

Coaching Writing

The computer lab hums with activity. Kids talk, keyboards click, and an ancient printer grinds out paperwork in the corner. The teacher and I move through the room in zig-zag fashion, swooping in from time to time to either ask a question or answer one. Most students are well prepared, with notes or handwritten text, but several also seem well behind the curve, still struggling to generate ideas.

Rachel stares intently at her computer screen, then wrinkles her nose. I drag up a chair beside her. "So how's it going?" I ask.

"I don't know," she says. "This part doesn't sound good."

"Which part?"

She's looking at the screen again. "It starts out okay," she says, her voice trailing off. "Do you think it's any good?"

"What are you trying to do?" I ask. Now we're both reading the screen.

"Like we talked about in class: 'The bigger the issue, the smaller you write.' That was such a cool idea."

"So you're trying to use a story opener for your essay?"

"Right. I just thought—oh, I don't know."

I let a couple of beats go by. "Your strategy seems fine, Rachel. What's the idea you want to explore?"

Now she looks at me. "The assignment—reflecting on your writing process."

"Okay, but what do you want to *say* about it?"

"Getting started. How much trouble I have."

"That's a great idea to explore. Do you have it down in your notes?"

"Not yet."

"What interests you about the 'getting started' stage?"

"Like if I can get started, it's not that bad, you know? But if I get stuck, it's, like, hopeless."

I'm wondering how much to lead. "I see. So you're thinking about describing the problem—how you *usually* approach a writing assignment—and what happens when you get stuck?"

"Right."

"I notice you don't have any notes to work from."

"Usually I just write it out."

"Are you stuck now?"

Rachel hesitates. "Pretty much."

"Hmmm. So the just-writing-it-out strategy isn't working, and some thoughts and feelings are stirred up. What are they?"

She laughs. "Like being frustrated? Wanting to quit?"

A hand goes up down the aisle. It's time to move on. "Believe me, I know the feeling. But let's say you make a list of those thoughts and feelings so you can write about them. Could be you'd get yourself *unstuck*. What do you think?"

Rachel shrugs. "I guess."

"Give it a try, and I'll come back to see how you're doing. Then we'll look at that other paragraph." As I slip into the downstream current, Rachel flips open her notebook and wrinkles her nose again.

And so it goes. Conferences like this provide scaffolding for students as they struggle to generate ideas, organize texts, or make revisions based on peer feedback. In fact, for most teachers who help students with writing, mini-conferences are central to the game. Why? Because good conferences can reveal whether students are thinking about—or avoiding—the key issues of content and process in writing.

Although part of my conference with Rachel focused on content—her desire to write about the "getting started" part of writing—much of it dealt with process. Ironically, Rachel was still using a strategy that had not served her well in the past. So it seemed useful to encourage a substitute strategy of making a simple list.

Like someone who knows all about healthy lifestyles but strays from the path of regular exercise and good nutrition, Rachel already understood the value of prewriting tools, because they were part of her teacher's curriculum. All she needed was friendly encouragement to use what she knew.

Visualizing the Writing Process

Our aim in this chapter is to consider the challenges faced by Rachel and her classmates—and understand how good teaching might support their learning. Like other chapters, this one assumes that **scaffolded instruction** enables learners to internalize new writing skills and achieve content area insights.

This chapter builds on earlier ideas about expressive writing, as well as the design of assignments and rubrics. As you now know, informal expressive writing is often ungraded—the work students use to understand the concepts and issues in your field. Such writing promotes active learning—a rehearsal of ideas—that students draw upon when challenged with more complex tasks, as described in Chapter 6. In this chapter, we focus on helping students succeed with graded academic assignments.

Glancing back to the four writing domains (Figure I-1, p. 9) in this book's Introduction, you'll recall that expressive writing supports the upper domains. Such domains include *informational/functional writing,* or basic "report" tasks; *literary/poetic writing,* the "imaginative" work often assigned in English classes;

and *argumentative/persuasive writing,* the "analytic" thinking expected in debate and Advanced Placement programs. Having taken some risks with expressive writing, most students are more motivated to take on process writing assignments in the upper domains.

Here I'll share some basic ideas about writing process, a frame of reference for the key terms you can use with students. When you use terms like *prewriting* and *revising*—and such terms are also used by teachers in health, industrial arts, history, and other content areas—students take notice.

Figure 7-1 is a **recursive writing process** model. The term "recursive" means that to move *forward* in writing (improving the content or form) writers typically have to move *backward* to earlier steps. In other words, careful academic writing isn't usually a one-draft event. Generally, we have to do more research, or tinker with organization, or delete some words in favor of others. It's a kind of cognitive dance, and a physical one too.

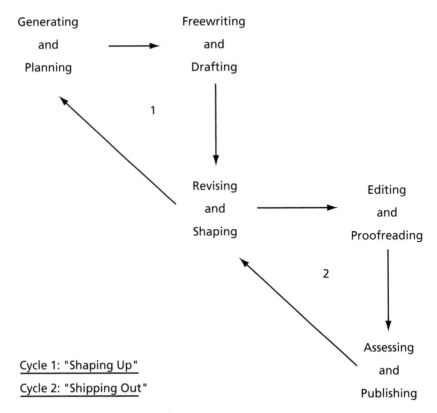

Cycle 1: "Shaping Up"

Cycle 2: "Shipping Out"

FIGURE 7-1   How Writing Develops

Source: Strong, W. (1996). *Writer's toolbox: A sentence-combining workshop.* New York: McGraw-Hill. © 1996 The McGraw-Hill Companies, Inc.

As you study this illustration, notice that it depicts two "cycles" of activity—"shaping up" and "shipping out." The cycles are connected, but students need to consider them separately so that they see what to do first, second, third, and so on. Without such a map, it's easy to become overwhelmed and discouraged.

And what about those "backward pointing" arrows in the writing process model? These arrows emphasize, as Paul Valery once put it, that writing is "never finished, only abandoned" (Murray, 1990, p. 197). After all, what writer doesn't hope for another edition—another chance to "get it right"?

In explaining Cycle 1 to students, emphasize the idea of concentrating first on *content* by generating an array of ideas through prewriting strategies. Students often try to take shortcuts, just like Rachel in the opening scenario. Explain that the work of developing good solid content—finding something to say—is really "job number 1" for a writer. It's content that enables a writer to develop a draft, and the draft sets the stage for more content. Why? Because as writers read their drafts, often with the help of partners, they can see "holes" in their work—missing points that should be included. And that's where revision, the heart of the writing process, comes in.

In explaining Cycle 2, focus on the idea of concentrating later on the *form* of writing. Explain that "form" refers mainly to organization, the sequencing of paragraphs, the "flow" of ideas. Point out that good ideas, when presented in a confused way, become muddled ideas. Encourage students to "preview" the organization of their reports in an introductory paragraph. Challenge them to move paragraphs around to improve readability. Explain why strong conclusions matter. Finally, have students focus on the basic mechanics of their papers—the spelling, usage, and conventions that are part of "good form." This, of course, is the editing step before "shipping out" the paper for teacher evaluation, or actual publication.

As you post such a model in your classroom, discuss it, and model a strategy or two, some students may say, "Hey, this isn't an English class."

"No, it isn't," you reply. "But I value good writing—and you should too. That's why I'm asking for your best revised work on our next assignment. Remember, *revision makes you smarter.*"

"You mean this writing counts on our grade?" someone will ask.

"You see? You're getting smarter already!"

Understanding the Model

Now that you have an overview of the two-stage model, let's explore its details. As you read these descriptions of specific writing process strategies, think of your own writing and the extent to which you already use them. Also, think about how you might scaffold these strategies in the context of your own classroom teaching.

Prewriting techniques of **generating and planning** include, among others, listing ideas; clustering or "webbing" them; sketching, drawing, and doodling; talking to others and reading; asking and answering questions; and outlining.

Remember that *open talk*—students thinking aloud with each other before they begin to write—can often help them discover a way into their topics.

Of course, it's one thing to assign writing, and another to teach it. Top-notch teachers prime the pump. By showing students how to outline quickly their responses to an essay exam, for example, these teachers boost writing quality. They also prompt students to revisit learning logs, or they set up think-pair-share activities, or they model Venn diagrams for comparison/contrast writing. And they remind their classes that ungraded expressive writing can serve as prewriting for many graded tasks.

Another aspect of generating and planning is to prompt thought about purpose and audience before students invest a lot of time in drafting. To many students, writing means simply "pleasing the teacher." However, modeling a process of question-asking about broader aims and other audiences—and following this modeling with work in small groups—helps make academic writing a real communication task.

Freewriting and drafting create direction for a text. You can compare drafting to riding a bike—and suggest that bike-riding requires momentum. As a rule of thumb, encourage students to relax and work fast, focusing first on *content*. However, some students will need a clear mental map before getting started, and perfectionists often equate drafting with "making mistakes." It's helpful to acknowledge and discuss such points. As psychologist Howard Gardner has pointed out, Beethoven required many drafts to achieve his magnificent music. Mozart, on the other hand, planned so extensively in his head that his efforts seemed like brilliant first drafts:

> Like Mozart, Beethoven was a fluent and skillful improviser, but he composed only with much more overt difficulty. In addition to keeping a notebook replete with discarded themes and false starts, Beethoven would score a piece numerous times—revising, rejecting, crossing out in his impetuous and messy hand. While Mozart's rapidly produced scores seldom contained erased passages—and indeed were practically of "camera-ready" quality—Beethoven's sketchbooks chronicled painful, even tormented sieges of creation. Certainly Beethoven's agonies during the throes of creation—rather than Mozart's seemingly seamless composing activity—served as the model of the suffering romantic artist in his garret.
>
> (1982, pp. 359–360)

Since many students procrastinate, offer "process points" to get them started. Also, emphasize that drafts are the raw material for revision—and that after the draft is written, it always helps to put it aside for a day or two before revising. Finally, resist the temptation to "grade" the rough drafts of your students. Such grading almost always reduces their motivation to revise.

In many ways, **shaping and revising** are at the heart of the writing process. In revision, the emphasis is still on content—getting the ideas right—but organization and development are also high priorities. Of course, to improve logic or add examples, the writer often returns to basic questions: What's my message? Where am I going with this? How can I present it more clearly? The model of recursive writing presented earlier suggests that a writer may go back to the stage of generating and planning in order to draft additional text—providing illustrations for a theme, for example. Or the writer may move chunks of the text around, tweaking the "fit" of various paragraphs.

It's in the revising stage that **peer response** can be helpful. As the writer gives voice to intentions and shares a draft, well-trained peers can offer valid advice. Thus revising becomes a collaborative effort, and candid feedback helps the novice writer see the text as having real effects on real readers. But as important as peer responders may be, the writer is always the "first reader" of the text, the one who must sort through advice, deciding what to act upon and what to ignore.

Although **editing and proofreading** may occur at any time, it makes sense for novice writers to have such a focus after their content and organization are solidly established. Editing refers to strategic decisions about particular words and sentence constructions as well as to the process of cleaning up errors in spelling, punctuation, and usage. Writing research suggests that less-able, "blocked" writers are preoccupied with editing at the early stages of writing, when they should be thinking about finding, developing, and organizing their ideas. It's this myopic focus on the details of text that prevents them from attending to the larger issues of content and structure. For regular writers—those who often don't take the time to proofread—it seems useful to "expect more." For example, giving students a five-minute "reminder minilesson" on frequently confused words—its/it's; your/you're; there/their/they're—can set the stage for them to proofread their papers, looking for these common errors.

Sharing good work with others makes the process worthwhile. So **assessing and publishing** are the final stage of the writing process. Such processes are always intertwined in the real world. A letter to the editor, a job resume, an advertisement, an interoffice memo or company report, a dissertation proposal—all of these texts are shared with readers and assessed by them. In classroom writing assignments, the teacher serves as the main assessor, but there are many different levels of publication for student writing, ranging from an audience of one to an audience of many. As students' work is posted on classroom bulletin boards—or on electronic ones via the Internet—the opportunities for assessment multiply.

Guiding Cycle 1 Activities (Prewriting)

To help students get started with process writing tasks, try supporting their work with checklists. Simple checklists, given in advance of your in-class workshops and conferences, are much like the grading rubrics in Chapter 6, except that students often help create them.

Let's say, for example, that your language arts class has been reading fables. Drawing from what students already understand about fables, you might list features of the fable genre at the board. Of course, these features define a fable writing task—and a corresponding checklist—for students.

A Fable for Today
1. The characters are animals with human qualities.
2. There is some kind of problem or conflict.
3. Animals may talk to one another in a fable.
4. Action grows out of the problem or conflict.
5. A clear "moral" comes at the end of the fable.

(Strong, 2001)

Or let's say that your science class has been researching the causes and effects of global warming, and you've asked them to use a letter format to share findings with a broader audience. Students have the option of writing a personal letter, a letter to the editor (for a newspaper or magazine), or a business letter (to a specific corporation or government agency). You might have this kind of checklist:

A Global Warming Letter
1. The letter (personal, letter to editor, business) is formatted correctly.
2. It makes a central point (thesis) about global warming.
3. At least three points of evidence (proof, reasons, examples) are given.
4. The letter has a clear beginning, middle, and end.
5. Words and ideas are appropriate for the chosen format.

Or let's imagine you're teaching general math, and you want to help students analyze data sets. You post the nation's current nutrition guidelines, and then you give learners the data sets from several fast-food chains (available at local stores or via the Internet). In the computer lab, students work in teams, each focused on a specific type of fast-food product (for example, chicken sandwiches, french fries, or quarter-pound hamburgers). Products are compared on variables such as fat content, cholesterol, carbohydrates, and sodium, so that "consumer rankings" can be developed on the class web site. A checklist like this one would be helpful:

A Web Site Article (Your Contribution)
1. Develop a 2 × 2 matrix listing fast-food restaurants and nutrition variables.
2. Transfer all data for a single type of product to your matrix for analysis.
3. Now, rerank the restaurants from best to worst on your product's variables.
4. Explain your rank order in writing (some variables may conflict).
5. Submit your writing to the Web Site Editors, supported by your matrix.

Or let's say you're a social studies and history teacher who has teamed up with colleagues in the English department. As high school juniors read Mark Twain's *Huckleberry Finn* and Mildred Taylor's *Roll of Thunder, Hear My Cry,* you draw upon key ideas in American history and social studies. For example, in your assignment for Twain's novel, you ask students to imagine Huck and Jim as very old men in the twentieth century, exchanging insights about race relations. You provide a checklist to further define the writing task:

A Dialogue between Huck and Jim
1. Create a setting and situation for your dialogue.
2. Weave modern historical facts (persons, events) into the dialogue.
3. Show how Huck and Jim see race relations in the twentieth century.
4. Also show the present relationship between Huck and Jim.
5. Use correct writing conventions for dialogue (quotation marks).

Or let's suppose your psychology class has been studying Freud's theory of human personality, and you've asked students to describe a personal experience that they feel comfortable sharing (for example, whether to go to the mall with friends or study for a major exam) in which the constructs of the Id and Superego were in dynamic tension, attempting to influence the Ego. Your checklist might look like this:

A Freudian Narrative
1. The narrative is based on a real event, not a fictional one.
2. A clear setting and situation are provided.
3. Two "inner voices" compete as the narrative develops.
4. One voice wins out, and a resulting action (consequence) is described.
5. A final paragraph reflects on the meaning of the story.

Clearly, checklists provide specific direction for students as they begin writing. But they also set the stage for productive talk in response groups, enabling students to get feedback from each other. Let's now examine how response groups can contribute to process writing activities.

Guiding Cycle 2 Activities (Revising)

The point of small response groups—three to five students—is to support and encourage revision. As a group offers helpful responses, the writer begins to see what's working in a text and what's not; then the writer gets ideas from others on how specific points might possibly be approached. Thus, good peer response takes the pressure off the teacher to be the sole judge and arbiter of writing quality.

Small response groups work best when each writer prepares photocopies of a draft. If this isn't possible in your classroom, organize students into groups of three, with the writer in the center and a peer responder on each side. The responders follow the text as it is read aloud by the writer. Here are some general guidelines for students:

How to Get Feedback on Writing
1. Read your work aloud twice.
2. Don't "defend" your work.
3. Take notes on what others tell you.
4. Ask questions to clarify what others say.
5. Thank people for their comments.
6. Never apologize for the piece you're going to read.

How to Give Feedback on Writing
1. Listen for the overall effect in the first reading.
2. Make notes/comments during the second reading.
3. Tell what you liked best about the writing.
4. Identify a place in the writing that may need work.
5. Comment on content and organization first, then mechanics.
6. Be specific by "pointing" to places on the actual page.

(Strong, 2001)

Before students work in response groups, it's vital to model the process and discuss these guidelines. Emphasize the value of *positive* feedback, because if students feel threatened by their groups, the process will be undermined immediately. By investing some time in training, you can avoid pitfalls.

To model the process, I recommend a "fishbowl" strategy. Set up a small response group as an inner circle and have students circle their desks to watch the action inside. Explain your purpose—to have live demonstrations of positive roles and negative roles. Then hand out role cards to response group players and "observation sheets" to students on the outside.

Fishbowl Observation Sheet

Directions: Name the four students in the inner circle, making sure to identify the writer. Then focus on what the three responders say and do. Take notes on their positive comments and behaviors—and also their negative ones. Use your notes in the debriefing session that follows. To earn points today, please hand in this sheet at the end of class.

Round 1

Mark	○ ○	Alisha
Sonia	○ ○	Carlos

Round 2

Laura	○ ○	Andy
Shauna	○ ○	Marcus

Round 3

Sam	○ ○	Michelle
Dana	○ ○	Will

As volunteers in the response group play roles in response to short pieces of anonymous writing from other classes, students on the outside take notes, usually with quiet intensity. Over several days, all students get to be in the fishbowl.

Role cards are fun to create. The positive ones include the Cheerleader (pointing to good points in the text), the Questioner (asking thoughtful open-ended questions), the Helper (offering specific useful tips for revision), the Encourager (expressing confidence that the writing is worth revising), and the Leader (keeping the group on task). Each positive role card should have general advice about being friendly, businesslike, and positive in verbal and nonverbal behaviors.

By contrast, the negative roles include ones like the Criticizer (naming all the weak parts of the text), the Dominator (monopolizing the feedback), the Mush-mouth (rambling on, mostly incoherently), the Clown (fooling around, deflecting attention from response), the Detailer (focusing on nitpicky points, not ideas), and the Sleeper (self-explanatory). Students playing these roles are invited to frown, sneer, and make rude, belittling comments about the writing or the writer.

After about five or ten minutes of role-playing response, pause to debrief. The observers will point out "good," or helpful, comments and contrast these with "lame" responses. After a round of such training, students volunteer for the response group inner circle—and a chance to show off their acting skills. Of course, all students are "playing roles," so there's no cause for bruised egos.

Does role-playing encourage negative behaviors in real response groups? Not usually. Instead, your students internalize standards of good conduct from the *contrast* between positive and negative roles. As you challenge students to think about real response groups, you'll discuss your expectations and the fact that good response represents a pooling of intelligence. Students buy into the process when they see how honest, thoughtful collaboration helps everybody do better.

I encourage students to use this simple Common Code for marginal notes:

+ = Good (use more + signs as necessary)
✓ = Some kind of problem here ("check this")
? = Confusion for me at this point
= Expand, say more, elaborate

Afterwards, try modeling a real response group with help from volunteers. Again, the fishbowl strategy is used, but now students are being themselves. The outside observers pay close attention, using an observation guide that lists positive aspects of response. As teacher, you lead the debriefing follow-up.

Response Group Training

Directions: Observe students in the fishbowl as they offer workshop response. Pay attention to *what* is said and *how* it is said (tone of voice, body language). Evaluate each person's feedback: 3 = very helpful; 2 = helpful; 1 = not so helpful.

Criteria for Effective Response	Jim	Sue	Joy	Ted
Faces the writer and seems interested				
Makes positive comments to support writer				
Points to specific places in text with ideas				

(continues)

Criteria for Effective Response	Jim	Sue	Joy	Ted
Is friendly but businesslike with suggestions				
Asks questions and listens to the response				
Stays on task and doesn't get distracted				
Uses descriptive, nonjudgmental language				
Other:				

Source: Strong, 2001, p. 138

Following a few rounds of the second stage of training, students know what you expect, so now it's time to get to work. Cruise the room as small groups meet. Be alert to off-task behavior or insensitive criticism, and reinforce students for responding well to the work of others. Early on—and especially with difficult classes—have responders jot down key points before elaborating orally. Make sure to set time limits for group work (ten minutes of response for a one-page paper) and conclude the response group sessions by asking writers to draft their plans for revising. Such closure makes the activity purposeful.

Students must understand that feedback sometimes confirms hunches and sometimes provides a challenge to content, organization, or writing style. It's after a period of nondefensive "listening" that writers figure out what's best for their papers.

Prompting Self-Assessment

The book makes few absolute pronouncements, but this is one of them: *Self-assessment is the key to writing progress.* In other words, once students get deeply involved in reading their own writing—and trying to improve it—we have the conditions for true insights. So, if our goal is to make self-assessment a habit of mind for young adults, how do we actually motivate and nurture such behavior?

To introduce the idea of "self-assessment," you might show several photographs of typical teenagers and ask students a few basic questions: How do they know what's "hot" and what's not? How much time do they spend each morning checking out how they look? Why do they do this?

You're leading toward a simple point—that the process of assessing that sexy, good-looking product in the bathroom mirror isn't all that different from slowly rereading a text that will go to one's peers and eventually to one's teacher. Many students wear cool outfits and fix their hair in special ways to make good impressions on their friends. They also check their writing with care because they value what others think—and because they don't want to look like fools.

Contrast a clearly developed student paragraph from your content area with a scrawled, inarticulate one, the kind students often rip from their notebooks. As you did with the photographs, ask students about their "first impressions." What judgments do they make (or inferences do they draw) about the authors of the two paragraphs? Do most of us make snap judgments about intelligence, level of education, and character based on first impressions? Of course we do.

This kind of lesson sets the stage for having students reflect on their own self-assessment strategies in writing. You might try an inventory like the following one.

Directions: Reflect on your attitudes toward writing and the approaches you usually take. Doing so will help you understand yourself as a learner. Keep this self-assessment on the inside cover of your working portfolio. Respond using this code: 1 = strongly agree; 2 = agree; 3 = disagree; 4 = strongly disagree.

1. __ I usually can write when I set my mind to it.
2. __ Figuring things out in writing is interesting to me.
3. __ When I write things down, I often learn more effectively.
4. __ I like to brainstorm lots of ideas before I begin to write.
5. __ I often jot down some kind of plan for my school writing.
6. __ I sometimes surprise myself with insights while writing.
7. __ I enjoy the feeling of sharing my writing with others.
8. __ I am willing to work hard at learning to write well.
9. __ Working with others helps me do my best writing.
10. __ I almost always know whether writing is good or not.
11. __ Having a quick conference with a teacher helps me write.
12. __ I generally know how to make my own writing better.
13. __ Rereading what I write is the way I improve my writing.
14. __ I whisper my writing to myself to check how it sounds.
15. __ I look forward to others' comments about my writing.
16. __ It's often fun to proofread and edit my own writing.
17. __ Learning to write is more important than the grade I get.
18. __ Even the best writers sometimes struggle with writing.
19. __ Writing well comes more from *doing* it than from inspiration.
20. __ Good writing skills will help me in my future life.

Source: Strong, 2001, p. 137

After students discuss their responses to these items, try sharing these three self-assessment strategies, which can lead to dramatic improvements in writing quality.

Strategy 1 (Reading Aloud)

When professional writers offer writing advice, they inevitably mention reading aloud. This strategy, like standing in front of a mirror, is basic to self-assessment. To demonstrate this strategy for students, prepare an acetate transparency of a draft paragraph you've written and then "think aloud" about it, making changes and corrections. Such a demonstration may take only five minutes, but to many learners, it will be memorable. Point out how reading aloud reveals clunky sentences or gaps in logic, but how it also helps you catch small mistakes. As you show students how to do what you expect them to do, you build self-assessing skills.

Strategy 2 (Reading Imaginatively)

Skilled writers flip back and forth between the roles of "composer" and "reader." The imagined reader can be someone real, one or more persons known personally, but often it's an audience *invented* by the writer. The point is that imagined readers serve as co-creators of the text. To illustrate this idea, take the paragraph from your reading aloud demonstration, and ask students to assume the role of voices in the writer's head. What questions do they have? What judgments are they making about the text? As these points are voiced, first take notes on them, and then tinker with the paragraph, making changes to the original. Students need to see how their imagined readers can help them revise.

Strategy 3 (Rereading with Care)

Although student writers might already read their writing aloud from an imagined reader's viewpoint, they sometimes don't reread with care. Such rereading involves letting the text "cool" for a day or two and then coming back to it. Typically, many students procrastinate until the last minute—a self-defeating strategy rather than a self-assessing one. In sharing the idea of careful rereading, you might compare it to an "appearance check" in the middle of a busy day—for example, making adjustments on hair style, deleting a gaudy fashion accessory, or adding a fresh cosmetic touch.

Bumps in Process Teaching

As we've already seen, checklists and rubrics assist assessment, especially when students help to define the standards. Another useful strategy is to use a few anonymous papers for discussion. As students look at model papers in relation to public criteria, they develop a more objective (less egocentric) frame of reference for self-assessment.

But let's be honest: Many students are so conditioned to traditional teacher and student roles that they resist writing process instruction. These are the students, like Kim in Chapter 2, who rush through writing tasks with little or no prewriting and who turn in papers with little or no revision. Given these realities, we shouldn't be too surprised when such students drag their feet during peer response and self-assessment. Expect such challenges, and don't be too discouraged by them. Just trust the process.

Change is as difficult for students as it is for us. If they're used to perfunctory assignments followed by top-down teacher grading, the dynamics of your teaching will feel incredibly *different* to them—and different can be scary. After all, you're asking for their real involvement, both intellectually and emotionally, and such a change requires a period of adjustment. Is this teacher for real? What are the risks here?

As a teacher, encourage self-assessment when you respond to student papers. For example, after reading literacy autobiography drafts (described earlier in this book), I offer my students a process for preparing final papers. Specifically, I ask them to (1) monitor their responses to my comments and advice; (2) put the paper away for a day and then develop a revision plan; (3) go to work on revision; (4) compare their old paper and their new one, looking for areas of improvement; (5) fill out a self-assessment rubric (scoring guide); and (6) develop a self-assessment cover letter that tells the "inside story" of the revision process.

The cover letters are always fascinating. It's not unusual for students to resist my advice initially; but then, after a day or so, their feelings tend to mellow. Still later, as they begin to revise, the writing usually becomes fun again, a process of rediscovery. By the time they compare the old draft with the final version, they're usually quite *proud* of the new product. And I've taught them the most important self-assessment lesson of all—what they *can* do.

Here's a typical self-assessment letter from science teacher Jeff Luke (personal communication, 2004):

> When I first read your evaluation of my [literacy autobiography] paper, I was a little disappointed. I thought that you would enjoy it more and critique it less. However, when I handed it in, I realized that it didn't fit the criteria for the assignment as well as it could. Seeing this, and also seeing the points you made in your cover letter to me, I decided to revise it.
>
> The first thing that I did was to think about my high school more (like you suggested). This got some ideas flowing which I actually jotted down on your cover sheet. This got me thinking about some college classes that influenced my attitudes as well (which I also jotted down).
>
> I thought a lot about how I was going to revise my paper. This thinking process spanned several days. I decided to add some of the things that I had jotted down and shorten the newspaper part of my paper. When I had actually done this, I realized that the "newspaper" theme did not really fit the rest of the paper. I tinkered with the opening and closing. Actually, I scrapped my old ones and did completely new ones. Although I am not sure how much I like the new ones, I feel they are better suited for the feel of my paper.
>
> It is hard to say how much thinking time went into revision, but total typing time was about three hours. I hope you like where the paper has gone.

This is the kind of clear, honest self-assessment that every teacher hopes for. With it, you get a pay-off for the time invested in coaching students to improve their writing. You'll learn more about responding to student work in Chapter 8, "Coaching and Judging Writing."

Managing Collaborative Writing

Visit real-world workplaces in a knowledge-driven economy, and you see people working in groups. Indeed, *teamwork* is probably the defining characteristic of today's corporate culture, whether in industry, finance, technology, government, or education. People have individual jobs, but they also participate in committees, task forces, and management groups to address issues relevant to their mutual survival.

And these teams write. They produce business plans, sales reports, engineering documents, and a bewildering array of other genre. If the teams are housed in schools, they produce grant proposals, accreditation materials, and Individual Education Plans, not to mention curriculum frameworks, web pages, and write-ups of committee recommendations.

But aside from the fact that collaborative writing is required within the modern workplace, such work can also be justified on purely practical grounds—namely, that it *reduces* the paper load for secondary teachers. Typical secondary teachers may work with 150 (or more) students per day. However, if students are organized into writing teams of three, the reading load is suddenly reduced to 50 papers—still daunting, but at least within the bounds of reason.

With a good collaborative task, the written product reflects the best thinking of a group, and all students have some hand in actual writing. For example, students in a choral music class might prepare program notes for the songs and composers in their annual Winter Solstice program. Students in an economics class might choose stocks and bonds and track their performance over a defined period, finally pooling their notes into a team-written paper. Spanish students might team up to assess the levels of computer literacy with the local Hispanic population, creating a report that is shared with the school board for community action.

As a practical matter, Dale (1997) recommends that each co-authoring group name a "primary writer" for each assignment. This person takes notes, integrates revisions and corrections into a fresh draft, and makes copies for team members. This key role should rotate during the semester. Dale also urges that "students not break the writing task into parts and parcel it out" (p. 45). Instead, the most productive groups write together and share in the big decisions of structure as well as the small details of phrasing and mechanics.

And what about grading? Dale (1997) suggests that the quality of the final co-authored product should be about 50 percent of the individual student's grade. The other 50 percent has to do with three kinds of assessments—moving among the groups and monitoring the contributions of individuals; reading students' learning logs and self-assessment forms; and collecting peer assessment forms. Such forms for classroom use are found in Dale's monograph *Co-Authoring in the Classroom* (1997).

While it's true that some students are adept at "faking it" in groups—hanging back and letting others do the work—it's equally true that competition for its own sake is hardly persuasive as an ultimate goal for education. Increasingly, individual success is linked to one's ability to work well with others—to cooperate and collaborate. Thus, collaborative writing makes sense as preparation for workplace realities and as a way to encourage self-assessment in writing. Keep collaboration in mind when you read Chapter 9.

WRITE FOR INSIGHT ACTIVITY

You've developed several "Write for Insight" expressive pieces while reading this book. Our next task draws upon those efforts. To assist your revision of this piece, let's share it in a peer response group. Although this process may be new to you, don't worry. Others are probably just as nervous as you are. Here's the writing task:

> Imagine you're chairing the "Writing Across the Curriculum" committee for your middle school or high school. A colleague has this to say just before he storms out of the first committee meeting: "Content area writing? Hey, give me a break! Kids learn handwriting in elementary school! I say you either know how to write or you don't—and the dummies need a special ed teacher, not me. And besides, isn't writing in the English department? I've got plenty to do teaching my subject, so don't add writing on *top*! Look, no offense, but I'm out of here!"
>
> Write a crafted email letter to your colleague. Try to communicate respectfully while also broadening this teacher's perspective on writing. To set up this task, you may find it helpful to list your key points. Are there any analogies or personal examples you might use to address your colleague's "either/or" point-of-view? What tone will help you accomplish your aims? Following is a checklist you can use when sharing your text with others or assessing it on your own.
>
> ### Email Letter to Colleague
> 1. The letter shows professional respect in its approach.
> 2. The letter summarizes the issue (or "problem") to be discussed.
> 3. The letter outlines alternative ways to think about the issue.
> 4. The letter invites further dialogue about the issue.
> 5. The letter demonstrates excellent control over writing mechanics.

Based on the response group feedback, revise and share your email letter with your instructor. Afterwards, discuss whether the process helped you improve your writing. If so, why? If not, why not?

8 Coaching and Judging Writing

The language must be careful and must appear effortless. It must not sweat.
—Toni Morrison

Responding to Writing

It's late on a Tuesday night after a day of on-campus classes, school visits, and a hundred-mile trip to meet with a cohort of experienced teachers. Now, my email messages are stacked up like planes on final approach to Chicago's O'Hare airport.

Among them are several **microthemes**—part of my effort to monitor students' reading before each class. In these, I ask teachers-to-be to summarize key points and react personally. This task is my humble alternative to traditional quizzes, long used by teachers to motivate required reading. After quick responses to several microthemes, I know what students are thinking and use this information to prepare for class. Students never know whether any given microtheme will receive response. All they know is that I keep electronic files—and no microtheme, no credit.

I click on an email from an affable young man who wants to teach English. So far this semester he's hung back a bit, with his arms folded across his chest. I like him and see his potential, but his microtheme rocks me back in my chair.

> TRhe isue of grammar and the way in which it is to be taught is particularly perplexing to me. I have personaly found it discouraging that that the last "grammar" class I remember was taken in 7th grade taught by a large unbpleasant woman who told us that she became a teacher to exact revenge upon her teachers by punishing her inoccent and unsuspecting students. Fortunatly for me however, I must have been a member of the dominant culture of power because the language I learned at home enabled me to pass every grammar test ever thrust upon me. Still, I am unable to preform simple grammatical tasks. For instance, if I was asked to define what an adverb was my response whould be a talented display of "b.s." and evasion. For this ineptitude I find myself disturbed about teaching grammar. I am actualy not sure that anyone realy knows or can define correct grammar. This makes me both angry that I was not taught more implicitly, and asking the question: "Why does it realy matter?" If you want an earfull about why it realy matters, I would be happy to elabortrate.

(Name withheld, 2003)

Rereading it, I hesitate. I know that email invites loose, off-the-top-of-the-head thinking. But do I respond only to the content of the message and ignore its lack of proofreading? What *is* its content exactly? Does this level of literacy define the kind of teacher I'd want working with *my* grandchildren? While my main interest is ideas, this expressive writing seems to deserve fuller coaching. I finally conclude that I can't simply file it away, with an easy click. And so here's how I reply, addressing the student by name.

> OK, here's a challenge. Look back at your microtheme to see how many errors in grammar, usage, and spelling you can find. I want to help you answer the question of "Why does it realy [sic] matter?"
>
> Your question is important, and answering it will help you see some reason for studying and applying language principles and, equally important, encouraging your students to get involved in such study. Otherwise, you risk going down the same path as the teacher you criticize—and giving kids negative views about language. I'd be surprised if you wanted THAT outcome!
>
> In short, I DO want you to elaborate, but I hope the elaboration might result in REAL conversation, one that involves respect for the person receiving your email. By "respect," I don't mean a deferential, brown-nosing attitude. I simply mean exercising a bit more care in communication!
>
> After all, your words say who you are and signal your attitudes toward the reader—whether a student, parent, or professor. You asked, "Why does it really matter?" I hope my honest response helps you think about your question.

Tough feedback? Yes. Are there risks here? Of course. But maybe there's a point when teachers have to resist acquiescing to "anything goes" conventions in written language. Maybe it's a disservice to students when we quietly abdicate standards of communication, the so-called "basic skills" of writing.

Of course, as professional teachers—not just assessors—we have to support our stance with age-appropriate coaching. For many students, such coaching means patient feedback on skills and some friendly encouragement to "hang in there." But for others—like this student, I think—it may mean a gentle kick in the butt.

I'm pleased to report a happy ending to the story. On the student's very next microtheme there was a dramatic turnaround—clear, interesting, thoughtful writing about the teaching of poetry. It wasn't perfect prose, but it showed a good-faith effort to summarize and react to textbook reading. And now I felt eager to respond to him.

> Great job! You're into this chapter, and you're seeing yourself in the classroom, dealing with kids. This raises a question in my mind: What do you think about poetry memorization and poetry performance? Are you for it or against it?

This student's answer to my question was almost immediate, a full page of detailed response. Now he was interested in working with *me,* and I was glad to know that.

Thinking about Assessment

This story focuses attention on **coaching** and **judging** activities—the oral and written feedback we give to student work. In this book, I've contended that expressive writing should often go ungraded, though we may need to reinforce it with points or smiley faces or sticky notes—or by having students *use* such writing in their formalized process writing assignments, the kind described in Chapters 6 and 7. So it's in the context of *graded* assignments that students generally need feedback about their writing skills. Let's explore this idea further.

Rhoda Maxwell conceptualizes school writing in three levels, arguing that each level dictates a different style of response. Level 1 is personal and expressive, its usual aim being for students to generate ideas and organize thoughts through journal writing, note-taking, and so on. If evaluation occurs, the focus will be on content only. Level 2—like my microtheme assignment—is more formal and organized, its function being for students to explain thoughts or inform others through homework, reports, and exams. Therefore, response focuses on both content and form, with skills addressed in relation to readability. Level 3, the most formalized (and infrequent) of school writing tasks, requires high-quality texts in forms such as poetry, letters to the editor, job resumes, and research papers. Our standards are exacting, revision is the norm, and in-class publication (or posting) is common. Most school writing should be at Level 1 or Level 2, Maxwell says, in order to have maximum instructional benefit. In her view, Level 3 is reserved for "only occasional use" (Maxwell, 1996, p. 44).

Maxwell's point about tailoring response to the level of the task makes practical sense. At Level 1, writing-to-learn tasks need only cursory reading, and sometimes not even that; at Level 2, the focus is mainly content accuracy, but with some attention to form and conventions; and at Level 3, there are explicit content standards, plus high standards for writing quality, usually accomplished through revision. It's only as we verbalize our *goals* for student writing that we can figure out how to respond usefully.

If you're a harried content teacher with plenty to do, giving feedback on writing may seem like a black hole for your instructional energy. Relax. No one expects you to take up the English teacher's workload.

Instead, this chapter outlines practical methods of response for times when you do have breathing room for assessment—or for occasions when parent volunteers can be mobilized to give you a hand. Believe it or not, many school districts have great "lay reader" programs to assist content area teachers. Typically, these programs are staffed by adult volunteers and trained by district personnel to help with the paper load.

Coaching versus Judging

When it comes to writing, we can serve either as **coaches** or as **judges**. Of course, the traditional role is the teacher-as-examiner, the adult who passes judgment on the quality of student work and "grades" it. A trickier role is the teacher-as-coach, the mentor who helps learners achieve their full potential through dialogue and revision. Students get confused when we send mixed signals about these roles.

In my opinion, it's silly to characterize one role as "good" and the other as "bad." Teachers frequently serve as judges as they assess the knowledge or skills of students at the end of a semester. Obviously, too, such judgments have far-reaching practical implications, ranging from report cards to college admissions. On the other hand, the judging role isn't the only one teachers play—or even the most important one. Good teachers, from Socrates forward, have helped their students meet expectations. They nudge, tease, cajole, and challenge students to accomplish important goals.

The roles of judge and coach are visibly separated in Olympic athletic events. While judges carefully assess performance skills in high-stakes competitions, nervous coaches retreat to the sidelines to chew their nails.

But in secondary schools, the roles become fluid and slippery. On one day, the teacher is a judge, assessing student work against the criteria of district, state, or national standards; and on the very next day, the same teacher is working side by side with students, helping them decide how to weave vivid examples into a text, find a better lead, or reorganize its paragraphs. Such shifting roles can present problems.

For example, you might meet with a student to review her research report. Like any good coach, you're positive and encouraging—pointing to strengths she can build on, inviting her self-assessment. There's a pause between the two of you.

"So it is good enough?" she asks. "What's it worth?"

And your heart sinks because you've been suckered again. You've had a coaching aim—to help her do good work and feel the pride of achievement—but her aim has been to get a judgment from you (a "grade") and do as little work as possible. You've been on very different wavelengths.

So how can this problem be addressed? Talk it through with your students. Explain that you're interested in education, not game-playing. Communicate that they're probably not well served by sloppy judging—that is, by low standards and the judge playing favorites—or by lazy coaching. That's why you'll wear a Judge's Hat when final papers are due and the Coach's Cap when you're setting up assignments and commenting on drafts-in-progress. Of course, you can contrast these roles by using an actual hat and a baseball cap as props.

Emphasize that the judge expects their best work, on time, with no excuses; but that the coach can be always be consulted on follow-up tasks to help them *learn* from mistakes. Thus, the judge strives to be honest and fair; and the coach strives to be helpful and encouraging. Finally, help students understand that coaching occurs "up front"—in advance of writing—as well as during their good-faith efforts to draft a paper.

We'll deal with both coaching contexts in this chapter. And later we'll turn to judging and grading, which will hold some unexpectedly pleasant surprises for you.

Getting Ready to Coach

To set up the advice that follows, let me review three common-sense principles of good assessment. Then we'll look at coaching strategies before academic writing and during it. This information will help you feel prepared to handle the process writing that comes your way—but also to feel less guilty about *not* correcting the essays that students toss in the trash can, never to be revised.

Principle 1 (Models)

To create positive contexts, give students a few samples of written work, ones that illustrate concretely and specifically what you want and don't want in their writing. Such samples come from previous classes—or from colleagues down the hall—and they are always shared without identifying names. As you point to specific features of strong and weak writing, your students will better understand your expectations. In sharing lab reports, for example, ask students for their responses to a well-formatted, thoughtfully presented report versus one that seems to have been thrown together at the last minute. Have students contrast the "telling details" of two (or more) reports. Share your responses to samples and the grade each would get.

Principle 2 (Rubrics)

In Chapter 6, "Designing Assignments and Rubrics," you learned about grading rubrics (the listing of text features and qualities). By openly sharing rubrics in advance, you help students anticipate your standards, particularly as sample papers are used to illustrate what you expect. Basically, you're teaching *to* the standards you've created. That is, instead of merely "assigning" writing—something the school's janitor can do—you're actually "teaching" it in a scaffolded, step-by-step way. For example, as students revise, they can use the grading rubric to assess papers in small groups—or an anonymous paper can be used in a large-group workshop. The rubric's framework helps students self-assess and helps you remain focused and fair in your feedback.

Principle 3 (Response)

When we respond to drafts in progress, our response should be *timely, focused,* and *balanced.* The aims of education are poorly served when papers stack up, instructional aims get forgotten, or comments become vague, mechanical, or just plain nasty. When students have to wait more than a week for response, their attention wanes. Feedback should center quickly on each student's demonstrated effort to meet the assignment's goals. Finally, comments should be balanced—offering praise for something done well, a suggestion or two, and closing words of encouragement. This three-part "sandwich" formula—praise, specific advice, and encouragement—helps students learn from your feedback.

These ideas deserve reflection. Why? Because it's easier to anticipate and avoid problems than to rectify the situations we inadvertently create for ourselves. I say this as one who has made countless mistakes in responding to student writing. I hope these pointers help you to avoid some response pitfalls.

Up-Front Coaching

Many students lack knowledge of basic academic "moves" for typical tasks. For example, developing writers often lack skill in setting up their responses to an essay question, or providing support for their views, or using language appropriate to the academic occasion. That's where "up-front" coaching linked to specific content area expectations can be tremendously helpful.

Let me explain. Chapter 1, "Writing from the Inside Out," describes my fourth-grade writing experience at a Catholic elementary school. But there's more to the story. In the intermediate grades, I was also taught a formula for catechism questions—namely, to begin each answer with key words from the question and then to write in complete sentences. So imagine my surprise when I moved to a public junior high school where few of my classmates knew how to do this. To me, writing short essays based on content knowledge in geography, English, or science was utterly natural because I had practiced it hundreds of times. To my friends, it was a new experience.

So imagine that your students don't have a clue about **thesis statements.** No, you're not an English teacher; but, yes, you do think it's useful for secondary learners to have some skill in presenting a problem, stating a thesis, and outlining their approach to an issue in an opening paragraph. How can you coach this skill?

You might begin by contrasting "knowledge dump" essays in your content area with ones that begin by identifying a problem, articulating a thesis, and framing a response. And then you might give students sentence-level practice in crafting (and responding to) thesis statements based on the models you provide. Here are a few in the area of science:

> Global warming does/does not present a serious threat at this time.
> Manned space flight to other planets is/is not worth the cost.
> Evolutionary theory should/should not be the basis for modern science.

Afterwards, you could convert expressive writing into thesis-training activities. We saw the "Take a Stand" activity in Chapter 3, "Exploring Expressive Writing," but students might also write up "award nominations" related to a content area (Mitchell, 1996). Here are some ideas:

> In English, awards could be based on character behavior in a novel, such as the most supportive person, greediest person, and so on.
>
> In physical education, students could nominate the most accessible sport, the sport that works muscle groups, and so on.

In social studies, students could nominate and give awards to people, eras, actions, and events.

(p. 95)

Of course, for each award nomination, students are actually framing thesis statements that invite supporting details like specific facts and content information.

It will come as no surprise that up-front coaching also works with *supporting information.* You contrast bare-bones essays with well-developed ones, offer content-related practice to develop the skill, and then ask students to apply what they have learned in essay exams and short papers.

And finally, such coaching helps address *proofreading and editing* issues. We can collect garbled or confused sentences from exams and papers so that students have raw material for proofreading practice. By putting anonymous sentences on handout sheets or transparencies, students quickly *see* the importance of editing and learn how to do it by using a "common code" for proofreading. This simple code, set above errors or in the text's margins, is one you'll also use:

✓ C = Check capitalization
✓ P = Check punctuation
✓ R = Check reference (pronouns)
✓ W = Check wording
✓ Sp = Check spelling

Here are just a few of the hundreds of sentences I've collected from short in-class essays in content area literacy classes. Remember, these sentences are written by junior and senior college students, not by middle school and high school students.

Proofreading and Editing Practice
- I possible have somebody eltse read your Paper for clairity, Grammar and spelling. Then make revisions as needed.
- May I suggested though no writing is ever finished or prefect. We are always changing are minds so lets not be afraid to change and recreate out writing.
- Read your paper to you mom or friend get their oppioion on it. We will also be reading papers in small groups so we can get peers oppinion. Then you make changes don't worry about spelling just change the organization and content of your paper.

After students are reminded of the need to proofread and edit careless errors, they are more inclined to look over their own papers more carefully.

Coaching as Response

As I pointed out earlier, even the best assessments don't address the critical question of effective instruction, or what I've characterized as coaching. Wandering up a row of desks, sometimes dropping in for a brief conference, the coach works in a more personal way than the judge. Good coaches do circle errors on drafts and do raise questions about organization, but grades aren't attached to this advice.

Understanding that learning is an individual matter, the coach uses "different strokes for different folks." A supportive coaching style works well with most students, but others need directive "no-nonsense" feedback, a little like my microtheme response in this chapter's opening vignette.

Before responding to the written text of any student, we need to ask ourselves some very basic questions. By having clear answers to these questions, we increase the likelihood of working smarter, not harder.

- **Is this an early or middle stage text?** Early on, ask questions about ideas and make suggestions on development. Later—assuming the ideas are clear—comment on form and organization, then urge some attention to conventions such as spelling, usage, or punctuation. Skill-deficient students may be coached by peers with better skills or referred to a number of Internet sites that help with writing.
- **What kind of reading is required?** Skimming a learning log may require only a check mark. Scanning an essay exam for specific content will probably result in points—for example, seven points out of a possible ten. A thoughtful read of a draft essay will probably lead to coaching comments in a "sandwich" formula—praise, specific advice, and final encouragement. And then there's the quick joyful read of home-run texts when you simply shout Hallelujah!
- **What form should our coaching take?** We can talk with students in class, or we can put oral suggestions on audiotape. We can make notes directly in the margins of student papers, or we can use separate sheets and sticky notes, leaving the student's text unmarked. We can respond electronically, layering in suggestions as the student's text scrolls down the computer screen. In what follows, I offer suggestions for traditional marking, but I encourage you to experiment with the previous ideas.
- **How can we signal what's working and not working?** In a quick first read of the paper, lightly underline parts of the text that read well and use a wavy underline for confusing or awkward parts. For a paragraph or two, you can either circle spelling and punctuation errors or use check marks to identify problems; but make sure to signal where your "close reading" stops. (The student must confer with peers or teacher to find out what's wrong and then apply this learning to the rest of the paper.) As students do so, they often see repeated errors (such as using commas between complete sentences). "Oh, I get it," they say.
- **How should we praise writing?** As a rule of thumb, praise should be sparing and specific, not gushing and global. Students will remember "Stunning image!" but often dismiss global comments such as "Effective use of language." Try using plus signs or smiley faces to mark an exact word choice or a finely crafted sentence. Use simple exclamations like "Wow!" or "Tell me more!" or "I'm hooked!" to let students know that their good writing gets results.

- **How should we criticize writing?** In the same way that porcupines make love—*very* carefully. Helpful criticism centers on one or two key points. Be clear and personal. Say "I'm lost here" or "Give an example" or "I don't follow this." Report your experience rather than speaking for readers in general. Comments like "Confusing" or "Unclear reasoning" sound like Olympian pronouncements. Show respect for students with open-ended questions ("How could you introduce this idea earlier?") and other requests ("For your final paper, please edit with care").

Here are some specific coaching tips, assuming that comments (or corrections) are made directly on the student's paper during drafting and revision stages of text development will—and that students resubmit final work.

- Remember: the job is to teach the student, not to fix the text.
- Know why you are reading and what your focus will be.
- Be alert to the student's self-assessment questions and requests.
- Use the student's name as you make comments or suggestions.
- Have a grading rubric as a frame of reference for your comments.
- Lightly underline strong parts; use a wavy underline for problems.
- Tell how the text affects you as a reader, not readers in general.
- Don't waste time with a text that falls below your basic standards.
- Try to "sandwich" your criticisms between statements of praise.
- Raise questions to prompt reflection about content or form.
- Couch advice in open-ended language (e.g., "Consider . . .").
- Try to use full, elaborated sentences in brief summary comments.
- Use the common code (see Chapter 7, "Managing the Writing Process") employed by peer groups.
- Circle (or check) misspelled words, punctuation errors, and so on.
- Limit yourself to a paragraph or two of close editing, then move on.
- Use smiley faces or other icons to signal your responses to text.
- Try using sticky notes so that you don't write on the student's text.
- Work as fast as you comfortably can; take breaks to stay focused.
- Ask students to jot down their candid responses to your comments.

(Strong, 2001, pp. 177–178)

And finally, I offer the expert strategies of Donald Daiker (1989), an award-winning teacher of writing, and Donald Murray, the godfather of the process writing movement in North America. Daiker allows himself *only* positive comments in a first reading, and Murray's favorite response to a student writing begins, "I like the way you ____ " (p. 111). Such practices deserve emulation.

Audiotape Coaching

Let me also make a brief pitch for the use of audiotape, recounting what biology teacher Bob Tierney did with his Neuron Notes homework assignment. You'll recall from Chapter 4, "Helping Basic Writers Succeed," that students wrote down their actual understanding of a concept or process, but without the support of books or notes. Bob emphasized that it was okay if students didn't understand a concept, but that they needed to acknowledge this fact in their writing. They received full credit if they wrote a Neuron Note, but no credit if they didn't. And here's how Bob Tierney handled the papers:

> My students, at the beginning of the year, provide me with a blank audiotape. I believe that the best response to student writing is the oral response, not the written reply. I put the tapes in a bag, by period, and when they turn in a Neuron Note, I reach into the bag, find the tape, and then find the student's paper. As I read the paper, I talk to the student. I am able to coach each student, one on one for the upcoming test. I do not provide answers. Like [the legendary Harvard naturalist] Louis Agassiz, I ask questions that allow the student the exhilaration of their own discovery.
>
> (2002, p. 16)

Using another audiotape approach for essays, you can have students activate the "line numbering" feature on their word processors. Thus, all the papers you receive will have their lines numbered in the margin. As a reader, you first skim the text, underlining strong sections with straight lines and weak sections with wavy underlines. Then you drop a labeled audio cassette into the tape recorder and begin your comments in a friendly, upbeat way. In a personal, conversational tone, you point out strengths of the text, note errors, and give advice. Of course, you use the line numbers as points of reference for your comments.

The audiotape approach is interesting because it's very personal and because papers have *no* correcting marks on them when they are returned! The student's task is to listen to comments, make revisions and corrections on the working copy, and then resubmit the paper for a final (graded) reading. Of course, students should also submit a self-assessment sheet with their final paper, describing changes and improvements.

What I like about audiotape is that it forces active response to teacher advice. In other words, the *student* jots notes in the margin, or checks the punctuation mistakes, or draws reorganizing arrows. If your school has a set-up for audio playback in its media center (playback units plus headphones), audiotape response is certainly worth a try—if nothing else, as a change of pace in your feedback strategy.

Getting Ready to Judge

To clarify your role as judge and grader, it helps to have explicit criteria for writing tasks. One such set of criteria—widely used standards with validity—is the Six Trait Analytical Model developed by the Northwest Regional Educational Laboratory. By using a framework like the one in Figure 8-1, also available in a set of teacher-friendly rubber stamps (**www.nwrel.org/comm/catalog/**), you can help students better understand the standards used to assess their essays.

Standards like these, scored on a five-point scale, can influence students' thinking when used in workshops, response groups, and self-assessment activities.

FIGURE 8-1   Six Trait Analytical Model

	Ideas	Organization	Voice
5	The paper is clear and focused. It holds the reader's attention. Relevant anecdotes and details enrich the central theme or storyline.	The organization enhances the central idea or storyline. The order, structure, or presentation of information is compelling and moves the reader through the text.	The writer speaks directly to the reader in a way that is individualistic, expressive, and engaging. Clearly, the writer is involved in the text, is sensitive to the needs of an audience, and is writing to be read.
3	The writer is beginning to define the topic, even though development is still basic or general.	The organizational structure is strong enough to move the reader through the text without undue confusion.	The writer seems sincere, but not fully engaged or involved. The result is pleasant, or even personable, but not compelling.
1	As yet, the paper has no sense of purpose or central theme. To extract meaning from the text, the reader must make inferences based on sketchy details. The writing reflects more than one of these problems.	The writing lacks a clear sense of direction. Ideas, details or events seem strung together in a loose or random fashion—or there is no identifiable internal structure. The writing reflects more than one of these problems.	The writer seems indifferent, uninvolved or distanced from the topic and/or the audience. As a result, the writing is lifeless or mechanical; depending on the topic, it may be overly technical or jargonistic. The paper reflects more than one of these problems.

	Word Choice	Sentence Fluency	Conventions
5	Words convey the intended message in a precise, interesting and natural way.	The writing has an easy flow and rhythm when read aloud. Sentences are well built, with strong and varied structure that invites expressive oral reading.	The writer demonstrates a good grasp of standard writing conventions and uses conventions effectively to enhance readability. Errors tend to be so few and so minor that the reader can easily overlook them unless hunting for them specifically.
3	The language is functional, even if it lacks punch; it is easy to figure out the writer's meaning on a general level.	The text hums along with a steady beat, but tends to be more pleasant than musical, more mechanical than fluid.	The writer shows reasonable control over a limited range of standard writing conventions. Conventions are sometimes handled well and enhance readability; at other times, errors are distracting and impair readability.
1	The writer struggles with a limited vocabulary, searching for words to convey meaning. The writing reflects more than one of these problems.	The reader has to practice quite a bit to give this paper a fair interpretive reading. The writing reflects more than one of the following problems.	Errors in spelling, punctuation, usage and grammar, capitalization, and/or paragraphing repeatedly distract the reader and make the text difficult to read. The writing reflects more than one of these problems.

Equally important, scores on a rubric can help students understand where they need to invest time and effort. Note that this condensed version of the six-trait rubric yields descriptors for Ideas, Organization, Voice, Word Choice, Sentence Fluency, and Conventions.

My next piece of advice might cause you to raise your eyebrows.

Whenever you wear the Judge's Hat, I urge you to work swiftly—*not* marking up papers or correcting usage errors or offering advice on organization. Why? Because that's the job of the coach—and because the timing of your feedback, after the paper is completed, will be absolutely wrong. *Remember: The optimum time for coaching is when students are working toward a final product, not when the product is completed.*

Think about it: After the train has left the station, are you really all that interested in knowing what you could have (or should have) done to be on board? Pay attention to your students. Once they get their grades, many will ignore your advice and careful corrections. In other words, when the students' minds are elsewhere, your marking efforts are pretty much wasted.

"Wait a minute," you might be thinking. "If I *don't* correct my students' writing on that final product, they'll assume everything is okay. And they'll question their grades." And now we get to the root of the problem.

Instead of giving students the coaching they need at the right time—when the paper is being developed—most of us try to use after-the-fact feedback and corrections to justify some grade or another. Thus, we're confused about what we're doing and why.

I'm saying that *grading* (a judging activity) has little to do with *advising and correcting* (a coaching activity). Students should receive grades based on the quality of their Ideas, Organization, Voice, Word Choice, Sentence Fluency, and Conventions. The scale-point descriptors give students feedback on their writing performance, but it's usually not helpful to use that performance as a teaching moment. Think about it. Do we see Olympic judges (or coaches, for that matter) rushing to the side of competing athletes to point out their mistakes? Of course not. The hard work of coaching comes in between the assessments, not during them.

For some teachers, the advice to not correct final papers is utter heresy. "I have to mark *something* and give *some* comment," they tell me. As an unreformed English teacher, I understand completely. So my admonition is to limit your comments and to tie them closely to the criteria for the assignment. Here's an example of what I'm advocating by way of grading feedback:

> Jody, you've done a nice job on your "Real World Math" paper. Check out those good scores on Ideas, Organization, and Voice. Other areas need work. I marked a paragraph with three run-on sentences, so pay attention to this. I enjoyed your paper's creativity. Score: 23/30.

Judging Portfolios

Portfolios are collections of your students' best work. Today, increasing numbers of secondary school and college programs encourage the keeping of portfolios, because they showcase learning over a semester or year. Moreover, portfolios clearly reduce the corrosive effects of high-stakes grading as described in Chapter 2. But, perhaps most importantly, portfolios extend the amount of time that teachers can coach, rather than judge student work. Final grading gets delayed.

The mechanics of portfolios are straightforward. Typically, students keep a **working portfolio,** a folder or notebook that warehouses all of their academic work over a semester—the good, the bad, and the ugly. From the working portfolio, they select several examples of their very best work, called *artifacts,* which go into a **presentation portfolio.** Before submitting the presentation portfolio for assessment, students must prepare a *cover letter* that discusses the artifacts and the growth (or learning) they represent.

Thus the presentation portfolio and cover letter constitute each student's case for getting a passing grade in the course. Of course, the teacher has shared explicit (minimum) standards for the portfolio—the number of artifacts, the types of artifacts—that relate to course goals. For example, a health education teacher might have students include their three most insightful learning logs, their most thoughtful in-class essay, the two (out of three) exams that represent their best work, and their most engaging piece of collaborative research writing. To create a cover letter, students examine all their work over a semester, select artifacts that show what they can do, and then lay out their case. In this way students get deeply involved in ongoing self-assessment, an essential frame of mind for lifelong learning.

Of course, rubrics can be developed for portfolios, just as they are developed for individual assignments. Such rubrics provide a kind of checklist of expectations. But to scaffold the portfolio task for students, it helps to have exemplars of good portfolios from previous classes. For all their differences in style, such portfolios always share certain common features, such as an array of top quality artifacts and detailed cover letters. It's also useful to set up a series of portfolio checkpoints, so that procrastinating students aren't scrambling at the last minute to pull it together.

Portfolios represent a real leap of faith, a partnership approach to assessment. As teachers, some of us take security in traditional teacher/students roles—the fact that we're in charge and students must please us to get the grades we dispense. However, portfolio assessment changes this dynamic. It forces us to see students as individual learners again, not as grade points on a distribution curve.

Students find it difficult to fake their portfolios. Inevitably, their focus shifts from whining and making excuses to laying out their best work and making their best case. And grading gets easier because the standards are explicit and public.

Coaching as a Lifetime Sport

Let's recall the student whose story opened this chapter. Our aim is to help such students internalize self-assessment strategies—or what some teachers call "think-for-yourself" skills. Helping students self-assess is a lifetime sport. But as I pointed out in Chapter 2, the school's hidden curriculum can often work against our coaching.

Consider having an explicit policy on feedback: *I read only papers that have been proofread by the student author and one or more peers.* As students sign this contract, you gain some protection from being "used" by lazy ones.

The best time for coaching, I've emphasized, is *before* the final paper comes in. Of course, big classes mean that secondary teachers must limit the amount of time for feedback. Earlier I also mentioned the rubber stamp kit from the Northwest Regional Educational Laboratory. Using this kit, you can mark the point where you have to stop. Obviously, some coaching is better than none, and students get the message that their revision matters.

When it comes to feedback, problems arise from trying to do too many things at once. For example, we might want to give advice about using vivid examples (probably a prewriting lesson), finding a clearer voice (a drafting lesson), organizing better (a revision lesson), and checking sentence mechanics (an editing lesson). Overloaded circuits result if we succumb to this temptation.

My advice is to work smarter, not harder. Repeating earlier advice, praise what the student is doing well and "sandwich" a suggestion or two within your note. And then move on!

Given these points, it will come as no surprise that I urge *balance* when commenting on student papers. Traditional approaches emphasize criticism over praise, form over content, and directions over questions. Unfortunately, such feedback typically has an unhappy legacy—discouragement. The approach offering the best hope for ongoing growth in writing balances praise *and* criticism, content *and* form, questions *and* directions.

Finally, after making a good-faith effort to coach students, using response groups and occasional conferences, none of us should feel guilty about asking them to rely on their own resources for exams and in-class papers. In other words, there comes a time to step from the role of coach to the role of judge. The point of this switch is to assess what students can do *on their own,* without the support of peers and teacher.

Explaining (and, if necessary, re-explaining) your roles of coach and judge will be a first step in setting up a positive work environment. As learners see you move back and forth between these roles, they begin internalizing such roles for themselves. And if you're lucky, you'll get a surprise note years later from some grownup who wants to communicate, belatedly, the effects of your coaching. Perhaps you'll have forgotten that student's name and face, but he or she won't have forgotten your coaching.

Believe me: good coaching matters.

WRITE FOR INSIGHT ACTIVITY

This chapter deals with the ideas of "coaching" and "judging" as applied to your work with student writing. It makes the point that students can easily get confused when we send mixed signals about these roles.

Let's assume that you're interesting in heading off such confusion—and let's also assume that you want to use writing as your mode of explanation. Having a thoughtful, rational policy about such issues—one that both students and parents can understand and support—will help to make your life as a teacher more positive and effective.

Develop a one-page classroom handout that communicates your expectations for the written work that students submit in your content area. Remember, the audience for this text is both students and their parents. Describe how you plan to approach drafts-in-progress and final papers. Use language that students and parents are likely to understand. Express your desire to help students develop quality writing, but also speak about *their* responsibilities to work with each other and you.

For obvious reasons, make sure to use your spell checker and grammar checker as you shape this text into its final form. After developing this one-page classroom handout, share a copy of it with your instructor and your classroom colleagues.

CHAPTER

9 Researching Outside the Box

We do not write what we know; we write what we want to find out.

—Wallace Stegner

A Research Story

Sometimes questions hook us.

For me, a research quest began not long after September 11, 2001, when I was asked to prepare a keynote talk for Colorado teachers on the theme of "Taking Stories to Heart." I wanted to think hard about the personal side of research—how narrative can help students negotiate the thinking challenges posed by informative, practical writing and persuasive, argumentative writing.

And so I'm prowling the library's shadowy fourth floor, not far from long rows of government archives, where I find a book whose cover is the color of wheat stubble in winter. Its title reads *Tell Me a Story*, and my heart leaps. But then I read the subtitle, "A New Look at Real and Artificial Memory," and my heart sinks. Roger Schank may have programmed computers at major universities, but it's not likely he'll help frame a rationale for taking stories to heart. I crack open the preface any way.

> We assess the intelligence of others on the basis of the stories that they tell and on the basis of their receptivity to our stories. . . . We have a memory full of experiences we can tell to others. Finding the right ones, having the right ones come to mind at the right times, having created accounts of the right ones in anticipation of their eventual use in this way, are all significant aspects of intelligent behavior.
>
> (1990, pp. xi–xii)

The book feels weightless in my hands. According to Schank, two aspects of intelligence are critical for both humans and computers: "One is having something to say, to know something worth telling, and the other is to be able to determine others' needs and abilities to know what is worth telling them" (p. xii).

Schank has a little taxonomy of stories—personal experience, secondhand accounts, official stories, and so on. His mention of children reminds me of stories I used to tell my kids, including the one about my Olympic skiing medals and how the move to Utah had been to protect them from the unhealthy pressures of celebrity status. My skiing story had many twists and turns, including the mystery of my missing medals, and my children often tried to trap me in some contradiction.

It's like I'm sleepwalking now, still reading, pausing on the landings between each floor, then out the library door into the sunny Utah cold. That night I'm in the bedroom, considering Schank's assertion that human memory is story-based and that stories are prior experiences that we learn from. I can't help but read aloud to my wife.

"Wow!" she says. "Read that last part again."

And so I do, pausing for emphasis: *"Learning from one's own experiences depends upon being able to communicate our experiences as stories to others"* (Schank, 1990, p. 12).

Over the next week, I reread Schank's argument about the role of stories in shaping memory and intelligent behavior. He explains how stories compress experience into chunks of memory and how, over time, these chunks tend to get smaller with each retelling. To tell a story is to create the gist of an experience that we can recall and use whenever we need to. Intelligence amounts to accessing the right story at the right time.

And that's the point, I find myself thinking. Stories scaffold our lives. They intensify life, make it memorable, help us live it over and over. They connect us—to ourselves and others. So the rationale for taking stories to heart is all about memory.

> *We need to tell someone else a story that describes our experience because the process of creating the story also creates a memory structure that will contain the gist of the story for the rest of our lives.* Talking is remembering. It seems odd, at first, that this should be true. Certainly, psychologists have known for years that rehearsal helps memory. But telling a story isn't rehearsal, it's creation. The act of creating is a memorable experience in itself.
>
> (Schank, 1990, p. 115; italics in original)

My fingers on the keyboard, the morning light through the blinds—these become part of my gist, useful for memory. And I find myself thinking about students with slack, bored faces, because their experiences so often go untold, unwritten, unremembered.

There are two kinds of memory, then—the *semantic* kind that is organized hierarchically, and that amounts to shared world knowledge about biology and literature and really cool rock groups—and then there is *story-based* memory, the kind activated as we process our experience. Semantic memory is like Chinese boxes—concepts nested within concepts. But story-based memory involves the creation of gists, ones that we mull over so we can be reminded of them later. Put another way: stories are the glue for making our world knowledge personal, connected, and accessible to self.

Intelligence, according to this view, is a set of behaviors linked to stories. People labeled "intelligent" get reminded of the relevant stories in their repertoire more often. They adapt old stories to new situations or problems. They connect new and confusing experiences to old stories—actively seeking to make sense, to figure things out and make a new story. They generalize or explain from their stories, including the stories in which things to do not go according to expectations. They use stories to plan future action. They tell or write elaborated stories, ones that share insights not obvious in the original. And of course intelligent people also seek to know the story behind the story, betraying a trait called curiosity.

Eventually I travel to Colorado, where I tell three stories to illustrate these points. What I say finally is that, yes, five-paragraph themes have their place and, yes, it's important for kids to write simple reports, but that it's in **research stories** like this one that we express our intelligence insightfully. After all, in sharing our insights we come to know what we really know. Indeed, we *are* the stories we tell.

Personalized Research

My research story dramatizes my interaction with ideas. The narrative creates a current that carries the ideas and information forward. In other words, personalized research is a cognitive tool for developing intelligence and insight.

So I again return to this book's basic theme, that writing can empower personal knowledge construction. But unlike earlier chapters, this one deals with research tasks that students mostly define for themselves, sometimes by teaming up with others. The aim of such writing, as with the traditional research paper, is *higher-order thinking*. To engage in such thinking, students document and analyze others' ideas, then synthesize and evaluate those ideas in meaningful ways.

However, personalized research isn't constrained by rigid expository formats and the dry voice of academic detachment like that of the papers some students cavalierly download from the Internet. Instead, these are papers "outside the box" of typical conventions, ones that invite *genuine* research. Of course, to achieve this aim, students are asked to pursue questions of real interest—and not to waste their time (and ours) by doing fake inquiries that result in fake writing.

You may object, saying that personalized research can't possibly prepare students for the rigorous demands of college writing. However, this argument is based on the premise that the traditional research paper now accomplishes this goal. Respectfully, I must question such a claim, based on my 35 years in higher education. Indeed, I'd say that far too many college students have perverse and cynical conceptions of research writing, often construing it as a meaningless patchwork of quotations. This is hardly a helpful or positive frame of mind for college work.

Your second concern may center on motivation—getting students involved in authentic research when some are either sleeping in class or neurotically seeking approval. Motivation is a tough issue, but it *does* help to tell the truth: that life is too short (and education too important) for self-deception and going-through-the-motions fakery. In this dialogue you can challenge students to explore content-related topics of personal interest, their real questions and curiosities. Explain that research writing may be a requirement, but this doesn't mean it has to be boring. In fact, such writing is a chance to have some fun and come alive intellectually.

This chapter examines how to teach research-based writing without distorting its underlying values. Students conduct interviews as well as review print sources in the library or via the Internet. We'll explore three contexts for personalized research—the Saturation Report (Bernstein, 1997; Olson, 1997a, 2003), the I-Search Paper (Macrorie, 1988, 1997; Olson, 1997b), and the Multigenre Research Project (Romano, 1995, 2000). These tasks invite description and narration as well as explanation, analysis, and evaluation. Each is adaptable across content areas, and each has the potential to engage the creative and intellectual abilities of students.

Toward the end of the chapter, I'll discuss how to approach research writing from a traditional angle while also discouraging cut-and-paste mindlessness. Of course, by inviting real-world formats—such as a feature article for a science magazine or history journal—even traditional papers become more lively. Also, high-quality multimedia presentations can fuse image, sound, and text to make student research public.

Finally, a key issue for *all* teachers is academic honesty. Therefore, this chapter concludes with basic strategies and Internet resources for dealing with rampant plagiarism and research fakery.

The Saturation Report

Let's examine some features of the Saturation Report, as developed by high school teacher Ruby Bernstein. Such a report involves:

- Writing about some place, some group, or some individual that you know well or can get to know firsthand. You "saturate" yourself with your subject.
- Writing a nonfiction article using fictional techniques. There will be scenes, characters and characterizations, dialogue, and a subtle, rather than overt, statement.
- The appeal of information of information and facts. You are writing nonfiction, and the reader will want to "know" about your subject; in short, be sensitive to this thirst for facts on the part of your reader.
- Author identification. Your point of view can be quite flexible. You can be an active participant in the action; you can remove yourself; or you can come in and out.
- Microcosm. You are focusing on some particular subject, but in so doing you are saying something more. As you capture an isolated segment of today's world, you say something about the total world.
- Implication. Much of what you attempt to "say" in your article (because of your use of fictional techniques) will be said through implication—through dialogue and through your manipulation of details.
- Reporting. You will observe your subject with a keen eye. You note interesting "overheard" conversations. You might want to interview someone.
- Form. You might write your article in pieces—conversations, descriptions, interviews, facts—and then piece it together, finding the best form for your subject (time sequence and so forth). A "patchwork"—working sections together with no transition—can be quite acceptable.
- Choice of subject. You can pick some subject from the present or recreate some subject from your past.

(1997, p. 137)

In contrast to traditional research, the Saturation Report challenges students to exercise both narrative and expository techniques. Bernstein asks them to show personal involvement as they report the information gleaned from research. In other words, the mind-numbing "knowledge dump" paper simply doesn't pass muster in Bernstein's class. She expects more, and she gets it.

Here's how Bernstein frames the Saturation Report assignment.

> This paper will bring together some of the techniques you have practiced: use of descriptive detail, dialogue, narrative, close observation. For the saturation report you may do one of the following:
>
> 1. Teach or be taught a task
> 2. Visit a place.
> 3. Capture an event.
> 4. Vividly describe a person.
> 5. Show your job in action.
>
> No matter what you do, you will need to bring in an abundance of notes in which you have recorded your feelings, your detailed observations, conversations you have heard, people you have spoken to, and descriptions. After all your visiting, looking, and listening, bring your notes in (more than you need, please), focus on your subject, and then write. Remember that your paper should make some kind of statement about a lesson, place, event, person, or job. That statement may be stated or unstated as your material demands.
>
> (1997, p. 137)

Thinking outside the box, let's imagine math students in writing teams. Their challenge is to explore how math is used in the modern workplace. Their parents may be sources of information, but they could also arrange to visit local businesses, construction sites, and professional offices to investigate real-world applications. Imagine seventh graders sitting down with a factory manager and learning the inside story of math. Imagine tenth grade girls linking up via email with female engineers in the aerospace industry. The reports written from such real-world experiences can resonate with students for the rest of their lives.

Or let's think about health education students doing Saturation Reports on human health stories—families and individuals who struggle with Alzheimer's disease, diabetes, alcohol or drug addiction, obesity, physical disabilities, and other problems. Human dramas surround us. As students respectfully depict the saga of human stories, taking care to protect privacy, they develop compelling reasons for learning more about a specific condition and communicating what they learn. Research has a human face.

Building on Bernstein's ideas, Catherine D'Aoust (1997) adapted the assignment to include historical figures, asking students to do background reading and focus on a key moment in a famous person's life, weaving in elements of setting, action, and interior thoughts. Carol Booth Olson (1997a) further developed the task to allow students the option of witnessing a person, place, or event, with the goal of creating a "you-are-there" effect for the reader. Olson (2003) requires students to document at least three sources, using in-text citations and a reference list in APA style.

A Student Saturation Report

Here's an excerpt from "Just the Facts," an eight-page Saturation Report by Missy Tierney, one of Olson's students. In this paper, we go inside the media frenzy surrounding the indictment, trial, and execution of Julius and Ethel Rosenberg, both convicted of espionage during the ramp-up to the Cold War in the early 1950s. While most Saturation Reports have a single viewpoint, this one has two voices—that of Ethel Rosenberg as she is strapped into the electric chair at Sing Sing Prison on June 19, 1953, and that of a reporter/narrator who has covered the Rosenberg drama and has helped hype the story at his editor's urging. In the following monologue, while the reporter watches final preparations for Ethel Rosenberg's death, we get the behind-the-scenes story.

> Over the past three years I feel like I've traced Ethel's every movement. Every emotionless gaze, straightening of shoulders, pursing of lips and unfeeling blink has been documented into my notebook. It's almost eerie to see that she hasn't changed that demeanor since the first day I saw her at their tiny apartment in the Knickerbocker Village (Neville, 1995, p. 16), through her testimony, to the reading of the verdict, and even now she sits there in the electric chair. But first impressions always stick. That first encounter, observing her coldness and detachment, set the tone for the stance that I and other members of the press took through this ordeal. And even though the charges brought against her should not have been enough to put her in that chair, the impressions she gave to the press and public were sufficient to convict her.
>
> I should have known that when my editor stormed through the office door three years ago, hair on end, tie undone, shirt unbuttoned, cigar in tow, he wasn't going to be the bearer of glad tidings.
>
> "We've got to keep on top of this Rosenberg scandal," he barked at me. "All of our competition's already on the case. The *Times, Herald Tribune, Post, Journal-American,* and *World-Telegram and Sun* are on assignment. Hell, the *Jewish Daily Forward* and the *Daily Worker* are even runnin' the Rosenbergs as headlines (Neville, 1995, p. 35). The *Daily Mirror* has got to keep up. The police only arrested Julius yesterday, but that means the FBI's been on their track (Neville, 1995, p. 17). But this has all the makings of a great story! Espionage, the reds, brothers, sisters, the atomic bomb. Our readers will eat it up. Now, the wife will be granting interviews at her apartment tomorrow. Looks like you've got yourself an assignment."

With her narrative, Missy Tierney had skillfully set up a scene that will show the first press interview with Ethel Rosenberg. But now she can also fold in relevant factual information about the political context—how "all of the major newspapers were featuring stories on McCarthy, Korea, and Russia," and how syndicated columnist Bob Considine "had whetted the public's appetite for 'patriotic' news." Of course, the reporter/narrator is swept along by the political tide. In order to "suggest Ethel Rosenberg's involvement in the trading of secrets about the atomic bomb," he acknowledges writing about "the messy state of her apartment, her pithy answers, her aloof attitude, and her seeming incapacity to show emotion." And here we again pick up the story.

> The following day, I picked up a copy of the *Journal American* and *Daily News* to compare my colleagues' accounts with my own. Emblazoned across the top of the *Journal American* was the headline "Doubts FBI Charge: Wife Defends a Spy Suspect" (Philipson, p. 375). The angles of their articles were almost identical to mine. And mine, I couldn't help notice as I glanced over my name in the by-line of the *Daily Mirror,* had an awful lot of text taken straight from the "commentary" side of my notebook.
>
> The newspaper articles that covered Ethel Rosenberg from that day forward followed the same formula as those my colleagues and I published after that first interview. An eye-catching headline with the word "spy" was inevitably included, along with text that we liberally peppered with words like "cold," "emotionless," "Communist," "guilty," and "unfit mother." Looking back, that first interview must have set the tone for the way the press treated Ethel. I don't think any of us realized how much clout we had in influencing public opinion. No, there wasn't enough evidence to convict Ethel, let alone send her to the chair. But these days, a drop of suspicion is evidence enough.

Clearly, such powerful prose has been informed by lots of background research. This Saturation Report concludes with an unforgettable description of the execution—"I'll never forget my last sight of her, slumped in the oak chair, smoke rising from her pores, and the last morbid stench of burning flesh"—followed by the reporter's thoughts and his decision to publicize a wrongful execution.

The I-Search Paper

It's a warm Saturday afternoon in October as I write these words. I've just come in from a walk along the river, where the leaves are turning yellow and asters bloom in purple profusion. Earlier today, I purchased *The Best American Essays 2003* (Fadiman and Atwan, 2003), and I've now spent a few autumn hours getting acquainted with several fine writers. Scan these opening lines. Do they share any common features?

- My daughter, Olivia, who just turned three, has an imaginary friend whose name is Charlie Ravioli. Olivia is growing up in Manhattan, and so Charlie Ravioli has a lot of local traits: he lives in an apartment "on Madison and Lexington," he dines on grilled chicken, fruit, and water, and, having reached the age of seven and a half, he feels, or is thought, "old." But the most peculiarly local thing about Olivia's imaginary playmate is this: he is always too busy to play with her.

(Gopnik, 2003, p. 107)

- The patient needed a central line. "Here's your chance," S., the chief resident said. I had never done one before. "Get set up and then page me when you're ready to start." It was my fourth week in surgical training. The pockets of my short white coat bulged with patient printouts, laminated cards with instructions for doing CPR and reading EKGs and using the dictation system, two surgical handbooks, a stethoscope, wound-dressing supplies, meal tickets, a penlight, scissors, and about a dollar in loose change. As I headed up the stairs to the patient's floor, I rattled.

  (Gawande, 2003, p. 83)

- It was a silver Seiko watch with a clasp that folded like a map and snapped shut. The stainless-steel casing was a three-dimensional octagon with distinct edge, too thick and ponderous, it seems now, for a thirteen-year old. Four hands—hour, minute, second, and alarm—swept around a metallic blue face. I received it for my bar mitzvah. . . .

  (Fisher, 2003, p. 61)

- The first time I opened Peter Singer's *Animal Liberation,* I was dining alone at the Palm, trying to enjoy a rib-eye steak cooked medium-rare. If this sounds like a good recipe for cognitive dissonance (if not indigestion), that was sort of the idea. Preposterous as it might seem, to supporters of animal rights, what I was doing was tantamount to reading *Uncle Tom's Cabin* on a plantation in the Deep South in 1852.

  (Pollan, 2003, p. 190)

What you probably notice is the vividness of these leads, their "voice." All of these nonfiction essays use techniques associated with fiction—description, dialogue, and characterization—and like most pieces in the volume, they're written from a first person ("I") viewpoint.

Truth be told, each article reveals the author's involvement in the topic being discussed. For Gopnik, the topic is children's psychological development and what Charlie Ravioli's behavior reveals about the disquieting character of urban life. For Gawande, the topic is an inside look at surgical training. For Fisher, the topic is our relationship to the relentless advance of modern technology. For Pollan, the topic is the animal rights movement and the grim industrialization of farming in America.

In the 1970s, legendary teacher Ken Macrorie saw the profound disconnect between good professional writing and the vacuous, pedantic prose rewarded in schools. Why is it, he asked, that so many teachers insist on voiceless research papers written in a dry, academic style? Why not invite students to think outside the box—and use the techniques of real writers?

Macrorie's antidote to the toxic influence of traditional research tasks was the "I-Search" paper (1988), a narrative rendering of research. Following the methods of good nonfiction, Macrorie encouraged students to tell the story of their research simply and clearly, showing their personal investment in knowledge construction.

He also urged young writers to drop the phony pretense of academic detachment. Of course, this frontal assault on traditional research writing was controversial. To many teachers, such ideas were a welcome breath of fresh air; but to others, they suggested the imminent collapse of western civilization.

Drawing upon Macrorie's I-Search ideas, Carol Olson (2003) developed a clear set of directions for communicating expectations for the "Personalized Research Paper" to students:

 ## Personalized Research Paper

Description

The personalized research paper is designed to teach both the writer and reader something valuable about a chosen topic and about the nature of searching and discovery. Unlike the standard research paper, in which the writer usually assumes a detached and objective stance, this paper allows you to take an active role in your search, to experience some of the hunt for facts and truths firsthand, and to create a step-by-step record of the discovery process.

Topic

The cardinal rule in the personalized research paper is to select a topic that genuinely interests you and that you need to know more about. The important point is that you choose the topic rather than having the instructor select a topic or a choice of topics.

Format

The personalized research paper should be written in three sections. These can be organized either explicitly, with subheadings, or implicitly. The sections are:

I   What I Know, Assume, or Imagine
II The Search
III What I Discovered

I: What I Know, Assume, or Imagine   Before conducting any formal research, write a section in which you explain to the reader what you think you know, what you assume, or what you imagine about your topic. For example, if you decided to investigate teenage alcoholism, you might want to offer some ideas about the causes of teenage alcoholism, give your estimate of the severity of the problem, create a portrait of a typical teenage drinker, and so on. This section can tell the story of how you came to be interested in your topic.

II: The Search   Test your knowledge, assumptions, or conjectures by researching your topic thoroughly. Conduct firsthand activities like writing letters, making telephone calls, initiating face-to-face interviews, and going on field trips. Also, consult useful secondhand sources such as books, magazines, newspapers, films, tapes, electronic sources, and so forth. Be sure to record all the information you gather. For a search on teenage alcoholism, for example, you might want to do some of the following: make an appointment to visit a rehabilitation center, attend a meeting of Al-Anon or Alcoholics Anonymous, consult an alcoholism counselor, or interview your peers; you would also need to check out a book on the subject, read several pertinent articles, and perhaps see a film.

Write your search up in narrative form, relating the steps of the discovery process. Do not feel obligated to tell everything, but highlight the happenings and facts you uncovered that were crucial to your hunt and contributed to your understanding of the information; use documentation when appropriate.

III: What I Discovered   After concluding your search, compare what you thought you knew, assumed, or imagined with what you actually discovered; assess your overall learning experience; and offer some personal commentary about the value of your discoveries and/or draw some conclusions. For instance, after completing your search on teenage alcoholism, you might learn that the problem is far more severe and often begins at an earlier age than you formerly believed. Perhaps you assumed that parental neglect was a key factor in the incidence of teenage alcoholism but have now learned that peer pressure is the prime contributing factor. Consequently, you might want to propose that an alcoholism awareness and prevention program, including peer counseling sessions, be instituted in the public school system as early as sixth grade.

Documentation   Include in-text citations and a list of works cited to document the research sources you consulted.

Source: Carol Booth Olson, *The Reading/Writing Connection: Strategies for Teaching and Learning in the Secondary Classroom.* Published by Allyn and Bacon, Boston, MA. Copyright © 2003 by Pearson Education. Reprinted by Permission of the Publisher.

Olson's prompt can help your students know what's expected in terms of process and product. However, many students will need more guidance. To download the prompt and a model student paper electronically, visit Olson's web site for her excellent book *The Reading/Writing Connection: Strategies for Teaching and Learning in the Secondary Classroom* (2003) (**www.ablongman.com/olson**) and find the pull-down menu for Chapter 9, "Alternative Approaches to the Research Paper." Look in the list to the left for the "Student Model of Personalized Research," a well-written paper on canine parvovirus. While there, make sure to check out the other support materials.

Multigenre Research Project

Like other papers we've discussed, the Multigenre Research Project involves deep immersion in a topic. But multigenre writing asks students to *transform* what they have learned into a collage of different types of text. In other words, besides including straight-ahead informational writing—usually in an introduction or prologue—the multigenre project may include poetry, fiction, letters, advertisements, dialogue in play format, or visuals. The idea is to interweave factual, emotional, and creative material to address a research topic. It's fun for students to write and exciting for teachers to read.

For example, middle school teacher Amy Anson (personal communication, 2003) wanted to teach historical research by having her students investigate a family ancestor. To set up the research, Anson stipulated that the ancestor had to have been dead at least ten years and that students had to have sufficient information to get deeply involved. A minimum of three research sources—biography, autobiography, journal, family history records, photographs, Internet, magazines, or interviews—were required. Students who couldn't meet these basic requirements for an ancestor were allowed to research a famous historical figure of their choice.

As scaffolding for research, Anson and her colleague Jacoy Blair created a "Fact Sheet" prompt that outlined basic questions and that students used for note-taking. One important feature of the Fact Sheet was the documentation of all facts, including title, author, and page number for books; web address and log-on date for Internet sites; and name of interview subject and date for all interviews.

Here are questions Anson and Blair used to spark student research. Of course, students were encouraged to go beyond these questions in pursuit of historical truth.

Fact Sheet
1. What is his/her full name?
2. When was he/she born?
3. Where did he/she live?
4. Who were the other members of his/her family?
5. What did he/she do (job, chores, responsibilities, etc.)?
6. Whom did he/she marry?
7. How many children did he/she have and what were they like?
8. What was happening in the world during his/her life?
9. What was happening in the country where he/she lived?
10. What kind of person (happy, mean, shy, etc.) was he/she?
11. What is something ordinary this person did?
12. What is something extraordinary (special) this person did?

(Anson and Blair, personal communication, 2003)

After students became deeply immersed in their material, Anson and Blair shared a writing framework. Students were asked to take imaginative risks and to choose a genre that could communicate the rich texture of a person's life. As minimum requirements, young writers had to include four genres from Column 1, two genres from Column 2, and two genres from Column 3. (Note that some contemporary genres are familiar to middle school students but would not have been available to ancestors or to other historical figures.) Of course, there are many genre possibilities beyond those listed below (see Figure 3-1, p. 46).

Multigenre Options

Short written genre (Choose four)	Long written genre (Choose two)	Visual arts genre (Choose two)
birth certificate	journal entry (one page)	game
wedding invitation	personal letter (one page)	fashion doll (clothes)
passport	childhood memory (one page)	wanted poster
obituary	conversation or dialogue (two pages)	clay sculpture
grocery list	song (two pages)	movie poster
recipe	interview (20 questions and answers)	map
post card	play (two pages)	scrapbook page
receipt	compare/contrast essay (two pages)	CD jacket
memo	magazine article (one page)	portrait
poem	movie preview (one page)	cartoon character
advertisement		book cover
tabloid cover		video game cover
radio announcement		
email		
home page		
photo caption (with photo or drawing)		
suitcase packing list (15 items)		

Source: Anson and Blair, personal communication, 2003.

To begin writing, each student used his or her Fact Sheet as a prewriting tool. The choice of genres coupled with the emphasis on creativity led to very high writing motivation. Later, as students engaged in revising their papers, Anson and Blair created a "Multigenre Reality Check," so they could discern the invented, fictional material in each paper from the content that was factually based. This basic disclosure statement, filled out by each writer, anchored their writing in research-based fact rather than allowing untethered flights of fancy.

Multigenre Reality Check

Made-Up Information (things you imagined or invented)	Filler Information (your inferences that don't change history)	Research Information (facts from your research notes)
1.	1.	1.
2.	2.	2.
3.	3.	3.
Etc.	Etc.	Etc.

Source: Anson and Blair, personal communication, 2003.

Having done their research and having imagined their way into a life history, students were eager to share what they had learned with classmates. They learned the *skills* of research—a goal of the state's core curriculum—but they also learned the *pleasures* of sharing knowledge, an equally important goal.

Challenging Advanced Students

Of course, multigenre research becomes more challenging in the upper grades. For example, high school teacher Warren Bowe asks students to choose topics in one of four areas: biographical (a deceased famous person); historical (a specific event in history); scientific (a specific discovery, invention, disease cure, etc.); or social (e.g., a specific organization founded to help people). Bowe's overview is a model of clarity:

> In this paper, you will choose different forms of writing and create a paper that clearly informs the reader about the topic you have selected. You will still use sources to investigate your topic, and you will use these sources to inform your readers. But you will expand on the ways you use this information. Within this one paper, you might write an editorial, a poem, and a letter, in addition to a "traditional" essay. But you won't just "make up" or create these pieces of writing out of thin air; instead, these creative efforts will be informed by, based on, and shaped by your solid research, just as any traditional research paper would be.
>
> (Bowe, personal communication, 2004)

Bowe's multigenre assignment stipulates several basic expectations (a typed document of at least 2,000 words, parenthetical documentation, annotated bibliography and Works Cited page, plus the inclusion of graphics and/or photos. He also asks for no repetition of information in the genres and for transitions among them; for five different writing formats and a minimum of six research sources; and for a half-page (minimum) reflection on each genre included. Clearly, such expectations cannot be met in a marathon writing event the night before the paper is due.

Bowe's multigenre rubric is linked to these expectations. It's based on a one-hundred-point framework in six sections, each of which has elaborating detail (not shown here).

1. Purpose	/20 possible
2. Word Choice	/10 possible
3. Organization	/20 possible
4. Documentation	/20 possible
5. Conventions	/20 possible
6. Layout/Presentation	/10 possible
Total Points	/100 possible = _____Grade

Finally, there's the dynamic teaching of Tom Romano (1995, 2000), who promotes multigenre research in secondary schools. In his teacher education classes, Romano insists on a minimum of ten sources—other than the Internet—to be cited in the bibliography and used in the paper. He also encourages primary material such as interviews, testimony, and observations. Consider the tone of Romano's admonitions to students, especially his emphasis on quality and his passionate insistence on originality:

> The Internet contains the good, the bad, and the ugly. It is democratic, but there is no screening for quality as there is in journals and books. So gauge the quality of what you find in cyberspace. And I definitely don't want you to simply paste material from the Internet into your paper. I want to see an original piece of work from you, one grounded in a thorough research understanding of your topic. I want to see you expand your learning and content knowledge about some subject; I want to see you stretch and refine your writing skills and powers of communication. I want to read your paper and be informed, but even more, I want to be *moved.*
>
> (Romano, personal communication, 2001)

As a savvy, veteran teacher, Romano knows how important it is for students to begin early and to avoid the pitfalls of procrastination. He therefore insists that they produce a "Multigenre Research Design" paper early in the semester. Because the design paper is worth 25% of the grade for the final project, students are motivated to knuckle down. Of course, Romano uses these papers to guide and assist students' research. Here are the seven points that frame each student's design paper:

1. What is your topic?
2. Describe what you know about your topic.
3. Tell what you want to learn about.
4. Describe the origins of your research. What sparked your interest in the topic? Why do you want to know more about it?
5. List at least a dozen questions you have about your topic.

6. Describe your plan for collecting information about your topic.
7. Provide a preliminary bibliography.

(Romano, personal communication, 2001)

Later, as students begin to convert their research notes into creative texts, Romano helps them frame introductions that will guide the reader into the paper. Students are coached in specific writing strategies that enhance the effectiveness of various genres. To help them better understand the standards for the assignment, they are also given model papers and grading rubrics. Here's a typical research rubric developed by teacher Karen Blanchette and cited by Romano (2000, p. 166):

Multigenre Research Paper Guide

5 genres present (minimum)	50 points	_____
6–8 typed pages	25 points	_____
Content/historical accuracy	100 points	_____
Mechanics/presentation	25 points	_____
Documentation/bibliography	50 points	_____
Total possible	250 points	_____

For tips on teaching—and many models of successful multigenre writing by students—I highly recommend two books: *Blending Genre, Altering Style: Writing Multigenre Papers* by Tom Romano (2000); and *Writing Multigenre Research Papers: Voice, Passion, and Discovery in Grades 4–6* by Camille Allen (2001).

Traditional Guided Research

If the idea of personalized research makes you nervous, consider a more traditional approach to research writing, one that defines the territory to be researched as well as methods of inquiry. Such an approach makes perfect sense if you're doing an inquiry unit—for example, a geology unit on rocks, a social studies unit on inventions, a science unit on marine mammals, a history unit on minority leaders, an art unit on famous impressionist paintings, or a vocabulary unit on word histories.

In **guided research**, each student takes an aspect of a topic being studied and becomes a class expert. For example, earth science students might be divided into teams—igneous, sedimentary, and metamorphic—representing the three classifications of rocks. Each team member would then choose a specific rock within the classification for research. The teacher could have an imaginative in-class activity or two for "getting to know your rock"—ideas like close observation, dialoguing with the rock, and imagining the rock's history. Then the teacher could provide a guide for research, suggesting a few Internet strategies but also teaching about direct quotation, paraphrasing, and citation conventions. Eventually, each report could become part of the team's oral presentation to the class and be posted on the "Hard Rock" web site.

The key to successful guided research is focus. Instead of taking on enormous topics like "Exploration of Space" or "The Issue of Abortion," students limit research to small issues. For example, an art teacher might provide a class with an overview of the impressionist movement in painting—its major figures and features—but students will probably get involved when they know a single painting in depth. Again, the teacher might organize the class into teams—Monet, Degas, Renoir, Van Gogh, and so on. Each team would explore the artist's work, with each member researching a single painting and preparing a report. Of course, the teacher could use questions to guide writing: In what sense is your painting representative of the artist's work? In what sense is it different, unique? What are its key technical elements? What story do you see in the painting? What drew you to this painting initially and how do you now view it? What do art critics say about the significance of this work?

Although this chapter has argued for "Researching Outside the Box," I do think that traditional research has its place, especially when supported by good teaching. What matters most is the *context* of student inquiries. Students notice whether we merely assign research writing or whether we take time to structure the process into stages, with explicit expectations. They notice whether we encourage teamwork. They notice whether we provide model papers and whether we're available for conferences. They notice whether we're open to real-world formats such as magazine articles with graphics, web sites, CD-ROMs, and high-powered multimedia presentations.

And even with traditional reports, it's important to let students know that their job is to interest us and teach us with their writing. We're like them. We hate being bored, and we like being stimulated. Tell students the truth—that quality research writing can not only earn a high grade but also make your day.

The Problem of Fakery

Here's a sure-fire way to get really depressed as a teacher: Simply type the words "research paper" into your Internet search page and click. What you'll immediately get are hundreds of commercial web sites that provide reports, term papers, and "custom writing" to the student market.

Of course, it's hardly a secret among informed teachers or work-averse students that the Internet can support intellectual dishonesty, as papers are downloaded with impunity, then handed in with a sly smile. This fact simply provides one more reason for emphasizing guided inquiries and for inviting Saturation Reports, I-Search Papers, and Multigenre Research Projects.

Sadly, the fakery problem is corrosive in two key ways: Not only does it deprive students of the opportunity for real intellectual development, but it also undermines the basic moral contract between teacher and students. And the problem is growing. For example, in a national survey conducted by *Education Week*, 54% of students admitted to Internet plagiarism, and 74% of students admitted to "serious cheating" during the past year (**www.plagiarism.org**).

Should such ethical issues be discussed in class? Absolutely. Students should know where teachers stand. They need to know what plagiarism is and why it's sleazy to use someone else's words and thoughts without attribution. A wonderfully helpful (and free) site for teachers is available via the "Research Resources" link at **www.plagiarism.org**. Here you can get student handouts that define plagiarism, give tips on avoiding it, and offer citation guidelines. I highly recommend this site for both teachers and students.

Beyond these information items, consider discussing plagiarism as the moral equivalent of a performance-enhancing drug, and note that the International Olympic Committee strips athletes of their medals when they take such drugs. To situate the Internet downloading issue starkly, you can relate how the careers of reporters and editors at the *New York Times, USA Today,* and other media outlets have been ruined because of plagiarism, fabrication, and intellectual cheating. Look students in the eye and let them know that you expect better of them.

Linked to **www.plagiarism.org** is a commercial web site, **www.turnitin.com**. This site makes a "digital fingerprint" of submitted documents and uses the Internet to cross-reference research across multiple databases. The incredible detection abilities of this site are purchased annually by individual schools or districts and even sometimes by enterprising teachers. According to research conducted by the company, implementing the Turnitin program at a large public university in California reduced plagiarism from 40% in 2001 to nearly zero in 2002 (**www.turnitin.com**, 2003). Clearly, this is a move in the right direction!

With Internet tools like these maybe teachers can get back to doing what we do best: helping students learn. Let's hope so.

WRITE FOR INSIGHT ACTIVITY

Choose one of the following tasks for your learning log. Then share this writing with your colleagues and instructor.

1. Tell the story of research writing you remember from middle school, high school, or college. What did you write about and why? What do you now remember about your topic and the research process? How does your experience—positive, negative, or neutral—now inform your thinking about involving students in research writing?
2. Using concepts from this chapter, develop a statement on how you think research writing should be approached in your content area. What kinds of topics do you see as interesting to students? What kinds of research formats or methods do you see as practical and educational? How might your imagined approach teach the "habits of mind" valued in your field?
3. Do research on the topic of "research papers" on the Internet. As you visit several web sites, take notes on the services being offered. Also visit the web site **www.plagiarism.org** to explore the resources available for teaching and take notes on these. Use your notes to write up a summary of what you learn—one that your colleagues might find interesting.

CHAPTER
10 Writing as a Means to Meaning

Inspiration usually comes during work, rather than before it.

—Madeleine L'Engle

Visible Despair

It's a warm Monday night in New Orleans as I sit at the well-elbowed counter of the Tastee Donut Shop, sipping lukewarm coffee and staring at a yellow notepad where my title, "Writing: A Means to Meaning," lies inert, congealed into little lumps of script. My thumbnail is well chewed. Somewhere out beyond me, there's music and honky-tonk toughness to be savored in the French Quarter, a place where the magnolia night air mixes with the aroma of a bad sewer system. My despair is visible, like the skin of tobacco smoke on doughnut shop mirrors.

Irony of ironies, I think. I've been getting ready for this moment all winter, while running in the evenings or standing in the shower afterwards. But nothing is happening. Like my students, I've got an assignment, but no plan for accomplishing it. I bemoan my procrastination, then kick myself for a dumb title.

My big idea will be that writing helps us *think*—to find out what we know and don't know by getting words down and revising them for precision. Consolidating experience, elaborating ideas, selecting and organizing, making connections—this, I'll say, is what makes writing a means to an end and therefore so basic in human terms. Now I'm desperate for something, *anything*, to get me started. My mind feels in disarray, like the center drawer of my desk.

The coffee is almost cold. Arrows and doodles and words litter my notepad. I wonder about my purpose. To inform? To entertain? To informally entertain? And then I picture a teacher audience in Oregon as I mumble an awkward apology at the podium.

The image makes me shiver from head to toe. *Start somewhere,* I whisper to myself. *Make sentences. Trust yourself to make meaning.* Peeling back a fresh yellow sheet, I glance around the Tastee Donut Shop.

It's in this glance that I decide to start where I am—in the here and now—as a way of getting to wherever I'm going. For now, it locates me in time and space, creating a narrative path. But it also commits me to a problem. At one level, it's how to get from New Orleans to an Oregon meeting; but at another level, it's how to *use* my experience to demonstrate the power of writing for thinking something through.

And so I begin.

Talk versus Writing

Just down the grayish-white counter are a half-dozen doughnut shop regulars, an interracial mix, both glazed and sober, who gossip with the manager. He is a nervous, wiry man with brown, slicked-back hair and skin the color of lard. Swapping well-rehearsed jokes, he jives with his customers—his gum-chewing, machine-gun patter a perfect mirror of theirs, polished to arrogant perfection.

The manager's helper, on extended break, is having a terrific time. He is a white man in his early forties, with narrow, weathered face, gray eyes, a gap where his front teeth should be. He sucks a cigarette, wheels around in his swivel seat, and howls at the yellow ceiling where big-bladed fans are folding the layers of air like kitchen mixers working the doughnut batter. His is the look of rural redneck poverty.

I'm writing like this—scribbling about the men, noticing how the waitress flirts with her boss, reading and rereading—when a simple fact begins to squeeze its way into my neocortex. The fact is this: In the 20 minutes it's taken me to get down 250 words or so, the men have exchanged thousands. I've gone through another cup of coffee and more yellow sheets, trying to get the detail right and capture the breathtaking repartee of raw street talk—the one-liners, put-downs, come-ons, and complaints. Next to them, I'm the one who is inarticulate.

But one big difference, I tell myself, is that while their voices are evaporating without a trace, a visual residue of mine remains. A paradox in this: Transcription slows me down, but it also makes my thoughts *retrievable*. In other words, because I'm able to reread—to go back into my words, pausing to reflect for seconds, minutes, hours, or days—writing becomes a different sort of cognitive event. Compared to back-and-forth conversation or an oral joke or story, writing is profoundly incremental. It provides a glimpse of a mind defining, elaborating, organizing—in short, *thinking*.

Writing as a different sort of cognition—this thought interests me as I think about it. I see in these words a kind of center for the message I'm after. And it's here, not surprisingly, that Janet Emig's seminal essay "Writing as Mode of Learning" (1983) begins to come back in pieces: her insistence that talking is an important form of prewriting but that writing is not simply recorded talk; her delineation of differences between talk and writing; and her discussion of the profoundly integrative nature of writing—its utility as a learning behavior.

And so I ask myself: What am I learning? Am I finding something to say in the process of getting it down? Is the physical act of writing helping me transcend my limitations of thought?

Suddenly, the plan for my writing clicks into place: I'll use the doughnut shop reality to illustrate Emig's key points—to *show* what she's saying. My method will be to shuttle between my experience and Emig's more general, theoretical points. The result, if I'm lucky, will dramatize my ideas about writing as means to meaning. An inner weight slides away, and I grin wildly at the guys in the Tastee Donut Shop.

Inside Writing Process

The words are coming now. Hand, eye, and brain are coordinated in a kind of dance because I'm working to accomplish my goal. When I glance away from the page, it's to make a choice in phrasing, to hear an inner voice, or to pause for planning. The voices of rereading and writing are now becoming one voice, hotly engaged in the forward momentum of ideas. Editing changes are instinctive. In a sense, I'm *becoming* my words. My voice flows down my arm, through my pen, onto yellow paper.

I take a breath. My whole body feels alert, responding to inner synapses. How can I explain this dance—this *felt sense* of my brain working? I turn to Emig:

> Writing involves the fullest possible functioning of the brain, which entails the active participation in the process of both left and right hemispheres. Writing is markedly bispheral, although in some popular accounts, writing is chiefly presented as a left-hemisphere activity, perhaps because the linear written product is somehow regarded as an analogue for the process that created it.
>
> (1983, p. 126)

These words resonate. My experience—the way I'm clicking right now—tells me her point is correct. Sometimes I analyze what I've said for connectedness or make a plan for the next sentence, but often intuition takes over. An image floats to the surface or connections between ideas reveal themselves unexpectedly. It's exciting.

"More coffee?" the waitress asks.

"Uh, no thanks—I've had more than enough."

"We got cake doughnuts on special."

"Thanks—not tonight."

So the writing process integrates hand, eye, and brain, I'm thinking—and it also integrates left and right hemispheres. I chew my thumbnail again. The central fact of serious writing, I hear myself think, is *confronting* the blank page. It's in the exploration of emptiness up ahead—getting from what is known, or just now being expressed, to what is unknown and yet to be put into words—that demands the mind/body integration called "writing." It's far more complex than a simple chaining of words and sentences. And it can't be explained by after-the-fact abstractions about such efforts.

Okay, I tell myself, but what *else* makes writing central to content learning? Even as I write this question, I know its answer: Careful writing forces me to be explicit about what is implicit—to spin out my meanings in detail. Like a spider, I must create out of myself—without any outside intervention—what something means to me. As I weave random threads of inner speech into "a deliberate structuring of the web of meaning," I connect what I already know to what I imagine or tentatively know (Vygotsky, 1962, p. 100). It's by making words known to myself and others—fashioning personal knowledge—that I learn what I didn't know I knew.

I learn what I didn't know I knew: These words sum up a bottom-line rationale for writing in content classrooms. Writing returns us to the basic or classical meaning of the word "educate": to draw out. Whatever else it may be, writing elicits meanings and provides balance in a factory-like system that pushes information at students. Allowing students to make sense of what they've been taught—to connect and apply and test the limits of their understanding—is also worth doing. Why? *Because knowing what you know means you really know it.*

So writing is a means—perhaps the best means available—to make knowledge personal, connected, and accessible to self.

Reflecting on Writing

Editing my mini-epiphanies, I sag a little. I've long ago paid my check at the Tastee Donut Shop, wandered back to the hotel, and worked late into the magnolia night. Now I'm winging toward home, wondering what else to say.

Outside the aircraft, the sun sinks low on the Utah horizon, as I watch the hydraulically controlled wing flaps during the plane's long glide toward Salt Lake City. It's a staggeringly complex system, and there are many such systems in the plane—a symphony of technology. Once again I'm struck by the fact that the everyday miracle of modern flight is possible only because of writing and mathematics and conceptual model-building. Indeed, without writing—a tool that enables us to construct, store, and access knowledge in libraries and databases—modern civilization wouldn't exist.

The Wasatch Mountains stand massive in the gathering twilight, their snow-capped ridges turning rose and gray. Thinking back, I see myself at the Donut Shop base camp, sipping coffee and taking tentative steps up the fog-shrouded terrain, eyes down, groping word by word. The ideas were slippery, and each paragraph-to-be presented treacherous, unsure footing. Over and over I came to dead ends where I tore a sheet from my notepad and started over. All around me was the dense fog of uncertainty and the empty space of the blank page.

Nevertheless, I kept at it, following my instincts and telling myself to push on. While climbing, I often glanced back at the terrain already covered, pausing to reread. As I did this, the fog *behind* me seemed to lift, even though it remained thick up ahead. And thus it was that a trail of meaning became my property, liberated from the fog, sentence by sentence. The sentences weren't much, but they got me started.

And there was more. In rereading, I also looked *ahead*, trying to find my way. At first, the abysses seemed impassable, but occasionally I'd glimpse a line of attack. Each time this happened—as I pushed on to a new point—the fog would clear for a moment, and I no longer had to worry about my word-by-word footing. Then I'd work my way toward another resting place—a ledge for rereading, a place to ponder my next moves. It was in these pauses—minutes, hours, even days—that I'd size up questions yet to be addressed. And finally I'd set off again, playing out a thick rope of words and hoping my audience was still with me.

The backward-glancing "plateaus," I now realize, made my writing different from the Tastee Donut Shop chatter. The doughnut shop crowd traveled as a pack, their talk repelling joyfully and randomly from point to point. But I was on my own in unknown territory, with imagined readers or listeners. It was my imagining of their questions that set the direction, like pitons, for my ascent up Discourse Mountain. And it was my responses, in sentences like this one, that created a trail of meaning.

Now, following a radar signal, the aircraft in which I ride approaches the runway at 150 miles per hour and touches down flawlessly, its braking systems activated. At this moment, I'm glad that the past teachers of aeronautical engineers insisted on clear, effective writing. Thanks to their good work, my head is no longer in the clouds.

Understanding Composing

For me, the most compelling analysis of the behavior described in this chapter is Sondra Perl's landmark essay "Understanding Composing" (Perl, 1985). Working with struggling writers, Perl came to question the textbook assertions about writing—a linear model of planning, drafting, and revising. She found through "think-aloud" audiotapes that composing was not a straightforward process, even for skilled writers. In fact, to move forward, writers continually went backward, frequently rereading, reorganizing, or rethinking their aims from the perspective of an imagined audience. To understand composing, Perl said, we must understand the recursive nature of writing.

Recursiveness, the "looping back" process, seems to occur in three basic ways. We may reread after every few phrases, or after every sentence, or after a semantic "chunk" of information. A second kind of rereading happens when we get stuck and go back to our topic, or to a key word in it, altering what we've written to fit the topic or even changing the topic to fit the emerging text. Finally, rereading takes place as we pause and "seem to listen or otherwise react to what is inside" (Perl, 1985, p. 30). What we attend to, Perl learned, is a *felt sense* (Gendlin, 1978)—a sense that is always there within, as a kind of inner compass:

> When writers are given [or take up] a topic, the topic itself evokes a felt sense in them. This topic calls forth images, words, ideas, and vague fuzzy feelings that are anchored in the writer's body. What is elicited, then, is not solely a product of a mind but of a mind alive in a living sensing body.
>
> When writers pause, when they go back and repeat key words, what they seem to be doing is waiting, paying attention to what is still vague and unclear. They are looking to their felt experience, and waiting for an image, a word, or phrase to emerge that captures the sense they embody.

Usually, when they make the decision to write, it is after they have a dawning awareness that something has clicked, that they have enough of a sense that if they begin with a few words heading in a certain direction, words will continue to come which will allow them to flesh out the sense they have.

(Perl, 1985, p. 31)

Perl notes that for some people, the felt sense is centered in their stomachs, whereas for others, it's a more generalized "hovering" attention throughout their bodies. In rereading, we ask whether our words are "right"—whether they capture what we are trying to say—and, if not, what seems to be "missing."

According to Perl, we match words to our "felt sense," and if we are on the right track, the sense deepens. We begin to feel totally *in* the moment, and our awareness of surroundings may virtually disappear. But sometimes, after rereading, we find that we've gotten off the track, or discovered a new one. If the words "feel" wrong in rereading, we change them so that they fit our emerging sense of what works.

Thus, felt sense provides a *means to meaning* by linking the physical reality of the body to the mental experience of composing language. In other words, felt sense is all about *paying attention*.

In my experience, paying close attention to inner cues and bodily sensations can't be rushed. On the other hand, it *can* be stimulated by inertia-breaking activities—related reading, conversation, drawing and doodling, list-making, freewriting, and so on. It was only because I surrendered imaginatively to the Tastee Donut Shop experience that I was able to explore what it might teach me

Happily, the insights of Perl's classroom research can now help middle school and high school students break through their "blocks" in composing. In a slim new book with an audio CD, *Felt Sense: Writing with the Body* (2004), Perl provides a flexible set of Guidelines for Composing. The Guidelines are "a set of questions that help writers cultivate a felt sense and then write with this felt sense as a guide" (p. 8). The audio cues in this instructional package are profoundly empowering, and they become even more powerful with repeated use.

Whether you choose to use the audio CD in class or to read the script that Perl provides is a personal decision. Your students will *love* the experience of finding meaning within and learning to trust their felt sense.

Writing Self, Reading Self

Being physically and imaginatively into writing means trying to satisfy a reader within, regardless of other audiences. In other words, when we are truly engaged, two facets of self—the Writing Self and the Reading Self—are deep in dialogue.

The Writing Self sets goals, plans strategy, transcribes thoughts into words, and then makes changes. Meanwhile, a discerning Reading Self monitors the text to assess its meaning, readability, tone, mechanics, and other features.

The interplay between these two facets of consciousness is a dance—and its main feeling, when the rhythms are strong and clear, is one of deep satisfaction, even joy. "Once words come in this connected way," writes Sondra Perl, "we often experience relief, excitement, surprise, even pleasure" (2004, p. 5). And on this same point, the renowned psychologist Mihaly Csikszentmihalyi is explicit: "Enjoyment occurs at the boundary between boredom and anxiety, when the challenges are just balanced with the person's capacity to act" (1990, p. 52).

But what if the goals are *not* clear, or if the Writing Self has no real investment in them? What if the Writing Self plays victim and permits negative past experiences to undermine self-confidence and the willingness to persevere? What if the Writing Self somehow develops the wrong-headed idea that "writing is easy for everybody but me"? Or what if the Writing Self substitutes the goal of "pleasing the teacher to get a grade" for the goal of a good-faith effort?

And what if the Reading Self carps self-critically, "You're not a writer, so you can't do this," or frets incessantly about what readers might think? What if the Reading Self has impoverished reading experience and feels uncertain when assessing whether certain words, sentences, or paragraphs "work" in context? What if the Reading Self ignores the conventions of incomplete sentences, or rushes through the text, not really imagining them being read by someone else? What if the Reading Self simply shuts down and refuses to engage in dialogue, leaving the Writing Self to go it alone?

The answer to these questions is obvious: Writing won't be experienced as an interesting, dynamic dance between facets of self, but rather as a boring, meaningless, even tortuous activity. And this is indeed the experience of many secondary learners. As students turn in papers without proofreading or self-assessment, they broadcast both their lack of motivation and their belief that it is the responsibility of teachers—and not their responsibility—to care about the content and form of their work.

In Chapter 2 we began with Churchill's quote: "First we shape our institutions, and then they shape us." So how does shaping happen? What are the negative conditions that warp the spirits of teachers and students alike?

- It occurs when we permit students to cling to self-defeating myths—first, that conscious knowledge of grammar is the secret to writing; and second, that good writing comes from "inspiration" or "inborn talent."
- It occurs when we rely on fill-in-the-blank worksheets instead of inviting students to construct (and share) personal knowledge through meaningful writing-to-learn activities.
- It occurs when we assign vacuous topics and give little encouragement or direction, but also when we try to "program" writing in lockstep fashion, ignoring choice and creativity.
- It occurs when we consign basic writers and ESL students to the margins of our room instead of supporting their efforts with peer tutors, scaffolded teaching, and modified tasks.
- It occurs when we become so obsessed with assessment that writing amounts to a paint-by-number activity, with rubrics defining the limits of imagination and language.

- It occurs when we read papers mechanically, offering little insightful feedback, or when we limit our attention to deficits in usage and mechanics, with no encouragement.
- It occurs when we remain silent about writing being a messy, highly idiosyncratic process for most of us—with finished texts leaving no clues to their construction.
- It occurs when we don't allow students opportunities for personalized research, when we tightly restrict the venues for publication, and when we ignore the possibilities of collaboration.

The truth of the matter, then, is quite simple: *Writing is hard, interesting work, and in the difficulty lies both the attraction and the joy.*

When we don't level with our students about this fact, we help them remain emotionally and intellectually detached—in effect, giving them tools for do-it-yourself frontal lobotomies. Of course, some students derive perverse self-stimulation from "playing the academic game"—figuring out what teachers want and engaging in fakery. But the costs of such cynicism are high because students then come to devalue their own thoughts, thereby twisting the knife in their own gray matter.

Our students deserve better, and so do we.

Teaching with Insight

So let's review a few of this book's key ideas to focus on the overarching theme of teaching with insight. Perhaps this summary list will offer some points of departure for faculty workshops, dialogue with your colleagues, or future reading and writing. More immediately, you might want to explore one or more points in the "Write for Insight" activity that concludes this chapter.

- The National Commission on Writing has called for a *doubling* of writing in secondary schools, urged attention to writing across the curriculum, and emphasized that "writing is every teacher's responsibility."
- Content area writing is a way for teachers to "work smarter, not harder." As students write, they learn more actively. Much of the expressive work in learning logs doesn't *need* a grade.
- Expressive writing helps learners connect personally to content learning. It also supports graded writing tasks in the three upper domains discussed in this book's Introduction (Figure I-1, p. 9).
- Inviting students to write learning histories is a useful activity in all content areas. Such writing tells a personal story that can inform classroom instruction in important ways.
- Many students have learned a "hidden curriculum" of writing by the time they reach secondary school. Such lessons often have to be unlearned for students to become insightful learners.

- As playful expressive writing develops fluency, it reduces the resistance many students feel toward content area instruction. Such writing can occur before, during, or after content lessons.
- Metaphorical thinking supports concept development. By having students talk and write metaphorically, we engage their imaginations and help them visualize key ideas.
- Students with special needs and ESL learners can improve writing fluency if they receive help with basic skills. Buddy systems are great tools to assist such students.
- Ten principles of assignment design help turn perfunctory writing tasks into interesting ones. Teachers can prepare their own rubrics or rely on generic ones such as the Six Traits assessment.
- Process writing works when teachers scaffold its instruction. As students come to understand process writing, they need prewriting support and response group training.
- Coaching and judging require different skills. Most teachers need to coach more and judge less—in other words, give more occasions for practice and fewer occasions for grading.
- The ideal time to coach students is during their practice time, *not* when the final papers come in. Judging (grading) of final papers should be done swiftly, using a rubric.
- Working portfolios provide a context for ongoing fluency development and content area insights. Presentation portfolios showcase a student's best efforts, thereby building self-assessment skills.
- By inviting students to research "outside the box" of traditional reports, we discourage the recycling of fake research from the Internet and encourage genuinely insightful learning.

And finally, there's one last point that takes us full circle, back to important ideas in this book's Introduction.

The Flow of Insight

In *Flow: The Psychology of Optimal Experience,* Csikszentmihalyi discusses attention, saying that "consciousness can be ordered in terms of different goals and intentions"—in other words, that it can be self-directed (1990, p. 28). "The mark of a person who is in control of consciousness," he writes, "is the ability to focus attention at will, to be oblivious to distractions, to concentrate for as long as it takes to achieve a goal, and not longer" (p. 31).

It's this ability that gives rise to optimal experience—the moments of total engagement that people throughout the world, in diverse fields of endeavor, report as "flow." The flow experience is familiar to athletes, artists, surgeons, mathematicians, dancers, woodworkers, gardeners, musicians, scientists, computer programmers—and many others, including writers. In flow, "we feel a sense of exhilaration, a deep sense of enjoyment"—and such moments usually occur, says Csikszentmihalyi, "when a person's body or mind is stretched to its limits in a voluntary effort to accomplish something difficult or worthwhile" (p. 3). In fact, we are "so involved in the activity that nothing else seems to matter" (p. 4).

My own experiences in writing—and those researched by Perl and discussed in this chapter—seem to be examples of flow. Indeed, the term "felt sense" is probably the same phenomenon with another name. But such experiences are hardly mystical. In fact, they are quite ordinary and accessible to middle school and high school students via Perl's "Guidelines for Composing" on audio CD (Perl, 2004).

As this book comes to a close, let's pause to think about school writing through the lens provided by Csikszentmihalyi:

> When people reflect on how it feels when their experience is most positive, they mention at least one, and often all, of the following. First, the experience usually occurs when we confront tasks we have a chance of completing. Second, we must be able to concentrate on what we are doing. Third and fourth, the concentration is usually possible because the task undertaken has clear goals and provides immediate feedback. Fifth, one acts with a deep but effortless involvement that removes the worries and frustrations of everyday life. Sixth, enjoyable experiences allow people to exercise a sense of control over their actions. Seventh, concern for the self disappears, yet paradoxically the sense of self emerges stronger after the flow experience is over. Finally, the sense of the duration of time is altered; hours pass by in minutes, and minutes can stretch out to seem like hours. The combination of these elements causes a sense of deep enjoyment that is so rewarding people feel that expending a great deal of energy is worthwhile simply to be able to feel it.
>
> (1990, p. 49)

"Clear goals," "immediate feedback," a personal "sense of control"—these conditions are essential. With such conditions, teachers create classrooms where "each day is made for discovery," as my student Linda put it.

Finding out where this book wanted to go has been a fascinating process of paying attention. While writing, I've been surprised by words and images that seemed to unfold, like long strands of DNA, from the nucleus of thoughts—and I've loved the many opportunities to rework language and clear away clutter. For me, there's been an active dialogue between a Writing Self and a Reading Self. To the good, hard-working teachers who have accompanied my reading, I offer sincere thanks. I hope that our trek through difficult terrain has made sense.

As I've tried to show, writing is far more than frozen talk. First, it's a snapshot of unique experience and insights, a way of giving voice to our personal story. Second, it's a way to make content knowledge meaningful as well as a way to probe what we *don't* yet know or fully understand. Third, it's a complex set of skills—an orchestration of hand, eye, and brain—that uses processes of two-channel thinking and decentering in order to select, connect, and sustain a flow of ideas.

And that's why writing for insight has the potential to make content learning infinitely *interesting*—to our students and to us.

May ongoing insights be your teaching legacy.

WRITE FOR INSIGHT ACTIVITY

Unlike other chapters in this book, this one is philosophical and reflective—without apology. Its big ideas provide a kind of capstone for the practical strategies discussed elsewhere. Select one of this chapter's ideas as the center for a final writing-to-learn entry that you might share with colleagues. Or, as a learning log alternative, ask yourself, "What can I do to help ensure that 'each day is made for discovery' in my teaching?" Then write for insight.

A Literacy Autobiography Case Study

By describing significant writing experiences and seeking their meaning, you improve the likelihood of being a teacher who promotes literacy among young people. According to teacher education research, "reflective practitioners" make the best teachers. So the idea is to tell a story—*your* story—and reflect on it. This writing will be a case study in which you are both the researcher and the subject of research.

One of your main audiences is yourself, as a writer looking in the mirror of experience to see what it means. Another audience will be your colleagues and instructor, people who are interested in what your story can teach. It's your task to recreate your experiences for both audiences—to "show it like it was"—and then to consider the significance of chosen events. Your paper will probably be about four or five double-spaced pages (1,000–1,200 words).

One problem you might face is remembering writing experiences. By using strategies shown herein, you'll access many memories. Another kind of writing problem is the selection and organization of memories. You'll need to sort and select what you see as the *most important* experiences to write about; the ones with emotional resonance, either positive or negative.

In preparing a first draft of your paper, you may refer to events involving specific teachers. Refer to these individuals by initials (for example, Mr. S. or Ms. L.), not by their real names. This technique is important to protect privacy. Also, your instructor may organize you into small response groups so that you can try out your text on colleagues and gain insights for revision. This process will be explained by your instructor. You should have three copies of your paper, plus the original, for work in response groups.

Questions to Consider

A few questions to prompt your initial thinking about your personal case study are listed here:

1. Who were your earliest influences as a writer? Were the influences positive or negative? What role did parents, peers, and other adults play in your development? Have the influences since the early ones helped or hindered

your writing? Who in middle school or high school was an especially positive or negative influence on writing? What specific incidents are vivid for you?

2. How have you felt about writing? Do your feelings vary, depending on the type of writing you're doing? Have your feelings changed as you've grown older? How would you *like* to feel about writing? What stops you or holds you back? To what extent is writing an activity that you do for pleasure and stimulation? To what extent is it work or drudgery? What kind of writing do you find boring or difficult? Why do you think this is so?

3. What kind of kid were you in middle school and high school? Whom did you "hang out" with? Go back to a photo album and see yourself as you were then; then try to develop a "profile" (character sketch) of yourself in relation to the group you identified with. How did the norms and expectations of the group relate to literacy activities and/or school? Do you still identify with the norms of this social group or are you now "moving on"?

4. To what extent does writing really help you learn? What do you know about using writing for personal learning? When and where did you learn these lessons? How do you get started when you have a writing project like this one to do? How do you sustain interest and concentration? How do you organize your time when it comes to drafting, revising, and editing? How successful (or competent) do you feel as an adult writer?

Some of those questions will be more interesting than others. Zero in on those you'd like to explore for only a few minutes. Work fast and don't worry about order or whether something is "profound" or well worded. First, just get your thoughts down. After doing this, look back over your work and circle words and ideas that seem to hold particular interest (or surprise) for you. You'll want to follow leads that help you answer the central question: *What literacy experiences have made me who I am today?*

Then, on a separate sheet of paper, try drafting with the focus you've chosen. Think back to incidents from your past that are pertinent to your case study, and use this material in developing your rough draft. Be prepared to read your draft aloud in a small response group. Toward the end of your draft, reflect on the meaning of your experience, as you understand it, and the possible implications for teaching.

Revising Your Literacy Autobiography

What features should you work toward to accomplish this assignment? Here are a few key features of a successful literacy autobiography paper:

- Has an adult voice—clear, honest, reflective—that uses the "I" pronoun in recalling important literacy experiences and sharing them

- Narrates selected literacy experiences (reading/writing memories) in an engaging way and discusses the connections among those experiences
- Describes your thoughts and feelings about reading/writing as a *learner* and relates those to your present attitudes, interests, skills, and so on
- Considers your role as a model of literacy (for your own children and for adolescent students)
- Uses standard English conventions (spelling, punctuation, and usage) associated with the professional status of educator

These criteria are organized into a simple rubric. Note the list of text features. Use this evaluation rubric as you share your work in small groups and self-assess your paper.

Text Feature	Awesome	Very good	Satisfactory	Needs Work
A reflective voice				
A focus on key literacy experiences ("themes")				
Linkage between past R/W events and present skills, attitudes, and interests				
Teacher as a literacy model (adult reflection)				
Standard English conventions				

Remember: your work should reflect your good-faith effort—and efforts of your writing partners—with respect to writing conventions (paragraphing, sentence structure, word choice, usage, spelling, punctuation, and so on). Your instructor is not your proofreader.

APPENDIX

B Graphic Organizers

A *graphic organizer* is an instructional tool used to illustrate a student or class's prior knowledge about a topic or section of text; specific examples include the K-W-L-H Technique and the Anticipation/Reaction Guide.

The graphic organizer in Figure B-1 is used to describe a central idea: a thing (a geographic region), process (meiosis), concept (altruism), or proposition with support (experimental drugs should be available to AIDS victims). Key frame question include: What is the central idea? What are its attributes? What are its functions?

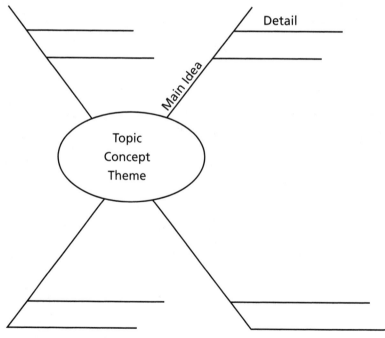

FIGURE B-1   Spider Map

This appendix copyright © 1988 North Central Regional Educational Laboratory, a wholly owned subsidiary of Learning Point Associates. All rights reserved. Reprinted with permission.

Initiating Event

Event 1

Event 2

Final Outcome

Event 3

FIGURE B-2   Series of Events Chain

The graphic organizer in Figure B-2 is used to describe the stages of something (the life cycle of a primate); the steps in a linear procedure (how to neutralize an acid); a sequence of events (how feudalism led to the formation of nation states); or the goals, actions, and outcomes of a historical figure or character in a novel (the rise and fall of Napoleon). Key frame questions include: What is the object, procedure, or initiating event? What are the stages or steps? How do they lead to one another? What is the final outcome?

The graphic organizer in Figure B-3 is used for time lines showing historical events or ages (grade levels in school), degrees of something (weight), shades of meaning (Likert scales), or ratings scales (achievement in school). Key frame questions include: What is being scaled? What are the end points?

Figure B-4 is used to show similarities and differences between two things (people, places, events, ideas, etc.). Key frame questions include: What things are being compared? How are they similar? How are they different?

Figure B-5 is used to represent a problem, attempted solutions, and results (the national debt). Key frame questions include: What was the problem? Who had the problem? Why was it a problem? What attempts were made to solve the problem? Did those attempts succeed?

Figure B-6 is used to show causal information (causes of poverty), a hierarchy (types of insects), or branching procedures (the circulatory system). Key frame questions include: What is the superordinate category? What are the subordinate categories? How are they related? How many levels are there?

Continuum Scale

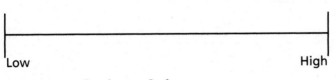

Low   High

FIGURE B-3   Continuum Scale

Compare/Contrast Matrix

	Name 1	Name 2
Attribute 1		
Attribute 2		
Attribute 3		

FIGURE B-4   Compare/Contrast Matrix

Problem/Solution Outline

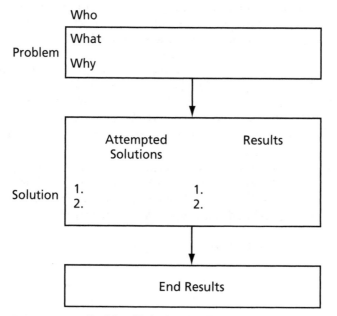

FIGURE B-5   Problem/Solution Outline

Network Tree

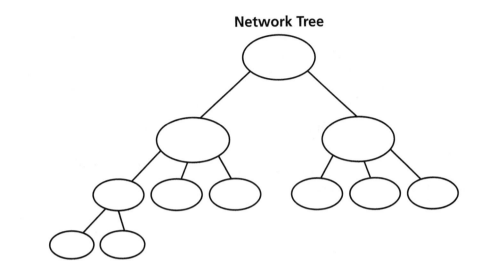

FIGURE B-6   Network Tree

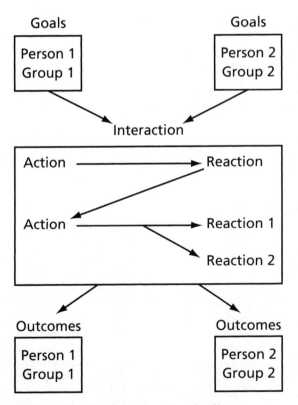

FIGURE B-7   **Human Interaction Outline**

Figure B-7 is used to show the nature of an interaction between persons or groups (Europeans settlers and American Indians). Key frame questions include: Who are the persons or groups? What were their goals? Did they conflict or cooperate? What was the outcome for each person or group?

Figure B-8 is used to show the causal interaction of a complex event (an election, a nuclear explosion) or complex phenomenon (juvenile delinquency, learning disabilities). Key frame questions include: What are the factors that cause X? How do they interrelate? Are the factors that cause X the same as those that cause X to persist?

Figure B-9 is used to show how a series of events interact to produce a set of results again and again (weather phenomena, cycles of achievement and failure, the life cycle). Key frame questions include: What are the critical events in the cycle? How are they related? In what ways are they self-reinforcing?

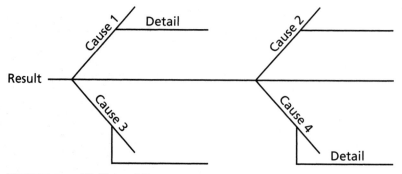

FIGURE B-8   Fishbone Map

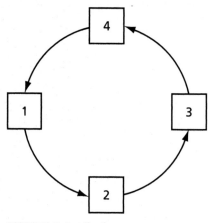
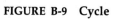

FIGURE B-9   Cycle

Bob Tierney's Trigger Words for Concept Teaching

Organize individual and group activities in which students use trigger words to develop extended metaphors that visually depict and/or explain (in writing) key concepts being studied. Students can choose trigger words or let serendipity (chance) be their guide.

skeleton	room	treadmill	oven	filter
valley	fruit	library	purse	molecule
maze	water	air	earth	money
tunnel	altar	diamond	army	computer
amoeba	anvil	bait	balloon	Bible
root	temple	window	star	typewriter
battery	armor	fountain	bed	seed
spice	bell	rock	album	robot
bag	tide	bank	weapon	farm
hinge	horse	image	junk	knot
algebra	alphabet	child	lamp	leg
menu	prison	monster	muscle	nest
pepper	pill	satellite	pod	ring
rainbow	rudder	safe	sauce	saloon
ice	index	key	ladder	landslide
liquid	manual	match	sex	data base
nut	frame	page	parasite	pendulum
port	prism	puzzle	radio	microscope
shadow	shovel	smoke	rash	horizon
lever	lock	machine	map	mattress
meteor	mist	moon	music	net
perfume	pipe	plant	pond	pore

rope	rug	sand	saw	screw
insect	kitchen	ladle	leaf	library
nail	meter	missile	motor	organ
ocean	sphere	paint	passport	glass
prison	pyramid	raft	record	river
shell	signature	herb	hose	icon
lode	magnet	marsh	meat	horoscope
nose	onion	palette	pebble	star
vise	pillow	plate	pool	stamp
robot	rose	sandwich	ruler	scale
vulture	joint	kite	lake	lens
mountain	needle	vertebra	violin	pacemaker
pocket	dung	powder	pump	radar
pulley	quilt	rag	ramp	rifle
script	shoe	siren	house	hieroglyph
milk	loom	mask	medal	lightning
soap	pen	knife	piano	planet
rain	halo	rubber	saddle	parachute
cup	school	program	ship	skin
umbrella	channel	crystal	woman	man
cope	cycle	plow	egg	hook
well	water	treasure	flag	guitar
girdle	glue	hair	template	harbor
zone	road	ball	zoo	trigger
caldron	cannon	chain	chord	cloud
drain	drum	tree	bomb	wing
flood	fog	fork	fungus	furniture
mirror	camera	wedge	wave	sandpaper
bridge	network	staircase	cave	box
folder	dust	eraser	statue	net
antenna	floor	flower	food	block
God	guillotine	bee	plug	blanket
trap	tube	spring	television	toilet
lamp	clock	crown	desert	chessboard

wallpaper	gate	diskette	broom	bottleneck
fossil	funhouse	window	glacier	ratchet wheel
funnel	book	brain	brakes	booby trap
buffer	weed	cancer	cell	cesspool
compass	circle	code	web	dress
factory	fairy	fan	farm	feather
foam	fly	fist	bird	bottle
game	garden	gear	ghost	plastic
circus	hammer	head	heart	family
current	detour	ear	button	face
fertilizer	field	finger	engine	floodlight
hole	color	dope	adult	forge
graph	gun	gutter	bruise	bug
blister	acid	candy	chorus	springboard
meatball	body	drill	eye	song
spotlight	pitcher	glove	hand	vegetable
table	tool	trail	vent	torch
target	telescope	fabric	sword	spectrum
spear	sponge	stomach	memory	dam
fish	fence	festival	film	fire
grave	lever	basement	square	sun
soup	spiral	shaft	market	torpedo
train	triangle	vacuum	ticket	thermometer
telephone	stove	tapestry	car	kaleidoscope

APPENDIX

D Content Area Writing Assignments

The following writing tasks in health, English, music, mathematics, history, and biology use the CRAFT approach described in Chapter 6, "Designing Assignments and Rubrics." These assignments have been adapted from the work of secondary teacher education students at Utah State University in Logan, Utah.

Health: Ask Dr. Abby Assignment (Tana Johnson)

Today you are Dr. Abby, a medical columnist. People from around town ask for your professional opinion on health issues. Following is a letter from the "Ask Dr. Abby" mailbag. After getting in groups of three, read the letter together and discuss how Dr. Abby should respond. Draw from your reading in health, from class activities, and from Internet research. You should share ideas as a group but write individually. In your Dr. Abby written response discuss possible causes of the problem and offer advice on how the problem might be addressed. Write in a clear, friendly style so that readers of your column can understand and act upon your advice. Your response needs to be about one page in length, double-spaced, and typed in a 12-point font.

> Dear Dr. Abby,
> My friend eats whatever she wants whenever she wants. I am about 20 pounds heavier than I would like to be so I really watch what I eat. Over the past year I notice she hasn't changed a bit, but I seemed to have gained more weight. It doesn't make sense. I wonder why she can eat whatever she wants and not gain a pound, but I pay attention to my diet and still gain weight. Is there anything I can do to better manage my weight? Thanks for any insight you can provide.
>
> Sincerely,
>
> Frustrated in Florida

After your response is complete, bring it to class and share it with your writing partners. Make sure each person in the group gets to read and respond to your Dr. Abby column. After peer response, make any necessary changes and hand in the final version.

Ask Dr. Abby Scoring Rubric

Discussion of possible causes of the problem (diagnosis)	/20 possible
Answering the question presented in the letter to Dr. Abby	/10 possible
Offering advice on how the problem might be addressed	/10 possible
Format expectations and writing mechanics (conventions)	/10 possible

Total /50 possible

English: *To Kill a Mockingbird* News Story Assignment (Alice Koehne)

You are a journalist for the *Maycomb Times*. The editor has asked you to follow up on an incident that happened during the past three years (the time span covered in *To Kill a Mockingbird*). Pick a major event from the novel and create a newspaper article from it. Make this story real by "interviewing" a character from the novel (what would this person say about the event or situation?) or by reporting what you "saw" first-hand (use your reading to depict how the scene appeared to you). Your article should add some depth or insight to the basic story.

Your story should be one page long and set in a two-column newspaper format. Your page will be published as part of our class newspaper, so make sure it's free of errors in spelling, punctuation, or usage. You will get help with these conventions when we meet in response groups. For now, concentrate on developing a solid, interesting news story, using the journalistic techniques we have studied. When you turn in your story, please include the final copy, rough draft, and any notes you took to brainstorm and set up your story. These provide evidence of your attention to writing process.

Mockingbird News Story Scoring Rubric
Grading scale: 5 = excellent; 4 = strong; 3 = good; 2 = adequate; 1 = needs work.

Demonstrates knowledge of specific event in novel	5	4	3	2	1
Provides clear news article writing and organization	5	4	3	2	1
Uses first-person narration or third-person "interview"	5	4	3	2	1
Shows evidence of engagement in writing process	5	4	3	2	1
Attends to grammatical correctness (mechanics)	5	4	3	2	1

Music: Bach to Kappelmeister Assignment (Royce Backman)

Imagine that you are Johann Sebastian Bach in the year 1720. You earn a meager living as the organist and choir director for a large church. In addition to these duties, your employer, the Kappelmeister of the church, expects you to compose an entirely new cantata for each week's service. After months of sleepless nights and hundreds of new compositions, the Kappelmeister suddenly demands your resignation, contending that your music is tiresome and too difficult for church patrons to understand.

That night, in a dream, you have a vision of the modern era. You see concert halls throughout the world, where great musicians perform your work. You see your music widely distributed via modern technology. You see your name used in the same breath as Beethoven and Brahms, who credit your influence. Waking up, you realize that resigning your post may well alter the course of history.

Write a letter to your Kappelmeister to share your dream. Use examples from your dream to persuade the Kappelmeister to change his mind about requesting your resignation. Contrast the Modern era you saw and the Baroque era in which you live, giving examples in areas such as music, industrial progress, and culture. You might even point to dramatic changes in instruments, traditions, and lifestyle. Of course, feel free to do background research to assist with your letter writing.

Letter Writing Scoring Rubric
Grading scale: 4 = outstanding; 3 = very good; 2 = adequate; 1 = needs work.

Uses examples to contrast the Baroque and Modern eras	4	3	2	1
Develops examples through vivid, colorful language	4	3	2	1
Presents clear, compelling reasons for keeping position	4	3	2	1
Has an effective organization of ideas in letter format	4	3	2	1
Shows strong control over writing mechanics	4	3	2	1

Mathematics: Wallpaper Puzzle Assignment (Megan Tanner)

You and your little sister/brother share a bedroom. Your mom agrees to let you wallpaper the room, but you and your sibling can't agree on wallpaper. So she decides to let each of you wallpaper half the wall space in the room. Since you are older and in a great math class, you have the responsibility of deciding how much space each of you gets. Your little sister/brother has no idea how to figure area, so it is your job to first figure this out and then to convince her/him that you are not cheating and using more than half the wall space for your wallpaper.

Your assignment consists of four major parts.

1. For prewriting, measure *all* the walls in your bedroom, using the worksheet provided, to figure the total area. You will divide this area in half to figure the wallpaper needed by each of you.
2. Write a paper that describes the process you used. Then describe how you will convince your little sister/brother that the area of a rectangle is length × width, and that you aren't cheating in your calculations.

3. Write a dialogue between you and your little sister/brother in which you describe to her/him how much wallpaper each of you gets to use. The dialogue needs to include an introduction setting up the scene.
4. Make a visual aid to help teach your little sister/brother. Attach this visual aid to the dialogue writing you turn in.

Wallpaper Puzzle Scoring Rubric

Criteria and Points Possible (50)	Comments and Points Earned
Prewriting assignment is completed (+5)	
Math calculations are accurate (+5)	
The process is described in detail (+10)	
Plan for teaching is given in detail (+10)	
Dialogue has setting and clear development (+10)	
Dialogue has visual aid attached (+5)	
Writing shows attention to conventions (+5)	

History: Family History Research Assignment (Katie Carone)

You have just been elected chairperson of the state historical society. As chairperson, one of your duties is to speak at the historical society's annual luncheon. Because this year's theme is "Looking at Legacies," you decide to research your own family legacy and include this information in your luncheon talk. The following writing process will help you accomplish your goal.

Step 1: Gather histories
Begin by collecting personal histories of three relatives or ancestors in at least two separate generations (parents, grandparents, great-grandparents). If you do not have access to two different generations of your family, you may research personal histories of nonrelatives. Gain access to primary sources (first-hand accounts) as much as possible. Use diaries, journals, personal letters, oral histories, autobiographies, and interviews. Make sure to use personal interviews for at least one of the histories.

Step 2: Organize information
With your materials collected, begin organizing so that you can compare and contrast the three lives to each other and to yourself. You can use strategies discussed in class (e.g., concept mapping, comparison charts or lists, a table) or create your own method. Part of this comparison will relate to historical events, living

conditions, lifestyle, personality, thoughts and feelings, joys and hardships, and so on. This chart should be attached to your final speech.

Step 3: Analyze and freewrite

What are the major similarities and differences in the three lives? How did historical events affect the lives of these people? What surprises have emerged as a result of your research? What lessons have you learned from researching these stories? Why is it important to keep "Looking at Legacies"? As you think about these questions, begin the process of free writing. For now, don't worry about spelling or grammar. Just get your answers to the questions down on paper.

Step 4: Write a speech

Focusing on the theme of "Looking at Legacies" and using your free writing, develop a three- to five-page speech to present at the historical society luncheon. Use your three histories as examples. Draw upon the comparisons and contrasts in Steps 2 and 3. Describe what you discovered as you delved into family history. Because you are the society's chairperson, members will expect to hear *why* the process of historical research is so rewarding. Of course, make sure your speech has an introduction, body, and conclusion. You will also want to proofread carefully before you turn in a final copy. (The paper itself should be double-spaced, in 12-point font, with one-inch margins.) Finally, don't forget to attach a list of research sources at the end of your paper.

Family History Scoring Rubric

Assignment Criteria	Points Possible	Points Earned	Comments
Research includes three relatives in at least two generations.	10		
Research involves primary sources and one interview (minimum).	10		
Research includes an organizational chart for family history materials.	20		
Speech is organized with introduction, body, and conclusion.	10		
Speech compares and contrasts the three lives in multiple ways.	40		
Speech meets form requirements and includes a list of sources.	5		
Speech shows good control over basic writing mechanics.	5		
Total points	100		

Biology: Science Fiction Assignment (Jeramy Cook)

As we have learned in class, plants and animals are both classified as *eukaryotes*, meaning they have much in common. However, there are differences between plants and us that are important to understand and remember. A good way to learn biology information is to have fun applying it. This assignment invites you to understand plant and animal differences through creativity.

For this assignment, imagine you are a science fiction writer who has come up with a wonderful idea for your next book. The character you envision has been born here on earth with many of the structures and functions of a plant, and you want to tell the story of how this person lives. Your story will describe the challenges this person faces as well as the benefits of possessing certain plant-like structures and functions.

You can have your character look like a human but with the cells of a plant, or the character can possess both plant and human traits. It's up to you. With this writing, use your imagination and be creative. But I also want you to show your understanding of the important structures and functions that make plants different from people. Remember, real learning involves more than just memorizing the parts of a plant or animal.

The following rubric will help you understand my expectations. Meanwhile, have fun, explore, and be nice to plants!

Science Fiction Criteria	Possible Points (100)	Your Points
Appropriate length (3–5 pages, typed, double-spaced)	10	
Character shows challenges of having plant traits.	20	
Character shows benefits of having plant traits.	20	
Paper shows and discusses some specific parts of a plant (e.g., cell wall, plastids, etc.).	20	
Paper shows understanding of the main differences between plant and animal cells.	20	
Paper shows control over writing mechanics.	10	

REFERENCES

ACT. (2004). *Crisis at the core: Preparing all students for college and work.* www.act.org/path/policy/pdf/crisis_report.pdf. Retrieved November 1, 2004.

Allen, C. (2001). *Writing multigenre research papers: Voice, passion, and discovery in grades 4–6.* Portsmouth, NH: Heinemann.

Applebee, A. N. (1981). *Writing in the secondary school: English and the content areas.* Urbana, IL: National Council of Teachers of English.

Beaman, B. (1985). Writing to learn social studies. In A. Gere (Ed.), *Roots in the sawdust: Writing to learn across the disciplines* (pp. 60–71). Urbana, IL: National Council of Teachers of English.

Bean, J. C. (1996). *Engaging ideas: The professor's guide to integrating writing, critical thinking, and active learning in the classroom.* San Francisco: Jossey-Bass.

Bean, J. C., Drenk, D. & Lee, F. D. (1982). Microtheme strategies for developing cognitive skills. In C. W. Griffin (Ed.), *Teaching writing in all disciplines* (pp. 27–38). San Francisco: Jossey-Bass.

Beers, K. (2003). *When kids can't read: What teachers can do.* Portsmouth, NH: Heinemann.

Bernstein, R. (1997). Using fictional techniques for nonfiction writing. In C. B. Olson (Ed.), *Practical ideas for teaching writing as a process at the high school and college levels* (pp. 135–138). Sacramento, CA: California Department of Education.

Blockson, C. L. (1987). *The underground railroad: First-person narratives of escapes to freedom in the north.* New York: Prentice Hall.

Boyer, E. L. (1983). *High school: A report on secondary education in America.* New York: Harper & Row.

Britton, J. (1970). *Language and learning.* Harmondsworth: Penguin.

Bruner, J. S. (1978). The role of dialogue in language acquisition. In A. Sinclair et al. (Eds.), *The child's conception of language* (pp. 241–256). New York: Springer-Verlag.

Camp, G. (1982). *A success curriculum for remedial writers.* Berkeley, CA: National Writing Project.

Catton, B. (1996). *The American heritage new history of the civil war.* New York: Viking.

Chopra, D. (2003). *The spontaneous fulfillment of desire: Harnessing the infinite power of coincidence.* New York: Harmony Books.

Claggett, F. (1996). *A measure of success: From assignment to assessment in English language arts.* Portsmouth, NH: Boynton/Cook.

College Entrance Examination Board (CEEB), National Commission on Writing in America's Schools and Colleges. (2003). *The neglected "R": The need for a writing revolution.* New York: College Entrance Examination Board.

Collins, J. (1998). *Strategies for struggling writers.* New York: Guilford.

Csikszentmihalyi, M. (1990). *Flow: The psychology of optimal experience.* New York: Harper Perennial.

Daiker, D. A. (1989). Learning to praise. In C. M. Anson (Ed.), *Writing and response: Theory, practice, and research.* Urbana, IL: National Council of Teachers of English.

Dale, H. (1997). *Co-authoring in the classroom: Creating an environment for effective collaboration.* Urbana, IL: National Council of Teachers of English.

D'Aoust, C. (1997). The saturation research paper. In C. B. Olson (Ed.), *Practical ideas for teaching writing as a process at the high school and college levels* (pp. 142–144). Sacramento, CA: California Department of Education.

Emig, J. (1983). Writing as a mode of learning. In D. Goswami & M. Butler (Eds.), *The web of meaning: Essays on writing, teaching, learning and thinking* (pp. 123–131). Upper Montclair, NJ: Boynton/Cook.

Fadiman, A. & Atwan, R. (2003). *The best American essays 2003.* Boston: Houghton Mifflin.

Fisher, M. J. (2003). Memoria ex machina. In A. Fadiman (Ed.), *The best American essays 2003* (pp. 61–66). Boston: Houghton Mifflin.

Fry, E., Kress, J. & Fountoukidis, D. L. (1993). *The reading teacher's book of lists* (third ed.). Englewood Cliffs, NJ: Prentice Hall.

Gallwey, W. T. (1997). *The inner game of tennis* (rev. ed.). New York: Random House.

Gardner, H. (1982). *Art, mind, and brain: A cognitive approach to creativity.* New York: Basic Books.

Gawande, A. (2003). The learning curve. In A. Fadiman (Ed.), *The best American essays 2003* (pp. 83–102). Boston: Houghton Mifflin.

Gendlin, E. (1978). *Focusing.* New York: Everest House.

Gere, A. (1985). *Roots in the sawdust: Writing to learn across the disciplines.* Urbana, IL: National Council of Teachers of English.

Gibran, K. (1923/1975). *The prophet.* New York: Knopf.

Goodlad, J. I. (1984). *A place called school: Prospects for the future.* New York: McGraw-Hill.

Gopnik, A. (2003). Bumping into Mr. Ravioli. In A. Fadiman (Ed.), *The best American essays 2003* (pp. 103–111). Boston: Houghton Mifflin.

Heilbroner, R. & Thurow, L. (1981). *Five economic challenges.* New York: Prentice Hall.

Hillocks, G. (1986). *Research on written composition: New directions in teaching.* Urbana, IL: ERIC Clearinghouse on Reading and Communication Skills and the National Conference on Research in English.

Johnston, P. (1985). Writing to learn science. In A. Gere (Ed.), *Roots in the sawdust: Writing to learn across the disciplines* (pp. 92–103). Urbana, IL: National Council of Teachers of English.

Lakoff, G. & Johnson, M. (1980). *Metaphors we live by.* Chicago: University of Chicago Press.

Langer, J. A. & Applebee, A. A. (1987). *How writing shapes thinking: A study of teaching and learning.* Urbana, IL: National Council of Teachers of English.

Macrorie, K. (1988). *The I-search paper: Revised edition of searching writing.* Portsmouth, NH: Heinemann.

Macrorie, K. (1997). The reawakening of curiosity: The research paper as hunting stories. In C. B. Olson (Ed.), *Practical ideas for teaching writing as a process at the high school and college levels* (pp. 152–155). Sacramento, CA: California Department of Education.

Marik, R. (1985). Teaching special education students history using writing-to-learn strategies. In A. Gere (Ed.), *Roots in the sawdust: Writing to learn across the disciplines* (pp. 72–91). Urbana, IL: National Council of Teachers of English.

Maxwell, R. (1996). *Writing across the curriculum in middle and high schools.* Needham Heights, MA: Allyn & Bacon.

Mellon, J. (1981). Language competence. In C. R. Cooper (Ed.), *The nature and measurement of competency in English* (pp. 21–64). Urbana, IL: National Council of Teachers of English.

Mitchell, D. (1996). Teaching ideas: Writing across the curriculum and the English teacher. *English Journal, 85,* pp. 93–97.

Moffett, J. (1983). *Teaching the universe of discourse.* Portsmouth, NH: Boynton/Cook.

Murray, D. M. (1990). *Shoptalk: Learning to write with writers.* Portsmouth, NH: Boynton/Cook.

National Center for Educational Statistics (NCES), National Assessment of Educational Progress (NAEP). (2002). *The nation's report card: Writing, 2002.* nces.ed.gov/nationsreportcard/writing/. Retrieved August 1, 2003.

National Commission on Excellence in Education. (1983). *A nation at risk: The imperative for educational reform.* Washington, DC: U.S. Government Printing Office.

National Commission on Writing in America's Schools and Colleges. (2003). *The neglected 'R': The need for a writing revolution.* New York: College Entrance Examination Board.

Neville, J. (1995). *The press, the Rosenbergs, and the cold war.* Westport, CT: Praeger.

Newkirk, T. (1985). *To compose: Teaching writing in high school.* Chelmsford, MA: Northwest Regional Exchange.

Northwest Regional Educational Laboratory. (1997). Six-trait analytical model. www.nwrel.org/comm/catalog/. Retrieved March 1, 2000.

Olson, C. B. (1997a). Preparing students to write the saturation report. In C. B. Olson (Ed.), *Practical ideas for teaching writing as a process at the high school and college levels* (pp. 138–142). Sacramento, CA: California Department of Education.

Olson, C. B. (1997b). A sample prompt, scoring guide, and model paper for I-search. In C. B. Olson (Ed.), *Practical ideas for teaching writing as a process at the high school and college levels* (pp. 156–161). Sacramento, CA: California Department of Education.

Olson, C. B. (2003). *The reading/writing connection: Strategies for teaching and learning in the secondary classroom.* Boston: Allyn & Bacon.

Page, B. (1987). From passive receivers to active learners in English. In J. Self (Ed.), *Plain talk about learning and writing across the curriculum.* Commonwealth of Virginia: Virginia Department of Education.

Perl, S. (1985). Understanding composing. In T. Newkirk (Ed.), *To compose: Teaching writing in high school* (pp. 28–36). Chelmsford, MA: Northwest Regional Exchange.

Perl, S. (2004). *Felt sense: Writing with the body.* Portsmouth, NH: Heinemann-Boynton/Cook.

Philipson, I. (1988). *Ethel Rosenberg: Beyond the myths.* New York: Franklin Watts.

Pirsig, R. (1974). *Zen and the art of motorcycle maintenance: An inquiry into values.* New York: Morrow.

Plagiarism FAQ. (2004). Retrieved November 8, 2004, from www.plagiarism.org/research_site/e_faqs_text.html.

Plessinger, A. (2004). The effects of mental imagery on athletic performance. Retrieved August 1, 2004, from www.vanderbilt.edu/AnS/psychology/health_psychology/mentalimagery.html.

Pollan, M. (2003). An animal's place. In A. Fadiman (Ed.), *The best American essays 2003* (pp. 190–211). Boston: Houghton Mifflin.

Pugh, S. L., Hicks, J. W., Davis, M. & Venstra, T. (1992). *Bridging: A teacher's guide to metaphorical thinking.* Urban, IL: National Council of Teachers of English and ERIC Clearinghouse on Reading and Communication Skills.

Research resources (2004). Retrieved November 8, 2004, from www.plagiarism.org/research_site/e_home_text.html.

Richardson, G. E. (1982). *Educational imagery: Strategies to personalize classroom instruction.* Springfield, IL: Charles C Thomas.

Rico, G. (1983). *Writing the natural way: Using right-brain techniques to release your expressive powers.* Los Angeles: J. P. Tarcher.

Rico, G. (1997). Clustering: A prewriting process. In C. B. Olson (Ed.), *Practical ideas for teaching writing as a process at the high school and college levels* (pp. 14–17). Sacramento, CA: California Department of Education.

Romano, T. (1995). *Writing with passion: Life stories, multiple genres.* Portsmouth, NH: Heinemann.

Romano, T. (2000). *Blending genres, altering styles: Writing multigenre papers.* Portsmouth, NH: Heinemann.

Rose, M. (1989). *Lives on the boundary.* New York: Penguin.

Rose, M. (1995). *Possible lives: The promise of public education in America.* New York: Penguin.

Schank, R. C. (1990). *Tell me a story: A new look at real and artificial memory.* New York: Scribners.

Schon, D. A. (1983). *The reflective practitioner.* San Francisco: Jossey-Bass.

Scott, M. A. (2002). Doing small things with great love. In S. M. Intrator (Ed.), *Stories of the courage to teach* (pp. 35–40). San Francisco: Jossey-Bass.

Shaver, J. P. & Strong, W. (1982). *Facing value decisions: Rationale-building for teachers* (second ed.). New York: Teachers College Press.

Sizer, T. R. (1984). *Horace's compromise: The dilemma of the American high school.* Boston: Houghton Mifflin.

Smith, F. (1998). *The book of learning and forgetting.* New York: Teachers College.

Strong, W. (1976). Assessing skills in reading. *Media and Methods, 12,* pp. 28–59.

Strong, W. (1986). *Creative approaches to sentence combining.* Urbana, IL: ERIC Clearinghouse on Reading and Communication Skills and National Council of Teachers of English.

Strong, W. (1994). *Sentence combining: A composing book* (third ed.). New York: McGraw-Hill.

Strong, W. (1996). *Writer's toolbox: A sentence-combining workshop.* New York: McGraw-Hill.

Strong, W. (2001). *Coaching writing: The power of guided practice.* Portsmouth, NH: Heinemann.

Tierney, B. (2002). Let's take another look at the fish: The writing process as discovery. In A. Bauman & A. Peterson (Eds.), *Breakthroughs: Classroom discoveries about teaching writing.* Berkeley, CA: National Writing Project.

Tierney, B. & Dorroh, J. (2004). *How to write to learn in science* (second ed.). Arlington, VA: National Science Teachers Association Press.

Topping, D. & McManus, R. (2002). *Real reading, real writing.* Portsmouth, NH: Heinemann.

Watson, T. (1985). Writing to learn history. In A. Gere (Ed.), *Roots in the sawdust: Writing to learn across the disciplines* (pp. 137–147). Urbana, IL: National Council of Teachers of English.

Wotring, A. M. & Tierney, R. (1981). *Two studies of writing in high school science.* Berkeley: Bay Area Writing Project.

U.S. Department of Education, National Center for Education Statistics. (2002). The nation's report card: Writing. Available at www.nces.ed.gov/nationsreportcard/naepdata/.

Vygotsky, L. (1962). *Thought and language* (E. Hanfmann & G. Vakar, Trans.). Cambridge, MA: MIT Press.

Yoshida, J. (1985). Writing to learn philosophy. In A. Gere (Ed.), *Roots in the sawdust: Writing to learn across the disciplines* (pp. 117–136). Urbana, IL: National Council of Teachers of English.

Zimmerman, P. (1985). Writing for art appreciation. In A. Gere (Ed.), *Roots in the sawdust: Writing to learn across the disciplines* (pp. 31–45). Urbana, IL: National Council of Teachers of English.

Zinsser, W. (1988). *Writing to learn.* New York: Harper & Row.

INDEX